Exploring

REVELATION

THE JOHN PHILLIPS COMMENTARY SERIES

Exploring
REVELATION

An Expository Commentary

JOHN PHILLIPS

kregel
PUBLICATIONS

Grand Rapids, MI 49501

Exploring Revelation: An Expository Commentary

© 1974, 1987 by John Phillips

Published in 2001 by Kregel Publications, a division of Kregel, Inc., P.O. Box 2607, Grand Rapids, MI 49501.

Library of Congress Cataloging-in-Publication Data
Phillips, John.
    Exploring Revelation: an expository commentary / by John Phillips.
        p.   cm.
    Originally published: Chicago: Moody Press, 1987.
    Includes bibliographical references.
    1. Bible N.T. Revelation—Commentaries. I. Title.
BS2825.53 .P47   2001   228'.07—dc21   2001033772
                                                    CIP
ISBN 978-0-8254-3491-4

Printed in the United States of America

7 8 9 10 11 / 15 14 13 12 11

Contents

Preface

"Where are we today?" That is the question uppermost in the minds of many people as they approach a study of Bible prophecy in general and of the book of Revelation in particular. They instinctively feel that the Bible should speak clearly to the special needs of our age. They are right; it should, and it does.

Yet most commentaries on the book of Revelation make little or no attempt to relate the dramatic scenes of the Apocalypse to the realities of today. There are two good reasons for that. First, many of the commentaries were written before the events of our age began to take shape. Second, most of the events described in the Revelation are yet future and belong to a different age.

Just the same, thoughtful people are insisting that if we are not living in the age of the Apocalypse, we must at least be living on the threshold of that age. So many significant things are happening. Consider the rebirth of the state of Israel; the rise of Russia to the status of a world power and her domination of the Middle East and key parts of Africa; the rise of the nations of Europe to increasing collective consciousness; the awakening of China and the nations of the Orient; the sudden wealth, importance, and influence of the Muslim, Arab world based on their control of much of the world's oil; the resurgence of militant Islam; the political and moral bankruptcy of the nations and their international institutions; the rise of a sodomite society; the constant, brooding threat of nuclear war; the rising tides of lawlessness; the apostasy of the professing church; the vast changes within the Roman Catholic church; the emergence of the drug culture; the revival of the occult; the staggering strides being made in science and technology; the trend toward totalitarianism; the ecological threat to the planet. These and similar pieces are all part of the jigsaw puzzle of our age. Thoughtful people believe that if any clue to the picture is to be found, it must be in the book of Revelation.

In this study we are going to attempt three things—to carefully and clearly outline the book of Revelation so that its chief movements can be clearly discerned, to expound the book verse by verse so that its details can be grasped, and to show where the trends discernible in today's world will end and how they relate to the book of Revelation.

Part One:

Visions of God (1:1-20)

INTRODUCTION TO REVELATION (1:1-3)

A. The Significance of the Book (1:1a-b)
  1. The Person of Christ Unveiled (1:1a)
  2. The Purposes of God Unveiled (1:1b)
B. The Signature of the Book (1:1c-2)
  1. The Marvelous Way He Received This Revelation (1:1c)
  2. The Meticulous Way He Recorded This Revelation (1:2)
C. The Singularity of the Book (1:3)
  1. It Embodies a Special Promise (1:3)
  2. It Embraces a Special Period (1:3)

I. THE COURSE OF THE AGE (1:4-6)

A. The Blessing (1:4-5a)
  1. The Substance of the Blessing (1:4a)
  2. The Source of the Blessing (1:4b-5a)
B. The Benediction (1:5b-6)
  1. The Grace That Accrues to Us (1:5b-6a)
  2. The Glory That Accrues to Him (1:6b)

II. THE CONSUMMATION OF THE AGE (1:7-8)

A. The Eventual Triumph of Jesus (1:7)
B. The Everlasting Triumph of Jesus (1:8)

III. THE CHARACTER OF THE AGE (1:9-20)

A. It Is an Age of Individual Witness (1:9)
B. It Is an Age of Instinctive Worship (1:10-18)
C. It Is an Age of Intelligent Waiting (1:19-20)

Part One:
Visions of God (1:1-20)

INTRODUCTION TO REVELATION (1:1-3)

The book of Revelation was probably written during the reign of the Roman emperor Domitian, about A.D. 95. The emperor had demanded that public worship be rendered to himself; he was to be worshiped as lord and god. Christians refused to obey, and the second great wave of persecution against the church was launched. The Christians were subjected to public ridicule, economic boycott, imprisonment, exile, and death. The book of Revelation was God's answer to that reign of terror. Christians could see, in a dimension never before revealed, that God was still on the throne.

A. THE SIGNIFICANCE OF THE BOOK (1:1a-b)

The book is said to be a "revelation," an unveiling. Some years ago, the city of Chicago was given an original sculpture by Pablo Picasso to adorn the plaza outside the new city hall. As the statue was being erected, it was heavily screened from the curious gaze of the passersby. When it was finished, it stood in the plaza thickly veiled. The day came when Mayor Daley unveiled the statue to the astonished gaze of Chicago and the world. There it stood in all its glory, the latest offering at the altar of art, Chicago's own gigantic Picasso. What Mayor Daley did for Chicago when he unveiled the statue, the book of Revelation does for us. It draws aside the veil.

1. THE PERSON OF CHRIST UNVEILED (1:1a)

John tells us that this book is **the revelation of Jesus Christ, which God gave unto him.** When Jesus came to earth the first time, it was in meekness, with His glory veiled. He came to be "obedient unto death, even the death of the cross" (Phil. 2:8). He was God manifest in flesh, and He showed it in a thousand ways that only the eye of faith could recognize. James, for example, brought up in the same Nazareth home with Jesus, failed to recognize Him as the Son of God. Jesus was perfect in character, perfect in conduct, in conversation. He was deity in humanity, yet was unknown as such to the children who shared that Nazareth home! His chosen disciples themselves only half believed Him. The world was so blind to who He was that it offered Him a cattle shed for His birth and a cross for His death.

One day, however, He is coming back with His glory unveiled to smash the opposition of the world and to wield a scepter of iron. He is coming back in pomp and power to reign, backed by the hosts of heaven. His deity, manifest even now to the eye of faith, will blaze forth like flaming lightning then. In the book of Revelation, the Person of Christ is unveiled, and we are given view after view of that glorious Man who fills all heaven with His praise.

2. *THE PURPOSES OF GOD UNVEILED (1:1b)*

This book was written by God **to shew unto his servants things which must shortly come to pass,** God has a plan for this earth. Threads of prophecy are found in all parts of Holy Writ, and together they make up a magnificent tapestry of truth. The book of Revelation draws all these strands of prophecy together and weaves them into a detailed picture of things to come. As the various threads are woven into the warp and woof of the book, we see the apostasy of the faith and the rapture of the church; we see wars, famines, and pestilences; we see the coming of the beast and the false prophet, followed by persecutions without parallel in history; we see the battle of Armageddon, followed by the golden age; and we see the eternal destinies of men.

The scenes in Revelation alternate between heaven and earth. Chapter 1 is set in heaven; chapters 2 and 3 are set on earth; chapters 4 and 5 are back in heaven; chapters 6 and 7 are back on earth again. The book begins in heaven and it ends in heaven. The scenes alternate as follows:

1. In heaven: Blessing from God (1:1-8)
2. On earth: John Imprisoned (1:9)
3. In heaven: The glory of Christ (1:10-20)
4. On earth: Letters to the Churches (2:1-3:22)
5. In heaven: The Lamb and the throne (4:1-5:14)
6. On earth: The seals broken (6:1-17)
7. In heaven: The 144,000; silence (7:1-8:6)
8. On earth: The trumpet judgments (8:7-9:21)
9. In heaven: The little book (10:1-11)
10. On earth: The two witnesses (11:1-13)
11. In heaven: Worship (11:14-19)
12. On earth: Israel persecuted by the beasts (12:1-13:18)
13. In heaven: The 144,000 in glory; angelic activity (14:1-15:8)
14. On earth: The seven vials; the two Babylons (16:1-18:24)

15. In heaven: The marriage of the Lamb; its consequences (19:1-16)
   16. On earth: Final judgments (19:17-20:10)
17. In heaven: The last judgment; the celestial city (20:11-22:21)

The reason for the alternating scenes is clear. In this last book of the Bible we have the full and final answer to the Lord's prayer: "Thy kingdom come. Thy will be done in earth, as it is in heaven" (Matt. 6:10). In this book we see God's will being decreed and declared in heaven, then we see that will being done on earth. The book of Revelation shows that no power in heaven, earth, or hell can frustrate the fulfillment of that plan. God's kingdom will come, whether men like it or not.

The book of Revelation is occupied for the most part with events that have little bearing on our lives—most of the events will take place after the church has been removed from the scene. But there are two abiding values for us in this book. As we study it, we can keep in view the Person of Christ and the purposes of God. This book will teach us to adore that Person and accept those purposes, and thus make its impact on our lives.

B. THE SIGNATURE OF THE BOOK (1:1c-2)

The writer of this book undoubtedly was John, the beloved apostle. It was not until the second half of the third century that his authorship was seriously questioned. Dionysius claimed that differences in style and grammar between John's gospel and Revelation demanded different authors. He therefore invented a new author for Revelation, one John the Presbyter of Ephesus. Of this man, history knows nothing. The author of Revelation signs his work with his bare name—John. Three times in chapter 1 and once again in the last chapter he does that. As the sole surviving representative of the apostles, he would be so well known that he would need to do no more.

   1. THE MARVELOUS WAY HE RECEIVED THIS REVELATION (1:1c)

Of the book, John says that God **sent and signified it by his angel unto his servant John.** The word "signified" literally means "to give a sign or signal." The book has been "sign-ified"; it is a book of signs and symbols. About half of the symbols are explained in the book itself. Lamps, for example, represent assemblies of God's people; stars represent angels; incense odors represent the prayers of saints. Where the symbols are not explained, other parts of the Bible must be searched for clues. It is an axiom of hermeneutics that God is His own interpreter.

A sign or a symbol can be far more accurate than any other type of language. Words tend to change in meaning with the passing of time. The word "prevent," for example, in 1 Thessalonians 4:15 means, in modern English, "to hinder" or "to stand in the way." When the King James Version was published in 1611, it meant "to come before" or "to get in first." What a difference this change in meaning makes to an understanding of the text! Symbols, however, are fixed. Ideas connected with such things as rainbows, clouds, mountains, seas, stars, the sun and moon never change. In a book dealing primarily with events that were in the remote future at the time of writing, it was necessary to make use of numerous symbols.

We must beware, however, of fanciful interpretations of Bible symbols. The view, for instance, that the mysterious creatures of Revelation 9:1-12 are helicopters is frivolous. The context proves it so. The locust-like creatures come up from "the bottomless pit" (the abyss). Revelation 20 makes it clear that the bottomless pit is one of God's prisons; during the millennial age Satan is kept incarcerated there. Helicopters certainly do not come up from the bottomless pit. Whatever else the creatures symbolize, they cannot be helicopters. Such a fanciful interpretation may be sensational, but it is not sound Bible exegesis.

2. THE METICULOUS WAY HE RECORDED THIS REVELATION (1:2)

John tells us that he **bare record of the word of God, and of the testimony of Jesus Christ, and of all things that he saw.** The expression "the word of God" underlines *the uniqueness of this communication.* The expression is often used in Scripture to define a prophetic message. Samuel said to Saul, "Stand thou still a while, that I may shew thee the word of God" (1 Sam. 9:27; see also 2 Sam. 7:4; 1 Kings 12:22). The expression occurs five times in Revelation. It stands for a prophetic message, and as such it is unique.

The expression "the testimony of Jesus" underlines *the uniformity of this communication,* for while the revelation of prophecy is often progressive, it is always uniform. God never contradicts Himself. The book of Revelation builds on the testimony of Jesus Christ. It expands and explains many of the things He taught in the Olivet Discourse, which in turn were based on statements in the book of Daniel and elsewhere in the Old Testament.

John wrote down only what he saw and heard. He was meticulous in recording the revelations which were made to him. We must be just as careful in reading this book as John was in writing it.

C. THE SINGULARITY OF THE BOOK (1:3)

There is something singular and special about the book that ends our Bible.

1. IT EMBODIES A SPECIAL PROMISE (1:3)

John says, **Blessed is he that readeth, and they that hear the words of this prophecy, and keep those things which are written therein.** This is the first of seven beatitudes in the Apocalypse, and this one is for today. The next two (14:13; 16:15) relate to the period of the Great Tribulation; the fourth (19:9) has to do with Armageddon; the fifth (20:6) points to the Millennium; and the last two (22:7, 14) refer to the celestial city. The blessing here relates to those who hear what the book has to say and to those who heed what the book has to say. Just to hear the book of Revelation read is a blessing. True, much of it is difficult to understand, but so constant are the glimpses of Christ in glory, so consistent the outworking of the will of God, so glorious the ultimate consummation, that just to hear the prophecies of this book being read is a blessing in a troubled world like ours. But we must also heed what is written. The word *heed* literally means "to watch over," or "to observe attentively." We must keep an eye on things in light of what the book has to say.

2. IT EMBRACES A SPECIAL PERIOD (1:3)

John tells us, *the time is at hand.* This book is not to be put aside because it refers to events in the future. Although the coming of the Lord is not presented to us in Scripture as immediate, it is always imminent. It is impending; it can happen at any time. It is an event that overhangs the ages. The events it predicts can happen at any moment. The only one of the twelve apostles who had no blessed hope that the Lord would come during his lifetime was Peter (John 21:18-19; 2 Pet. 1:14). At any time in history, God could have ordered events to precipitate the return of Christ. Throughout the ages, devout believers have considered themselves to be living on the threshold of the Lord's return and have been able to detect what they sincerely believed to be signs of the times in events taking place in the world around them.

When Islam burst upon the world, for instance, it must have seemed that the time was ripe for the end-time prophecies to be fulfilled. Here was a false prophet of convincing and tenacious power and a false religion being spread with astonishing success by the power of the sword.

The same must have seemed the case when Napoleon surged up out of the crimson seas of the French Revolution. He swiftly brought order out of chaos and proceeded to redraw the map of Europe. His dealings in the Middle East, his plans to occupy Palestine and rebuild Babylon, and his dealings with the pope must have fascinated Bible students. It must have seemed that the last days had arrived.

I can remember as a boy listening to my elders discuss the international situation. Mussolini had come to power in Italy. He campaigned in Africa, openly declaring that he intended to revive the Roman Empire. Speculation was rife that he must be the Antichrist.

But, on all those occasions, there was one important factor missing from the equation. Israel was not yet a sovereign State. Now she is, and the configuration of events mentioned earlier (see Preface) surely heralds the imminent return of Christ.

Primarily, however, Revelation deals with a special period. It tells of events that will take place in heaven and on earth during the climactic "day of the Lord" (1:10). If it could be truly said in John's day, "The season is near," how much more it can be said today!

I. THE COURSE OF THE AGE (1:4-6)

The book of Revelation begins with the words *Grace be unto you, and peace*—more like a Pauline epistle than an apocalypse! It begins with a blessing and a benediction.

A. THE BLESSING (1:4-5a)

1. THE SUBSTANCE OF THE BLESSING (1:4a)

Scarcely has John picked up his pen than a blessing is pouring from it to the page. We note first the substance of the blessing. We read, *John to the seven churches which are in Asia: Grace be unto you, and peace* (1:4a). This book deals primarily with judgment, yet God begins it with *grace*. In this book, wicked men get richly deserved judgment from God. The floodtides of His wrath, dammed back since Calvary, burst all their banks and pour forth in all their fury. Yet God begins Revelation by telling men they can have what they do not deserve—grace! Thus the converts of the dark and dreadful age soon to come will probably outnumber those of all the rest of history. John sees a multitude that no man can number, men and women who have washed their robes in the blood of the Lamb and who loved not their lives unto death. Grace!

And not only is there grace, but *peace* as well! Here is a book that deals with the very opposite of peace. It deals with bloodshed and war. It rings with the din and noise of strife. It tells of carnage and conflict, earthquake and famine, pestilence and woe. It tells of purges and persecutions that dwarf all those of history. Blood flows in crimson tides. This book tells of the crash of empire, of anarchy, oppression, terror, and despair. It tells of war in heaven and of war on earth. It tells of an incarnate beast, driven and indwelt by the devil, wreaking fearful vengeance on the saints of the Most High. Thunders roll, stars fall from heaven, plagues issue up from the abyss, demons take control of human affairs, armies are marshaled by countless millions of men. Yet God begins this book with a single word—*peace!*

The news that Britain had entered the Second World War came at eleven o'clock on a Sunday morning. In a certain church in Britain a man arrived just after the announcement had been broadcast. He stood up and told the congregation that the country was now at war. A crushed silence descended. Then another man stood up and gave out a hymn. It went like this:

Peace, perfect peace in this dark world of sin?
The blood of Jesus whispers "peace" within.

Peace, perfect peace, with sorrows surging 'round?
On Jesus' bosom nought but peace is found.

Peace, perfect peace, with loved ones far away?
In Jesus' keeping we are safe, and they.

Peace, perfect peace, the future all unknown?
Jesus we know and He is on the throne.

Peace, perfect peace, death shadowing us and ours?
Jesus has conquered death and all its powers.

It is enough! Earth's struggles soon shall cease
And Jesus lead to heaven's perfect peace.

It is with a similar purpose that the Holy Spirit begins this war-filled book with the word *peace!*

Moreover, grace and peace win through at last. For at the end of the book the storm clouds roll away, the drums of war are stilled. The earth itself is purged by fire, and there emerges a new heaven and a new earth, in which dwell righteousness, and where all is grace and peace. So much then for the substance of the blessing.

2. THE SOURCE OF THE BLESSING (1:4b-5a)

Our attention is next drawn to the source of the blessing. It is a blessing backed with all the authority of heaven itself, a blessing bestowed by the Father, the Spirit, and the Son. We read first of all that the blessing is *from him which is, and which was, and which is to come.* In the context, this can be none other than God the Father. He is presented to us as the One who transcends all time. He lives in the present, in the past, and in the prospective tenses of time. He cuts across all the ages of time.

To Him the past is very much alive. As Irwin A. Moon of Moody Institute of Science said,

All of us have looked up, on a clear night, and seen the sparkling, twinkling stars. But, how many of us have realized that we cannot see the stars as they now are? Every time we look, we are looking into the past, seeing them as they were. The nearest naked-eye star, Alpha Centauri, is about four light years away. The most distant naked-eye object, the Andromeda Galaxy, is about a million-and-half light years away. This means that the light has been traveling four light years or over a million years to reach us. As a result, we are looking into the past. But this works both ways. If you were on one of the stars you would—assuming an adequate telescope—see the earth as it was sometime in the past. From the star Sirius, you could see what you are doing nine years ago, because, in a profoundly true scientific sense, you are still doing it. Yes, everything you have ever done, you are still doing. The ghost of your past haunts the universe. But remember . . . God is omnipresent. This means that, for God, every sin you have ever committed, every evil thing you have ever done, you are still doing, and will continue to do forever, apart from God's forgiveness. Only the omnipotent, eternal God, who controls all the factors of time, space and matter, could ever remove sin."[1]

That, of course, is why the Bible says that "God requireth that which is past" (Eccles. 3:15).

The present and the future are very much alive to God as well. He reads the past, He rides the present, He rules the future. Some years ago an itinerant preacher was accosted in an English country lane by a gypsy. "Sir," she said, "if you cross my palm with silver I will tell you what the future holds for you." The preacher looked at the woman and said, "You mean to say you can tell me what I will be doing a year from now, even what I'll be doing this time tomorrow?" The gypsy nodded her head. "Well," said the preacher, "I don't believe for one moment you can tell me what I'll be doing this time tomorrow, but I'll make a bargain with you. You tell me what I was doing this time yesterday, and I'll cross your palm with silver twice!" Needless to say, the fortune teller declined the offer! The great eternal God, who dwells in all tenses of time, majestically gathers the ages into His hand and whispers a word of grace and a word of peace to His own. Come what may, He controls it all.

The blessing comes, moreover, from God the Holy Spirit, *from the seven Spirits which are before his throne.* Some think this expression refers to seven angelic beings, but since the blessing comes also from the Father and the Son, the expression must surely refer to the Holy Spirit. No created being could join thus with the Godhead. The expression "the seven Spirits" has to do with the perfection of the Spirit's Person and with the plenitude of His power. He is seen taking up a position before the throne because He is the executor of God's purposes. Until now, He has been the executor of God's purposes in grace; He is now to be the executor of God's purposes in government. Even so, the saints of God will know nothing but grace and peace from Him.

The blessing, furthermore, is from God the Son. He has three titles, which, taken together, reveal His relationship to the present age. We note first *how the age commences.* The blessing is from *Jesus Christ, who is the faithful witness.* He came to earth to be a witness to a dark and degenerate world, and His witness was both unprecedented and unpopular. He witnessed

1. Irwin A. Moon, *Time and Eternity* (Whittier, Calif.: Moody Institute of Science, 1962), pp. 14-15.

to *the name of God*. In Old Testament times, God was frequently revealed through His many and varied names, each of which unfolded an aspect of His character. Jesus taught men a new name for God, the lovely, intimate, heart-warming name of *Father*.

He witnessed to *the nature of sin*. The Old Testament had developed an extensive vocabulary for sin. It employs some fifteen words to depict its various phases. David used three of them in a single verse (Ps. 32:5). Yet the full horror and criminality of sin was not fully revealed until Jesus came. Sin ploughed His back and crowned Him with thorns; sin hung Him up on cruel nails amid the sneers and jests of mankind; sin broke His body and broke His heart; sin wrung from His lips the "orphan cry" upon the cross. Sin was revealed in all its naked, unmasked horror when Jesus came.

He witnessed to *the need for righteousness*. The law of Moses did that too, for the very slopes of Sinai quaked when the law was given. But Sinai's demands are dwarfed and beggared by the demands for righteousness gently but firmly revealed on the grassy, sunny slopes of the Mount of Beatitudes. Sinai dealt with sin's fruits; the Sermon on the Mount dealt with sin's roots. Moses dealt, for the most part, with the deed; Jesus dealt with the very desire.

He witnessed to *the nearness of judgment*. The Lord Jesus spoke more about hell than He did about heaven. In Matthew's gospel, for example, where we have the most complete record of the Lord's public utterances, for every verse in which He mentions the abode of the blessed, there are three verses in which He refers to hell.

As the faithful witness, He brought *the news of salvation;* He imparted the news to good and bad alike, to the woman at the well, and to upright Nicodemus; to the rich young ruler with his claim to have kept the law, and to Zaccheus, a treacherous, unscrupulous man. The age began with Jesus as the faithful witness.

We note also *how the age continues*. The blessing is from the Lord Jesus, **the first begotten of the dead**. He has tasted death, risen in triumph from the tomb, and ascended into glory, there to implement the plans and purposes of God for this age. "First begotten" is *protokos*, implying priority and sovereignty. He is the leader of all who will rise from the dead through Him to everlasting life. There is a Man in the glory actively engaged in promoting the interests of God for this age. He is building His church, and the gates of hell cannot prevail against it. Down from "the excellent glory" come the encouraging words: "Grace be unto you, and peace."

We are also told *how the age concludes*. The blessing is from the Lord Jesus, **the prince of the kings of the earth**. He who once came to be born in a barn and to die on a cross is coming back to reign—coming in pomp and power, with banners flying and with the heaven's armies at His back. The devil is to have his final fling! He will crown a monster conjured from the sea and the abyss. He will smooth the sand and build His clay castle of an empire. He will head the shaky structure with a nasty little tyrant armed with a few fancy fireworks and a bag of magic tricks with which to dupe the masses of mankind. This coming world dictator will throw out his puny chest, set up his image, wave his futile fists at heaven, and burst into wind-bag blasphemies against the Lamb upon the throne. "I am God," he will shout. "Look! My prophet and I can make my image speak! Worship me or perish!" Then God will laugh! Peal after peal of frightful laughter will ring out from the throne of God. And the walls will all come tumbling down—the whole rickety affair, all stuck together like Nimrod's Babylon with slime from the pit. Down it will come! God's King is still on the throne. He is the prince of the kings of the earth.

So, then, this book begins with a blessing. Men are offered grace and peace by the triune God. In its ultimate fullness, the blessing belongs to the saints of a coming age, who will face the swelling of Jordan and the time of Jacob's trouble. But, surely, if this blessing will stand the test of a time like that, how much more can we pillow our heads on it for the tests and trials of today. When times become all but unbearable, grace and peace are ours, secure for us within the veil.

B. THE BENEDICTION (1:5*b*-6)

1. *THE GRACE THAT ACCRUES TO US* (*1:*5b-6a)

The blessing has hardly been uttered when the saints breathe back an answering benediction. The benediction tells of the grace that accrues to us. It is grace that endures. The saints respond to the blessing with the cry, *Unto him that loved us.* The revised text puts it in the present tense: "unto him that loveth us." It is *grace that endures.*

An African missionary, walking down a forest path where a day or two before fire had swept, leaving desolation in its train. found the charred remains of a nest. In the nest was the carcass of a mother hen, burned to a cinder. Idly he kicked the ashes with his foot and, to his astonishment, out from under the heap ran some baby chicks! Mother love had taught that hen to give her life for her brood. That was creature love. What can we say of Calvary love—of the love that many waters cannot quench, the love that will not let us go, the love that suffers long and is kind? It is love that endures!

The benediction rejoices in *grace that emancipates. Unto him that . . . washed us from our sins in his own blood,* is the joyful shout of the saints. The revised text renders it "unto him that loosed us." In the word "washed," we see the metaphor of sin as a stain. If we use the word "loosed," the metaphor is of sin as a chain. As the old hymn puts it:

He breaks the power of canceled sin
And sets the prisoner free;
His blood can make the foulest clean,
His blood availed for me.

(Charles Wesley)

The benediction speaks of *grace that elevates. Unto him that . . . hath made us kings and priests unto God and His Father* is the further response of the redeemed. He has bestowed upon us all the majesty of a prince and all the ministry of a priest. He has given us power with men and power with God. What more could we want than that? That is the grace that accrues to us.

2. THE GLORY THAT ACCRUES TO HIM (1:6b)

The benediction speaks also of the glory that accrues to Him. It is personal, positional, perpetual glory. *To him be glory and dominion for ever and ever.* His is the glory that outshines the sun, the glory He had with the Father before the worlds began. It is a glory that one day will be acknowledged by all mankind, when He returns in splendor from the sky. The dominion will be His as well, for He will reign from the river to the ends of the earth. The vast domains, originally placed into the hands of Adam (Gen. 1:26) and wrested from him by the serpent (Matt. 4:8-9; Heb. 2:5-9), will be the Lord's for ever and ever. The expression "to the end of the ages," unknown to the classical Greek writers, occurs fourteen times in the book of Revelation and is one of its keys.

Thomas Chalmers was one of Scotland's greatest preachers. In his early days as an unconverted man, while pastoring a small congregation, he secretly wanted to be a professor of mathematics at the University of Edinburgh and devoted most of his time to that end. He wrote a pamphlet expressing the view that a minister could easily discharge his pastoral obligations in two days, leaving the remainder of the week free for the pursuit of any avocation on which he set his heart. Then came Chalmers's conversion and his spectacular God-blessed ministry. Much later in his career, Chalmers attended a conference of the leaders of his denomination. One of his fellow ministers, jealous of Chalmers's success, read to the assembled synod the pamphlet penned by Chalmers in his unconverted days. "Did you write that, sir?" he demanded. "Did you write that?" Chalmers was stung to the quick. "Yes, sir," he said, rising to his feet, "I wrote it, strangely blinded as I was. In those days I aspired to be a professor of mathematics at the University of Edinburgh. But what, sir, is mathematics? It is magnitude and the proportion of magnitude, and in those unregenerate days I had forgotten two magnitudes—I had forgotten the *shortness* of time, and I had forgotten the *length* of eternity."[2]

---

2. W. Garden Blaikie, *Thomas Chalmers* (Edinburgh: Oliphant, 1896), pp. 23-24.

Not for one moment has God forgotten those two magnitudes. God never loses sight of eternity. The saints, in their joyful benediction, telling out the glory that accrues to Jesus, cry: *To Him be glory and dominion for ever and ever. Amen.*

II. The Consummation of the Age (1:7-8)

When men write books of action and excitement, they build toward a climax. A good gripping tale must keep the reader in suspense. The author must build up the tension, the mystery, the sense of impending doom, and he must prolong the suspense as long as he can. Not so with God. The book of Revelation has mystery enough for a dozen tales of suspense and horror enough for the most spine-tingling tales. What terrible things lie ahead! What dreadful things must unfold in this book as page succeeds page. John sees it all—the apostasy of the church, the breakdown of law and order, the crash of the establishment, the growing horror of war and woe, the dreadful bloodbaths of persecution, the savage reign of the Beast. Then he sees how it is all going to end at last in bursts of brightest glory. He cannot wait to tell us! The end is so good, so wonderfully, wonderfully good! *Behold,* he says, *he cometh with clouds; and every eye shall see him.*

A. THE EVENTUAL TRIUMPH OF JESUS (1:7)

There can be no doubt about the outcome. There are two things about the eventual triumph of Jesus. First, *it will be visible.* John says, *Behold he cometh with clouds; and every eye shall see him, and they also which pierced him."* The clouds are the clothing of His glory. When God summoned Israel out of Egypt, He marched before them all the way through the desert, wrapped in a cloak of cloud. When Israel pitched the Tabernacle in the wilderness, God enthroned Himself, draped with a cloud, upon the mercy seat. When our Lord stepped from Olivet's brow to climb the sky to glory, He flung around His rising form a glorious robe of cloud. And when He comes back to do battle with the beast and to claim this robbed and ruined vineyard as His own, He will once again be draped with clouds.

One of the most stirring pages in English history tells of the conquests and crusades of Richard I, the Lionhearted. While Richard was away trouncing Saladin, his kingdom fell on bad times. His sly and graceless brother, John, usurped all the prerogatives of the king and misruled the realm. The people of England suffered, longing for the return of the king, and praying that it might be soon. Then one day Richard came. He landed in England and marched straight for his throne. Around that glittering coming, many tales are told, woven into the legends of England. (One of them is the story of Robin Hood).

John's castles tumbled like ninepins. Great Richard laid claim to his throne, and none dared stand in his path. The people shouted their delight. They rang peal after peal on the bells. The Lion was back! Long live the king!

One day a King greater than Richard will lay claim to a realm greater than England. Those who have abused the earth in His absence, seized His domains, and mismanaged His world will all be swept aside. Every eye shall see Him, including those who pierced Him.

His coming will be visible. Furthermore, *it will be victorious.* John says, *And all kindreds of the earth shall wail because of him. Even so, Amen.* Think what men will be doing when He comes. They will be engaged in the final follies of Armageddon, goaded on by the Beast and his demon guides. Suddenly the armies will be dazzled; they will look up; they will see Him. They will fling down their weapons and weep. And poor Israel, too, poor blinded Israel in her last extremity, will look up, see Him, and be saved. What a day of weeping and rejoicing that will be!

B. THE EVERLASTING TRIUMPH OF JESUS (1:8)

The King, returned at last, is none other than "the King eternal, immortal, invisible, the only wise God" (1 Tim. 1:17). His triumph will be complete and everlasting. Hitler vowed that his infamous Third Reich would last for a thousand years. It was born on January 30, 1933, and lasted for the grand total of 148 months! Jesus is to set up a kingdom that will last for a thousand years, and when that golden millennium has run its course, the kingdom will be dissolved, not by decline or decay, not by surrender to the force of superior arms, but because He wills it so and because the time has come to set up an everlasting kingdom that will never pass away.

This everlasting triumph of Jesus is based on the three great attributes of deity. First, He is *omniscient.* He says: *I am Alpha and Omega.* Alpha and Omega are the first and last letters of the Greek alphabet. The Lord Jesus is God's alphabet. The alphabet is an ingenious way of storing the accumulated wisdom of the race. Our literature is composed of various letters of the alphabet arranged in an endless variety of ways. Jesus is the Alpha and the Omega, the first letter and the last, the first and final source of knowledge, understanding, and wisdom. His decrees will be based on omniscience. He cannot be deceived, disputed, discredited, or disconcerted. He could not be when He came the first time to redeem; He cannot be when He comes the second time to reign. His dictates will be full, inexhaustible, and wise, based on infallible knowledge of all the facts, all the forces, all the facets directly or indirectly involved.

Second, He is *omnipresent.* He says: *I am . . . the beginning and the ending.* His omnipresence is stated here in terms of time, but it is just as true in terms of space (see Matt. 18:20). The Lord is present in the midst of any company of His people in any part of the world at any given moment of time. "Lo, I am with you alway," He says, "even unto the end of the world" (Matt. 28:20). This was David Livingstone's favorite text. At every crisis in his life he would write it in his diary and add: "It is the word of a Gentleman of the strictest and most sacred honor, and that's an end of it!" To be present everywhere, what an attribute for a King! No wonder His triumph will be everlasting.

Third, He is *omnipotent.* He says: *I am . . . the Lord which is, and which was, and which is to come, the Almighty.* The first part of this expression has already been used to describe the Father (1:4); it is now used to describe the Son. He is God in every sense of the word. He is "the Almighty," an expression that occurs only ten times in the New Testament, nine of them in Revelation.

The first time the title occurs in the Bible is in 1 Samuel 1:3. Elkanah, we are told, "went up out of his city yearly to worship and to sacrifice unto the LORD of hosts in Shiloh." The judges have come and gone, and failure is everywhere. But the Lord has not failed! He is "Jehovah of hosts, the Almighty." Come back to the Apocalypse. Again there is failure everywhere. The church has failed and, apart from a raptured remnant, has become completely apostate. The nations have failed and have fallen for the blandishments of the Beast. Israel has failed. But God has not failed, for Jesus is coming again. "All power is given unto me," He said as He prepared to leave the earth for heaven. The claim was not rhetorical; it was true! His triumph will be eventual, but it will also be everlasting.

III. THE CHARACTER OF THE AGE (1:9-20)

We are now told three things about the character of the age in which we live, an age that will end with the rapture of the church and the subsequent horrors of the Tribulation.

A. IT IS AN AGE OF INDIVIDUAL WITNESS (1:9)

John says, *I John, who also am your brother, and companion in tribulation, and in the kingdom and patience of Jesus Christ, was in the isle that is called Patmos, for the word of God, and for the testimony of Jesus Christ.* The church will not go through the Great Tribulation, "the time of Jacob's trouble" (Jer. 30:7; Matt. 24:21; 1 Thess. 5:1-9). But it is by no means exempt from persecution. Jesus warned us, "In the world ye shall have tribulation" (John 16:33). Paul said, "We must through much tribulation enter into the kingdom of God" (Acts 14:22). The apostles were no strangers to the hatred of this world. John, writing the Apocalypse, was a prisoner on a small, rocky, inhospitable island about fifteen miles from Ephesus, having been banished there by Domitian. Rome lay to the west; Babylon, Jerusalem, and the Euphrates to the east. Patmos itself lay in the arm of the Great Sea, the Mediterranean, which figures so largely in the Apocalypse. He was a prisoner on Patmos because of his witness to the word of God and for his testimony for the Lord Jesus. This underlines the first great characteristic of the age. It is an age of individual witness.

B. IT IS AN AGE OF INSTINCTIVE WORSHIP (1:10-18)

John was not only "in the isle"; he was "in the Spirit" too. He was in the fetters of Rome, but he was also at the feet of Jesus. He was not only witnessing; he was worshiping. He says, *I was in the Spirit on the Lord's day* (1:10).

Every Christian lives in two locations. John was in the isle, and he was in the Spirit. He had a human environment and a heavenly environment. Paul wrote to the "saints and faithful brethren *in Christ* which are *at Colosse"* (Col. 1:2, italics added). The one must not be emphasized at the expense of the other. To be so taken up with being in Christ that we forget we are at Colosse is to become mystic and to embrace wrong ideas about separation. To be so concerned with being at Colosse and forget that we are in Christ is to become materialistic, with wrong ideas about sanctification. The two locations must be kept in balance. It would have been depressing indeed for John to have been in the isle had he not balanced that by being also in the Spirit.

Keep the two locations straight. A Christian was once asked if he were going to heaven. "I live there!" he said. Was he right? A workman had a little store in which he cobbled shoes. He also had an apartment upstairs over his shop. Someone asked him about his situation. "I work down here," he said, "but I live up there!" That's it! John had learned the secret of a life like that. He was "in the Spirit," living a life of instinctive worship.

Scholars differ over the expression "the Lord's day." Some think it refers to the first day of the week. Generally, however, when the Spirit wishes to refer to the first day of the week, He calls it just that. The expression here probably refers to "the day of the Lord," the great day when God will take over and settle accounts with this earth. Peter and Paul both added to the extensive body of Old Testament truth regarding that day, and now John is caught up in the spirit to that great day. We are living in "man's day" (1 Cor. 4:13), in which man is exalting himself and seeking to rule God out of His universe. The "day of the Lord" is the coming day in which man will be abased and the Lord exalted.

John heard a voice and saw a vision. *"I . . . heard behind me a great voice, as of a trumpet, Saying, I am Alpha and Omega, the first and the last: and, What thou seest, write in a book, and send it unto the seven churches which are in Asia; unto Ephesus, and unto Smyrna, and unto Pergamos, and unto Thyatira, and unto Sardis, and unto Philadelphia, and unto Laodicea. And I turned to see the voice that spake with me. And being turned, I saw seven golden candlesticks"* (1:10-11). Since "writing maketh an exact man," John paid strict attention to what he heard and saw, for he knew he had to write down the impressions he received. Note the stages through which he passed in receiving this particular vision. *I heard*, he says, *I turned* (v. 10), *I saw* (v. 12), *I fell at his feet* (v. 17). It was instinctive worship.

There follows a ninefold description of the Lord Jesus. One, He is the *unknowable One.* John saw *in the midst of the seven golden candlesticks one like unto the Son of man, clothed with a garment down to the foot* (v. 13). No wonder this book is called "the unveiling of Jesus Christ" (1:1), for veiled He is when the Revelation begins. The imperial form is hidden from the eyes of men, draped in concealing folds. Once, long centuries ago, men stripped Him of His garments and gambled for His clothes, then hung Him naked on a tree. God came down at the hour of brightest noon and flung a robe of midnight darkness around the scene. Now, in yonder glory, John sees this same Jesus clothed in a garment that conceals Him from His shoulders to His feet. It reminds us how little He is known and how little He can be known. True, He is standing in the midst of the lampstands, symbolizing the churches. But how little He is comprehended, even by those who should know Him best. John, who had pillowed his head on Jesus' breast in the upper room (John 13:23) sensed at once that this One, standing in mystery amidst the lampstands, is as far removed from him as is the finite from the infinite.

Two, He is *the unemotional One.* He was *girt about the paps with a golden girdle* (v. 13). All His emotions are rigidly restrained. It is not that He cannot feel for Adam's ruined race, that He cannot be touched with the feelings of our infirmities. It is not that at all. When He was on earth, He wept at the tomb of Lazarus, He wept over Jerusalem, and He wept in Gethsemane. He wept for an individual, for a nation, and for the entire human race. The first and last miracles of His public ministry, as recorded in John's gospel, were at a wedding and a funeral, life's gladdest and life's saddest hours. He entered into both. It is not that He is incapable of emotion, but that those emotions are divinely restrained. That is the significance of the golden girdle. He is about to enter into judgment with the world, and He must be swayed by neither pity nor passion. For similar reasons, we blindfold justice and set her high, carved in polished stone, with scales in one hand and an upraised sword in the other. Justice must be impassive, imperial, impartial, impervious to all but truth.

Three, He is the *unimpeachable One*. We are told that *his head and his hairs were white like wool, as white as snow* (v. 14). Isaiah suggests the significance of this. "Though your sins be as scarlet, they shall be as white as snow; though they be red like crimson, they shall be as wool" (Isa. 1:18). He knows what sin and temptation are, for He has stooped beneath the weight of a whole world's sin.

The enterprising mariners who ventured first from the shelter of the shore to steer their flimsy vessels out of sight of land were haunted by many superstitious fears. One of those was the legendary lodestone mountain that had the power, they thought, to seize a vessel against all the tug of wind and tide and draw it to destruction on its shores. Sin is a lodestone mountain. We feel ourselves drawn by that mountain, against all the counter pull of effort and resolve, until we are shipwrecked on its shores. But sin was not attractive to Jesus when He came. He had a human nature; His body was made of clay. He was of the same mold and metal as mankind, but His nature was unfallen and divine. Sin did not attract Him; it repelled Him. The devil tried hard enough, long enough, and often enough to tempt Him into sin, but all in vain. There was nothing in Him to respond. "The prince of this world cometh," He said, "and hath nothing in me" (John 14:30). He was unimpeachable. And so John saw Him, the purity within gleaming like virgin snow in a crown of glory on His brow (Prov. 16:31).

Four, He is *the undeceivable One*. John says *his eyes were as a flame of fire* (v. 14). Fire burns and bores its way into the heart of the toughest timber and can even melt the strongest steel. The ancients knew no hiding place from the searching power of heat and flame. His eyes are as a flame of fire, and they flash with holy anger as He sees the wreck and ruin that sin has made of earth. When He was here before, His kind but searching glance could scan the very wounds that shame would hide. "When thou wast under the fig tree, I saw thee," He said to Nathanael (John 1:48). "Come, see a man, which told me all things that ever I did," said the woman at the well (John 4:29). "And Jesus knew their thoughts," said Matthew, regarding the Pharisees (Matt. 12:25). John sees His eyes now burning like fire as He sweeps the globe with His glance, seeing all.

Five, He is *the undeterrable One*. Says John, *his feet [were] like unto fine brass, as if they burned in a furnace* (v. 15). Once the serpent's fangs fastened on those feet, but now like red-hot bronze they will trample on the serpent's head and crush him and all his works forever. He is undeterrable. Nothing can stand in His way. It was the same when He lived on earth. He wended His way with unhurried calm up that skull-shaped hill to die and then went down to the netherworld to claim that world as His as well. Then, out from the grave He walked, past terror-stricken guards, through rock and

stone. No priest or prelate dared say Him nay, nor could the iron might of
Rome throw cordons in His path. In a not too distant day, those feet of
burnished bronze will rend asunder Olivet (Zech. 14:4).

Six, He is *the unanswerable One.* We are told that *his voice [was] as the
sound of many waters* (v. 15). Imagine arguing with Niagara Falls! Imagine
standing at the foot of the falls with some 12 million cubic feet of water
roaring down each minute and trying to argue with a thunderous voice like
that! A mighty waterfall pours out its thundering sound with a deafening roar,
unmoved alike by the apathy, the animosity, or the admiration of those that
hear.

One of the great mysteries of the present age is the silence of God. It is
not the silence of indifference; it is the silence of great sabbatic rest. Sir Robert
Anderson says, "When faith murmurs, and unbelief revolts, and men challenge
the Supreme to break that silence and declare Himself, how little do they
realize what that challenge means! It means the withdrawal of the amnesty; it
means the end of the reign of grace; it means the closing of the day of mercy
and the dawning of the day of wrath."[3] One day that voice "as the sound of
many waters" will break the silence with a roar, and all voices raised in angry
protest will be silenced, drowned out by His.

Seven, He is *the unparalleled One.* John says *he had in his right hand
seven stars* (v. 16). These stars are "the angels of the seven churches" (v. 20).
The symbolism suggests One who has complete control over all forces, known
and unknown, natural and supernatural, seen and unseen, that shape the
destinies of men. He holds these forces in His right hand, the hand of power.
The things that overtake us are not overlooked by Him; they are overruled by
Him. It is not that He is careless, for the hand that holds the stars still bears
the scars of Calvary's nails. He knows the searing pain of hammer, nail, and
wood. It is not that He is careless, but that He is in control. We will understand
it better bye and bye.

Eight, He is *the unconquerable One.* John says that *out of his mouth
went a sharp twoedged sword* (v. 16). The sword is the Word of God, "quick
and powerful" and piercing "even to the dividing asunder of soul and spirit,
and of the joints and marrow" and discerning "the thoughts and intents of the
heart" (Heb. 4:12). Nothing can stand before God's Word. Ten times in Genesis 1
we read, "And God said." Worlds sprang into space, darkness fled, the earth
arose and flung back the sea, life forms appeared in countless multitude. When
the Word was made flesh (John 1:14), demons, disease, and death fled. Whether it is the Word going forth to replenish the earth as in Genesis 1, or to
redeem the earth as in the days of His flesh, or to reclaim the earth as here in

---

3. Sir Robert Anderson. *Silence of God* (Grand Rapids: Kregel, 1965), p. 146.

this majestic scene, the result is always the same. Whether as Creator, Comforter, or Conqueror that mighty Word is invincible.

Last of all, He is *the unapproachable One*. John says *his countenance was as the sun shineth in his strength* (v. 16). Saul of Tarsus saw it and was blinded (Acts 9:3-7). When Jesus lived on earth, He was the most approachable of men. Little children could come to Him. Zaccheus the publican could come; Nicodemus the statesman could come; Simon the leper could come; the poor, lost woman of the streets could come. But no longer! We cannot look upon the sun shining in its strength; still less can we approach it. One pound of heat can raise twenty million tons of rock by twenty-five hundred degrees centigrade and turn it into incandescent lava. The sun is losing weight by radiation at the rate of 4,200,000 tons a second! You cannot approach a power like that. John sensed it instantly. He says, *and when I saw him, I fell at his feet as dead* (v. 17).

The character of the age is one of instinctive worship. John is in the Spirit, and he is at the feet of Jesus, the same gracious Savior he had known so well, although terrible now in His glory. John says, *"And he laid his right hand upon me, saying unto me, Fear not; I am the first and the last: I am he that liveth, and was dead; and, behold, I am alive for evermore, Amen; and have the keys of hell and of death" (vv. 17-18).* Hallelujah! What a Savior!

C. IT IS AN AGE OF INTELLIGENT WAITING (1:19-20)

There are certain *times involved in the unfolding of the divine purpose, times which only God can reveal*. This is suggested by the words *write the things which thou hast seen, and the things which are, and the things which shall be hereafter* (1:19). This seems to be a general index of the Apocalypse. Certainly it implies that there are times and seasons known only to God, now to be revealed to John. The Lord's return is always imminent, although certainly in John's day, it was not to be immediate. There must be an intelligent waiting upon God for the ripening of His purposes.

John is given to understand also that there are certain *truths involved in the unfolding of the divine program, which only God can reveal*. This is suggested by the words *The mystery of the seven stars which thou sawest in my right hand, and the seven golden candlesticks. The seven stars are the angels of the seven churches: and the seven candlesticks which thou sawest are the seven churches* (1:20). Where doubt can arise about the significance of a symbol, the Scripture itself explains it. If the meaning is not immediately clear, there must be an intelligent waiting upon God for fresh light from His Word. Sometimes that light is given at once; sometimes it takes months of study and searching and prayer before the mystery is resolved.

So then, the book begins with visions of God, particularly of God the Son. They show God in control of the course, the consummation, and the character of the age. They challenge us to witness, to worship, and to wait.

Part Two:
Visions of Grace (2:1–3:22)

I. INTRODUCTION: THE FULL CHURCH (2:1–3:22)

    A. The Churches Viewed Practically
    B. The Churches Viewed Perennially
    C. The Churches Viewed Prophetically

II. EPHESUS: THE FALLEN CHURCH (2:1-7)

    A. The Faithful Works of This Church (2:1-3)
        1. It Was Standing Up to the Task (2:1-2a)
        2. It Was Standing Up for the Truth (2:1-2b)
        3. It Was Standing Up in the Test (2:3)
    B. The Fatal Weakness of This Church (2:4-5a)
        1. The Vitality of Their Passion Was Gone (2:4)
        2. The Validity of Their Profession Was Gone (2:5a)
    C. The Forceful Warning to This Church (2:5b-7)
        1. Love Must Be Absolutely Paramount (2:5b)
        2. Love Must Be Absolutely Positive (2:6)
        3. Love Must Be Absolutely Personal (2:7)

III. SMYRNA: THE FEARFUL CHURCH (2:8-11)

    A. The False Trend at Smyrna (2:8-9)
        1. What Was Favorably Accented at Smyrna (2:8-9)
        2. What Was Foolishly Accepted at Smyrna (2:9)
    B. The Fiery Trial at Smyrna (2:10a)
        1. The Human Level of the Trial—Its Misery
        2. The Satanic Level of the Trial—Its Mystery
        3. The Divine Level of the Trial—Its Ministry
    C. The Final Triumph at Smyrna (2:10b-11)
        1. Sharing in Christ's Cross (2:10b)
        2. Sharing in Christ's Crown (2:10b-11)

IV. PERGAMOS: THE FALTERING CHURCH (2:12-17)

A. The Faithful Christians in This Church (2:12-13)
1. Their Loyalty to the Lord's Person (2:13*a*)
2. Their Loyalty to the Lord's Precepts (2:13*b*)
B. The False Creeds in This Church (2:14-15)
1. The Doctrine of Balaam (2:14)
2. The Doctrine of the Nicolaitanes (2:15)
C. The Fearful Crisis in This Church (2:16-17)
1. How the Lord Warned the Church (2:16)
2. How the Lord Wooed the Church (2:17)

V. THYATIRA: THE FALSE CHURCH (2:18-29)

A. What the Lord Detected About This Church (2:18-19)
1. What He Emphasized About His Person (2:18)
2. What He Emphasized About His People (2:19)
B. What the Lord Detested About This Church (2:20-23)
1. The Source of the Heresy (2:20*a*)
2. The Seriousness of the Heresy (2:20*b*)
3. The Stubbornness of the Heresy (2:21)
4. The Suppression of the Heresy (2:22-23)
C. What the Lord Determined About This Church (2:24-29)
1. The Overseer and His Fellows (2:24-25)
2. The Overcomer and His Future (2:26-29)

VI. SARDIS: THE FRUITLESS CHURCH (3:1-6)

A. The Notable Reputation of This Church (3:1-2)
1. The Church Is Fully Weighed by the Lord (3:1*a*)
2. The Church Is Found Wanting by the Lord (3:1*b*-2)
B. The Needed Reformation in This Church (3:3-6)
1. The Call for a Remembrance by This Church (3:3)
2. The Call to a Remnant in This Church (3:4-6)

VII. PHILADELPHIA: THE FEEBLE CHURCH (3:7-13)

A. The Call to Behold (3:7-11)
1. All Saints Are Under His Control (3:7-8)
2. All Sinners Are Under His Control (3:9)
3. All Situations Are Under His Control (3:10-11)
B. The Call to Behave (3:12-13)
1. The Divine Initiative (3:12)
2. The Divine Invitation (3:13)

VIII. LAODICEA: THE FASHIONABLE CHURCH (3:14-22)

A. The Dynamic Christ (3:14)
   1. He Is the All-Conquering One (3:14a)
   2. He Is the All-Convicting One (3:14b)
   3. He Is the All-Controlling One (3:14c)
B. The Deluded Church (3:15-17)
   1. Its Sickening Compromise (3:15-16)
   2. Its Sickening Complacency (3:17)
C. The Definite Choice (3:18-19)
D. The Dual Challenge (3:20-22)
   1. To Sinners in the Congregation (3:20)
   2. To Saints in the Congregation (3:21-22)

Part Two:

Visions of Grace (2:1–3:22)

I. INTRODUCTION: THE FULL CHURCH (2:1–3:22)

A. THE CHURCHES VIEWED PRACTICALLY

There are three ways to view the letters to the seven churches. The first method is basic. First and foremost, these are letters dictated by the risen Lord to seven literal churches in western Asia Minor toward the end of the first century of the Christian era. The letters contain a wealth of local allusion and color. *The formal church,* Ephesus, was located in a city that was once the chief port of Asia Minor. Its harbor was given to change because of its continual silting. What was water became land; what was land became water. This shifting character of the city is reflected in the Lord's letter for the Ephesian assembly. Once so strong in its love for Him, Ephesus is seen by Him as shifting away.

Smyrna was *the fearful church.* Smyrna itself claimed to be the birthplace of Homer, and its coins bore his image. It was a wealthy commercial city renowned for its faithfulness to Rome. The Lord's letter underlines the faithfulness as well as the fearfulness of the Smyrnan believers. The name of the city reflects the word *myrrh,* an aromatic spice that gives forth its fragrance when crushed and bruised, hence the reference by the Lord to suffering. In 600 B.C., the city was destroyed by the Lyddians, and for four centuries its name was lost to history. Ultimately it was restored and became again an autonomous Greek city. It was also practically obliterated by an earthquake, but again it revived. It "was dead, and is alive." The Lord refers to Himself in this letter as the One who *was dead, and is alive.*

Pergamos was *the faltering church.* The city of Pergamos has been described as a combination of a pagan cathedral city, a university town, and a royal residence. It was famous for its medical center and for its magnificent pagan temples. The temple dedicated to Asklepios, the god of medicine, was renowned. The most conspicuous object in this temple was a wreathed serpent, the symbol of medicine even yet. Asklepios was often referred to as "savior." It might be this fact that caused the Lord to refer to Pergamos as the place of Satan's throne, "where Satan dwelleth." On the other hand, the reference may be to the enormous altar of Zeus, which dominated the city and which could be seen for miles. This altar was one of the seven wonders of the ancient world.

In 133 B.C., Attalus III bequeathed the city to the Roman Empire. It was the first city to build a temple to the divinity of Julius Caesar (29 B.C.).

The Lord refers to Himself in this letter as *he which hath the sharp sword with two edges* (2:12). In Roman thinking, the sword was the symbol of the highest order of official authority invested in the proconsul of Asia. The "right of the sword" *(jus gladii)* was similar to the power of life and death. The governors of provinces were divided into a higher and a lower class, according to whether or not they were invested with this power. The Lord wears this symbol of supreme authority.

Reference is also made to a white stone. This may refer to the custom of marking days of festivity by a white stone and days of calamity with a black stone. Or it may refer to the custom in a court of law of marking the guilt of a person with a black stone and the acquittal of the accused with a white stone. Some see in the white stone a reference to the *tessera,* a white stone given to those invited to partake of a sacred feast within the temple precincts.

Thyatira was *the false church.* Thyatira itself was once a great military city. It was built by Seleucus I to guard the mouth of a long pass between the Hermus and Caicus valleys. Its tutelary god was Tyrimnas, depicted as a warrior armed for battle with a great two-edged axe. To the church in this city, the Lord depicts Himself as the One with flaming eyes and feet of military bronze. At this period in history, Rome ruled the nations with a rod of iron, smashing to pieces any kingdom which dared oppose her might. The Lord promises the overcomer authority to rule the nations with power greater far than that of either Rome or Tyrimnas.

Sardis was *the fruitless church.* The city was once the capital of Lydia, seat of the fabulously wealthy Croesus. Looked at from a little distance to the north in the open plain, Sardis had a haughty, unconquerable aspect, dominating the majestic, broad valley of the Hermus from its stronghold on a steep spur that stood out in bold relief from the great mountains on the south. But close at hand, the hill was obviously nothing but mud, slightly compacted, crumbling under the influences of the weather, ready to tumble from the slightest disturbance. It was an appearance without reality, an outward show of strength undermined by neglect and careless confidence. The history of Sardis had been one of glory, yet it was a glory tarnished by unreliability and failure. Twice during its history it had fallen to plundering enemies because of its lack of watchfulness. Likewise, the church at Sardis is characterized by the Lord as having a great name for being alive, whereas actually it was dead.

In Roman times it was the common practice for cities to keep a roll of its citizens. Unworthy citizens had their names erased from the register; those who performed some exploit had their names written in gold. A hint of this is seen in the Lord's promise to the overcomer not to erase his name from the book of life.

Philadelphia was *the feeble church.* The city was founded by Attalus, king of Pergamos, who intended to make Philadelphia a center of Greco-Asiatic civilization and a means of spreading the Greek language and customs in the eastern part of Lydia and Phrygia. It was a missionary city, founded to promote a unity of spirit, customs, and loyalty within the realm. It was a successful teacher. Before A.D. 19 the native tongue had ceased to be spoken in Lydia, and Greek was the only language of the country. The church in Philadelphia was a missionary-minded one, dedicated to the spread of the gospel.

Philadelphia commanded a key situation on the main line of communication between Rome and the central plateau of Asia Minor. Its strategic location made it possible for it to open or to close these lines of communication. The Lord reveals Himself in the letter to Philadelphia as *he that hath the key of David, he that openeth, and no man shutteth; and shutteth, and no man openeth* (3:7).

Twice during the first century the city was renamed, once in honor of Tiberius and once in honor of Vespasian. The Lord said of the church at Philadelphia that it had not denied His name.

Laodicea was *the fashionable church.* The city was renowned for its prosperity. More than once the city recovered itself from disaster without seeking imperial aid. When destroyed by an earthquake in A.D. 62 in the days of Nero, it declined the offer of help from the imperial government, boasting that it had need of nothing. Laodicean bankers were famous, even in Rome. They had the reputation of never adulterating the gold they issued to their clients. Laodicea was noted, too, for its raven-colored wool. It boasted a medical school and was renowned for the manufacture of a special eye ointment. All these things are reflected in the Lord's words to the church at Laodicea. The wealthly, boastful believers were instructed to buy from the Lord gold, tried in the fire, to anoint their eyes with eyesalve, and to acquire from Him raiment of purest white.

Primarily, then, the letters to the seven churches are historical and must be studied in that light. Some of the churches needed rebuking, some a word of encouragement, some a terse warning from the Lord. In each there is a word to the overcomer.

In each letter, distinctive features of His glory, as described in chapter 1, are chosen by the Lord and are applied to the spiritual condition of the church addressed. Ephesus, the formal church, is reminded of the *presence* of the Lord (*he that holdeth the seven stars in his right hand, who walketh in the midst of the seven golden candlesticks,* 2:1). Smyrna, the fearful church, is reminded of the *position* of the Lord (He is *the first and the last, which was dead, and is alive,* v. 8). Pergamos, the faltering church, is reminded of the *possession* of the Lord (He has *the sharp sword with two edges,* v. 12). Thyatira, the false church, is reminded of the *perception* of the Lord (He has *eyes like unto a flame of fire, and his feet are like fine brass,* v. 18). Sardis, the fruitless church, is reminded of the *power* of the Lord (He is the one with *the seven Spirits of God and the seven stars,* 3:1). Philadelphia, the feeble church, is reminded of the *prerogative* of the Lord (He *openeth, and no man shutteth; and shutteth, and no man openeth,* v. 7). Laodicea, the fashionable church, is reminded of the *Person* of the Lord (He is *the Amen, the faithful and true witness, the beginning of the creation of God,* v. 14).

B. THE CHURCHES VIEWED PERENNIALLY

The conditions existing in the seven churches of Asia Minor that were selected by the Lord to receive these letters are conditions that have always existed in local churches. The letters are relevant in all ages of the church's sojourn on earth. There have always been churches needing the message addressed to Ephesus, for example. There have always been churches facing persecution as at Smyrna or the inroads of worldiness as at Pergamos, false doctrine as at Thyatira, and tradition or lukewarmness as at Laodicea.

Ephesus sets before us the issue of *fundamentalism.* The picture is that of a church busy and outwardly sound but notably lacking in love, especially in love for Christ.

In Smyrna, the perennial problem to be faced is *ritualism.* Mention is made of "the synagogue of Satan" and of a deliberate Judaizing of Christianity. Judaism ended at Calvary when God rent the Temple veil. To attempt to clothe the church in the tattered remnants of a dead religion is roundly condemned throughout the entire New Testament. The tendency is bluntly called satanic.

The problem at Pergamos is *clericalism,* setting up a separate caste in the church to officiate in matters religious. This seems to have been at the root of Nicolaitanism. That which was called a deed in the letter to Ephesus is accepted as a doctrine at Pergamos.

Thyatira confronts the issue of *sacerdotalism.* The reference to Jezebel points us back to the Old Testament tyrant who officially introduced the abominations of Baal-worship, together with its idolatries, cruelties, and priestcraft, into Ahab's kingdom.

In Sardis the perennial problem is *liberalism.* Sardis had a great reputation as a live, dynamic, successful church, but it was actually dead. Great truths entrusted to the church had been forsaken and forgotten. Works are emphasized but, divorced from the truth, are unsatisfactory to God.

In Philadelphia we see the existence of *revivalism* in the church. Philadelphia represents the greatest recovery in the church since apostolic times. For this church the Lord has nothing but praise. The church is the very picture of revival. Throughout history the church has waxed and waned just as the moon does. It has known times of gradual decline even to the point where nothing but a remnant has remained—the Waldensians in one age, the Huguenots in another, the Lollards in another, the Anabaptists in yet another. Then, at times, the Spirit of God has visited the church with revival, and its light has waxed until the earth has been flooded with its rays, and darkness and superstition have fled.

At Laodicea we see *materialism,* another of the church's perennial problems. It has ever been the enemy's tactic to seduce the church when he could not subdue her. Whenever the church has ridden the crest of material affluence, its spiritual influence has been drowned.

C. THE CHURCHES VIEWED PROPHETICALLY

Many have seen in the letters to the seven churches a prophetic anticipation of the church's history from the close of the apostolic age to the end of the dispensation of grace. Each of the seven letters is seen as representing a different phase of that history.

We have *the post-apostolic church* reflected in the letter to Ephesus, particularly in the phrase "thou art fallen" (2:5). Even in apostolic times, a gradual cooling toward the Lord was evident. The drive, the dynamic that characterized the early years, was replaced by a more staid and settled form of Christianity. The church rested on her oars and began to drift. It tolerated trends and teachings that called forth urgent letters from Paul, Peter, John, and Jude, demanding a restoration of the gold standard in matters of belief and behavior.

The letter to Smyrna brings into focus *the persecuted church.* This is crystalized in the statement "tribulation ten days" (2:10). There were ten distinct outbursts of persecution under the pagan Caesars (Nero, A.D. 54; Domitian, 81; Trajan, 98; Adrian, 117; Septimus Severus, 193; Maximin, 235; Decius, 249; Valerian, 254; Aurelian, 270; and Diocletian, 284). The final outbreak lasted ten years. All former persecutions of the faith were forgotten in the horror of the last and greatest—the tenth wave of that storm obliterated all traces that had been left by others. The cruelty of Nero, the fears of

Domitian, the dislike of Marcus, the plans of Decius, the intrigues of Valerian—all fell into obscurity when compared with the concentrated terrors of
that final struggle resulting in the destruction of the old Roman Empire and
the establishment of the cross as the symbol of the world's hope. Eusebius was
a witness of this persecution. According to him, even the wild beasts refused at
last to attack the Christians, the bloody swords became dull and shattered, the
executioners grew weary; but the Christians went singing to their deaths with
hymns of praise, thanksgiving, and worship on their lips.

   The patronized church is brought into focus in the letter to Pergamos.
The phrase "the doctrine of Balaam" sums up what happened. Balaam was an
Old Testament prophet who taught Balak to unite the men of Israel with the
women of Moab. "If you cannot curse them, then corrupt them" was the
essence of his doctrine.

   In the history of the church, this had its counterpart. The young Constantine, a fugitive from the Roman court, was hailed by the army as emperor. He
sailed from Britain, marched over the Alps and, under the banner of the cross,
conquered Maxentius at Milvan Bridge near Rome. Constantine repealed the
persecution edicts of the former emperors and placed Christians in high positions in the empire. He generally corrupted Christianity with his patronage and
began that unholy marriage between church and state that effectively destroyed the church's proper character and wrecked its testimony.

   In the letter to Thyatira we have a forecast of *the papal church*. The
phrase "that woman Jezebel" (2:20) gives the clue to this. Jezebel was a pagan
woman married to one of Israel's worst and weakest kings. She became the
secret power behind the throne. In fact, the first instance in Scripture of the
secular arm being used to persecute the true people of God is in connection
with Jezebel. She made a priest-ridden paganism the national religion and filled
Israel with her idolatries and immoralities.

   Not long after the reign of Constantine, Rome became the effective center
of church affairs, and the Dark Ages of church history began. Corruption and
wickedness in the professing church rose to such height that the infidel
historian Gibbon could write, "The history of the church is the annals of hell."
The church became the home of heathendom. Pagan feast days became Christian festivals; pagan gods became Christian saints; pagan rituals received new
life as Christian rites; and pagan priests and nuns became the ordained servants of the church. In short, paganism was baptized and incorporated into
Christianity.

   In Sardis we have a prophetic glimpse of *the Protestant church*. The very
essence of Protestantism is summed up in the words "a name that thou livest,
and art dead" (3:1). The Reformation was brought in by godly and gifted men.
The names of Wycliffe, Hus, Luther, Melancthon, Zwingli, Knox, and Calvin

became household words. The new movement, however, was scarcely under way before it began to lean on the arm of princes and its impetus died out. There are things that remain, but the present state of Protestantism is largely one of utter deadness.

The practical church is seen in the letter to Philadelphia. The phrase "an open door" (3:8) epitomizes the period. It suggests the era of revivals and missions. Men like John and Charles Wesley, Moody and Finney, Carey, Livingston, Taylor, and Judson mark this period. God brought the church back to Himself and then thrust it forth to reach a lost world.

The present-day church is seen in Laodicea. Its character is summed up in the word "lukewarm" (3:16). Neither cold nor hot, neither one thing nor the other, it is a nauseating mixture of things. The present-day church is wealthy, worldly, and riddled with compromise, cults, and carnality. The Lord is outside the whole thing, calling to individuals to respond and to separate themselves unto Him. This church is to be spewed out of the Lord's mouth. This is exactly what will happen when, at His coming, the true church is caught up to be with Him and the apostate church is left behind.

The first four stages described above are successive; one gives place to the other. From the fourth to the end they are contemporaneous; each stage comes into existence after the one before, but each one runs on side by side to the end.

Those who wish to study the prophetic aspect of the seven churches further might wish to read Church History by Andrew Miller (re-published by Scripture Truth, Fincastle, Va.). The author takes the letters to the seven churches as his text and uses them as the basis for his fascinating, fact-filled, full-length study of the Christian church.

II. Ephesus: The Fallen Church (2:1-7)

The church at Ephesus is the only church in the New Testament to which two apostles addressed letters. When Paul wrote to Ephesus, it was the climactic church of the day. Of all the truths revealed through Paul, none excel the truths revealed in the epistle to the Ephesians. There are two notable prayers in that epistle. In the first, Paul prays that the Ephesians might have more light, and in the second he prays that they might have more love. "That ye, being rooted and grounded in love, May be able to comprehend with all saints what is the breadth, and length, and depth, and height; And to know the love of Christ; which passeth knowledge" (Eph. 3:17-19). When John wrote to Ephesus, it was the crisis church of the day. *I have somewhat against thee,* said the Lord, *thou hast left thy first love* (2:4). The furnace was still there, but the fire had gone out. There was still a measure of warmth, but the coals no longer had a bright, red luster; they had merely a dull and dying glow. With

that slow but certain cooling of passion for Christ, distance had crept in. Paul
wrote to the saints, John to the angel.

A. THE FAITHFUL WORKS OF THIS CHURCH (2:1-3)

Like any other fundamental church, this church was busy. It had an active
program and a full round of meetings.

1. IT WAS STANDING UP TO THE TASK (2:1-2a)

The Lord, standing in the midst of the lampstands, holding the seven stars
in His right hand, acknowledged that the church was standing up to its task.
He said, *I know thy works, and thy labour, and thy patience.* James would
never have written to Ephesus his stinging rebuke "Faith without works is
dead." This church was full of good works. It had a magnificent program.

Suppose you had attended this church one Sunday morning as a visitor
from Corinth, Jerusalem, or Rome. You have just joined, at an early morning
hour, with the other believers in the Communion service. Now brother Tychi-
cus rises to give the announcements for the week. They might go something
like this: "Immediately after this service will be a prayer meeting. The sisters
will meet in the annex next door, the brethren will meet on the patio outside.
At eleven o'clock the family Bible hour will begin, and the Sunday School
division of the family hour will meet in the school of Tyrannus across the
street. The adults will meet here. The gospel will be preached this morning by
our brother Alexander from Cyrene. Our aged brother is the son of the well-
known Simon who carried the cross for our Lord and who joined in Paul's
original commendation to the mission field. We are privileged to have our
brother Alexander with us today. He will also speak tonight at the evening
service at seven P.M.

"This afternoon at 2:30 there will be a street meeting to be conducted
outside the Temple of Artemis. Christians in the fellowship will recall that this
weekend brings many pilgrims to Ephesus to partake in the pagan festival of
Artemis. We suggest that those who, like Gideon's twenty-two thousand, are
afraid to get involved, should stay home. We only want those who are activated
by holy boldness to attend.

"The young people's meeting will convene at 4:30 P.M. Brother Simon Ben
Joseph from Jerusalem will be giving an illustrated talk on the Holy Land.
There will be a choir practice after the service this evening. Brother David ben
Korah has written a new Christmas cantata. All choir members should make a
special effort to attend since parts for this cantata are to be assigned this
afternoon.

"The tract club will meet in the home of brother Hermes tomorrow night.
A new tract has been received from brother Marcellus of Rome. All who can

wield a pen will be needed to begin making copies of this tract for distribution. The weekly prayer meeting will be held Tuesday evening. We need to pray earnestly for the activities of this church. Last week attendance at the prayer meeting was very poor. The weekly Bible class meets one hour after sundown on Wednesday evening. We are studying the apostle Paul's epistle to the Romans. Those who possess a copy of this scroll are requested to bring it to the meeting.

"There will be an elders' meeting at the close of the Bible class. All elders should make a special effort to be present. We are going to have an interview with James of Antioch who claims to be an apostle. A deacons' meeting will be held at the same time to consider the proposal that we install some new pews in the auditorium. The ladies' Dorcas meeting will be held this week in the home of sister Phoebe. The sisters are sewing for brother Gaius and his family serving the Lord in Egypt.

"The youth challenge rally will be held Saturday near Bonfire Square. We are expecting young people to be with us from Sardis, Thyatira, and Philadelphia. The youth challenge speaker will be our honored brother Fortunatus, who was recently condemned to die in the arena at Rome but who was reprieved at the last moment. There will be a potluck fellowship supper on Saturday. The sisters will see my wife about the food. Let us try to bring our unsaved friends and neighbors to that supper. There will be a testimony meeting after the meal.

"I think that is all the announcements. Oh, what's that, my dear? Yes! I should have mentioned that there will be a baptism class for new Christians after the prayer meeting on Tuesday evening."

The church at Ephesus was standing up to the task. It was busy. There was plenty of activity, but there was no blessing. When Paul wrote to the Thessalonians, he could commend their work of faith, their labor of love, and their patience of hope (1 Thess. 1:3). The church at Ephesus had works, labor, and patience, but it had lost the faith, the hope, and the love.

2. IT WAS STANDING UP FOR THE TRUTH (2:2b)

The believers at Ephesus repudiated *moral evil*. The Lord wrote, *I know . . . how thou canst not bear them which are evil.* The kind of thing that took place at Corinth would not have been tolerated at Ephesus. No man who was unscrupulous in business, impure in his conversation, known to be living in immorality, habitually intoxicated, given to fits of rage, unfaithful to his pledges, or convicted of lying would have lasted in the Ephesian fellowship. He would have been judged and excommunicated with due dispatch. True, there would be a certain hardness in the procedure, but high standards of discipline would be maintained.

The believers at Ephesus repudiated *ministerial evil*. The Lord said, *I know . . . thou hast tried them which say they are apostles, and are not, and hast found them liars.* People showing up at Ephesus with high-sounding claims to ministerial position met with short shrift. Even Paul would have needed a letter of commendation to be received at Ephesus! False doctrine, at least along certain lines, did not dare to rear its head.

    3. *IT WAS STANDING IN THE TEST (2:3)*

The Lord has one more thing to commend. He says, *Thou . . . hast borne, and hast patience, and for my name's sake hast laboured, and hast not fainted.* It was not at all easy going at Ephesus. The believers came in for their share of opposition and criticism from the world. But they did not give up easily. They kept on year after year, despite lack of fruit and poor results. They may not have been very fruitful, but they were certainly faithful. They struggled on, and God commended them for it.

    B. THE FATAL WEAKNESS OF THIS CHURCH (2:4-5*a*)

When Paul wrote to Ephesus, he reminded the believers of their exalted position in Christ. "You are risen," he said. Quickened together with Christ! Raised with Christ! Seated in the heavenlies in Christ! That was their position. John simply says, "Thou art fallen."

    1. *THE VITALITY OF THEIR PASSION WAS GONE (2:4)*

I have somewhat against thee, because thou hast left thy first love, says the Lord. With eyes aflame, the Lord says that one large debit consumed all their credit. The spiritual coin of poor insolvent Ephesus never saw the mint of love. It is possible to serve the Lord for a variety of motives—for the praise of men, for prestige or position, for the sake of reputation, because it is simply the thing to do, because of a sense of duty. If service for God is not born of a devoted passion for the Lord Jesus it is worthless.

    2. *THE VALIDITY OF THEIR PROFESSION WAS GONE (2:5a)*

Thou art fallen. Thus, in one terse, tragic statement, the Lord sums up the problem. When Rehoboam came to the throne of Israel, he acted like the fool he was. To humble him, God allowed the Egyptians to invade Judea and to carry away as spoil the golden shields that Solomon had provided for the Temple guard. Rehoboam took the loss in his stride. He made shields of brass instead. They would do! They looked like gold. The shields would shine in the sun just the same (1 Kings 14:25-27). That is what had happened at Ephesus and what has happened to many a fundamental church. The enemy has made off with the gold of devotion, and we make do with the brass instead. "Sounding brass and tinkling cymbal" is the way Paul describes Christian duty devoid of love (1 Cor. 13:1).

    "The love of which I speak is slow to lose patience—it looks for a way of being constructive. It is not possessive: it is neither anxious to impress nor does it cherish inflated ideas of its own importance. Love has good manners and does not pursue selfish advantage. It is not touchy. It does not keep account of evil or gloat over the wickedness of other people. On the contrary, it is glad with all good men when truth prevails. Love knows no limit to its endurance, no end to its trust, no fading of its hope, it can outlast anything . . . In this life we have three great lasting qualities—faith, hope and love. But the greatest of them is love" (1 Cor. 13:4-13, Phillips*).

C. THE FORCEFUL WARNING TO THE CHURCH (2:5b-7)

Apart from repentance there can be only one end. The testimony of the church will have to be extinguished. The lamp will be allowed to go out.

1. LOVE MUST BE ABSOLUTELY PARAMOUNT (2:5b)

The Lord warns the Ephesian church, **Repent, and do the first works; or else I will come unto thee quickly, and will remove thy candlestick out of his place, except thou repent.** No love, no light is the rule. Love is to be paramount; nothing less will do. If there is no real love for the Lord Jesus, the reason for the assembly's existence has vanished. A local church that is functioning without love for the Lord is worse than useless. It gives a wrong impression of what Christianity is all about, and it is best removed.

2. LOVE MUST BE ABSOLUTELY POSITIVE (2:6)

The Lord, even while reproving, has a further commendation to make. **This thou hast, that thou hatest the deeds of the Nicolaitanes, which I also hate.** Love must be a positive emotion; theirs was a negative emotion at best. Their love for the Lord, such as it was, manifested itself in a hatred of evil. All too often those who have forgotten how to love specialize in hating error. Error must be hated, of course, but there is something wrong when the Lord has to endorse the negative because he cannot find the positive. Even the endorsement He does give comes almost as an afterthought.

3. LOVE MUST BE ABSOLUTELY PERSONAL (2:7)

The Lord saw the corporate Ephesian church in a fallen condition. He appeals to the individual, **He that hath an ear, let him hear what the Spirit saith unto the churches; To him that overcometh will I give to eat of the tree of life, which is in the midst of the paradise of God.** Love is a personal matter. We are saved one by one; we must be restored one by one. No hint is given that the entire Ephesian church would respond to this letter, but the hope is that individuals would. When Adam fell, he lost Paradise, and he lost access to the tree of life. Here is a fallen church. It too has lost the paradise of

*J.B. Phillips, *The New Testament in Modern English*.

bliss that comes from walking with God. The Lord's call here is a call to individual believers to get back to the daily quiet time with Himself. There is no other way to restore a lost love and a lost life. It is tragically possible to have a saved soul and a lost life.

III. Smyrna: The Fearful Church (2:8-11)

He was just three years old when his father died. It was little loss to the boy, for his father had been a killer, a bully, and a cheat. His mother took over the family trade and continued the boy's education. She murdered his step-father with a dish of poisoned mushrooms. He was reared in squalor and proved a notable son to his parents. While still young, he committed his first murder, killing a teenage boy who stood in his way and watching him die with callous indifference. He married at fifteen but soon had his wife killed. He married again and slew his second wife too. In order to marry a third time, he murdered the husband of the woman he wanted. His mother annoyed him; so he arranged her murder, first by guile, but when that was unsuccessful, without pretense. He was an ugly man with a bull neck, beetle brows, a flat nose, and a tough mouth. He had a pot belly, spindly legs, bad skin, and offensive odor. At the age of thirty-one he was sentenced to death by flogging. He fled to a dingy basement and, in the house of a slave, cut his own throat. He gave the infant church its first taste of things to come. His name was Nero. He was the first of the persecuting Caesars of Rome.

When John wrote from Patmos, Nero had come and gone. Another Caesar, Domitian, was on the throne. He was a suspicious and blasphemous tyrant. The time had come for the second round of official persecution to begin. In his second letter, John addresses a church that was soon to face the bitter hatred of the world. The church at Smyrna became the cameo of the church under fire.

A. the false trend at smyrna (2:8-9)

The Lord begins the letter by introducing Himself as the One who has already conquered death, *the first and the last, which was dead, and is alive.* Death has been robbed of its sting, the grave stripped of its power.

1. what was favorably accented at smyrna (2:8-9)

As usual, the Lord begins by accenting the positive. *I know thy works and tribulation,* He says. First he underscores *the persecution at Smyrna* and brings comfort with the words "I know!" It is encouraging, to say the least, when facing some dark hour of trial, to have a friend in a position of high authority to take you by the hand and say, "I know, I sympathize, I understand, I'm standing by you in this. You can count on me." There is no sob, no tear, no heartache, pain, or fear that the Lord does not share. He has faced life to the full, drunk its sorrows to the dregs. He knows!

Smyrna was a burning bush of a church. The saints of all ages, coming across this letter and contemplating the persecution being faced at Smyrna, have borrowed the language of Moses and said, "I will now turn aside, and see this great sight" (Ex. 3:3). Here was a company of believers who "quenched the violence of fire . . . had trial of cruel mockings and scourgings, yea, moreover of bonds and imprisonment: they were stoned, they were sawn asunder, were tempted, were slain with the sword: they wandered about in sheepskins and goatskins; being destitute, afflicted, tormented; (Of whom the world was not worthy:) they wandered in deserts and in mountains, and in dens and caves of the earth" (Heb. 11:34, 37-38). The Lord says, "I know."

The Lord next underlines *the poverty at Smyrna*. He says, *I know thy . . . poverty (but thou art rich)*. The Lord Jesus is no stranger to poverty. "He was rich, yet for your sakes he became poor, that ye through his poverty might be rich" (2 Cor. 8:9). During a time of great economic depression, a Christian who in his prosperous years had given away large sums to the Lord's work and who had been rendered destitute by the economic collapse, was asked, "Aren't you sorry now that you gave so much away?" "Oh, no," he replied, "that is all I really have." The saints at Smyrna had lost whatever material possessions they once owned, but in the sight of the Lord they were wealthy. They had invested their treasures "in heaven, where neither moth nor rust doth corrupt, and where thieves do not break through nor steal" (Matt. 6:20).

2. WHAT WAS FOOLISHLY ACCEPTED AT SMYRNA *(2:9)*

The church at Smyrna was tolerating false doctrine. The Lord says, *I know the blasphemy of them which say they are Jews, and are not, but are the synagogue of Satan.* The basic error at the core of such a trend is the error of failing to distinguish between Israel and the church. From earliest times in church history, attempts have been made to graft various forms of Judaism onto Christianity. The two systems are mutually exclusive, as Paul clearly recognized even before his conversion. That is why he persecuted the church. Yet in doctrine and in practice, the church has tolerated the alien Judaistic graft. Some wish to graft on lawkeeping; others are fascinated by ritualism and by the sacerdotalism of the Old Testament; others wish to deny any factual distinction between Israel and the church and seek to make the one an extension of the other.

The church at Smyrna was harboring some form of extreme Judaistic error. Those propagating the heresy are said to belong to the synagogue of Satan. As God has His assembly in the world, so does Satan. The enemy sets up his groups to oppose the truth and to propagate falsehood. Satan was active along two lines at Smyrna. Within the fold, he was Satan, the adversary, the one who sets up heretical teachings in opposition to the gospel. Outside the fold, he was the devil, the accuser, the forger of the lies and innuendoes that inspired the pagan persecutions.

The Lord never minimizes the seriousness of error. Some of His strongest language was directed against false religious teachers. They are called "children of the devil," "wolves in sheep's clothing," "a generation of vipers." To Smyrna, He describes the clique within the assembly as the synagogue of Satan. He says that the propagators of the error are blasphemers. That is forceful language. We must not dilute it, for error is a serious matter.

B. THE FIERY TRIAL AT SMYRNA (2:10a)

The fiery trial soon to be intensified at Smyrna is viewed in three ways: from the human, the satanic, and the divine perspectives. Each perspective emphasizes a different aspect of human suffering—its misery, its mystery, and its ministry.

1. THE HUMAN LEVEL OF THE TRIAL—ITS MISERY

The Lord says, *Fear none of those things which thou shalt suffer.* There is a natural shrinking from suffering. The Lord encourages His own to face boldly the hatred and the violent opposition of the world. History tells us that the saints of God in those days of the early church responded nobly to the challenge.

History tells of a man who, at the age of ninety-two, chose abuse and death in a dungeon rather than deny the Lord; of a fifteen-year-old boy who could be deterred by no sort of cruelty from confessing Christ; of a young woman slave who showed almost superhuman strength under the most cruel tortures and who was thrown finally in a net to a wild beast; of Polycarp, the last of the saints to have known and talked with the apostle John, who was burned at the stake. Interestingly enough, Polycarp was bishop of Smyrna. He suffered martyrdom during the reign of Marcus Aurelius.

The long history of the church has been one of constant persecution. Many of those whose names have become household words in the family of God have had to suffer severely for their faith. John Knox, for example, labored at the oar of a French ship as a galley slave at one point in his confrontation with Mary Queen of Scots. He was a man of iron who could be neither coaxed nor cowed into submission. One day when at the oar, John Knox was presented by a priest with an image of the virgin mother and was required, as a blasphemous heretic, to do it reverence. John Knox took the image in his hand and looked at it. "Mother? Mother of God?" he snorted, "This is no mother of God; this is a piece of painted wood, more fit for swimming than worship." And he pitched it overboard!

Nor is the twentieth century without its roll of martyrs. The church in all ages has suffered fiery trials. Who can calculate on the human level the misery of it? "Do not fear," says the Lord. The Lord has promised grace sufficient for every need. He does not give martyr grace until martyr time.

2. THE SATANIC LEVEL OF THE TRIAL—ITS MYSTERY

Satan detests the church and has been its inveterate enemy since the moment it burst upon his startled sight at Pentecost. He was not prepared for that. The church was a secret concealed in the heart of God from a past eternity. The church has been the object of Satan's persistent attacks from the very beginning. Saints at Smyrna were about to bear the brunt of one of his attacks. "Behold, the devil shall cast some of you into prison," says the Lord.

C. S. Lewis, in his *Screwtape Letters,* provides a flash of insight into Satan's dread and hatred of the church. He has Screwtape dictate a letter to Wormwood, a junior demon, castigating him for losing a soul to the enemy, Christ. He advises Wormwood on how to make the best of an unfortunate situation and draws his attention to the church. He suggests that he make much of some of the peculiar people who make up the local congregation—of their mannerisms, their dress, their lack of culture and finesse. Then, in a flash of honesty, Screwtape, the senior demon, admits his uneasiness about the church. He admits that it is fortunate that humans have never seen the church as she is seen by the powers of darkness, for in reality she is "spread out through all time and space, rooted in eternity, and terrible as an army with banners."[1] That, Screwtape confesses, is a sight to make the boldest tempter tremble.

Satan knows well enough the high dignity and the high destiny of the church. He sees it enthroned in heavenly places with Christ, far above all principalities and powers and every name that is named. When he is hurled from heaven to earth, from earth to the abyss, and from the abyss to the lake of fire, the church will still be enthroned on the dizzy heights from which he fell. *Behold, the devil shall cast some of you into prison,* says the Lord. There is no mystery about that. The mystery is that He who upholds the universe, who holds the seven stars in His right hand, who controls all the factors of time and space, that He permits it! That is the mystery of it.

3. THE DIVINE LEVEL OF THE TRIAL—ITS MINISTRY

God never permits the saints to suffer without a cause. In this case there are two comforting factors that show God sovereign even in Satan's permitted onslaught on the saints. First we note the divine *reason* for this fiery trial. It is simply *that ye may be tried.* The church is to be tested, the chaff to be separated from the wheat. Next we note there is a divine *restriction* to it. *Ye*

---

1. C.S. Lewis, *Screwtape Letters* (New York: Macmillan, 1961), p. 15.

shall have tribulation ten days. The exact period is marked. On the other side of the trial, the church would be stronger than ever. Tertullian, who lived in the midst of persecution, said, "The blood of the martyrs is the seed of the Church." It has been an axiom from that day to this. When Saul of Tarsus made havoc of the Jerusalem church, the saints fled far and wide, taking the gospel with them and spreading it abroad. The devil, in his blind rage against the infant church at Jerusalem, simply took the precious gospel seed, stored in the Jerusalem granary, and cast it to the four winds of heaven. Wherever it came to rest, it took root and sprang up in a mighty harvest. That is one of the ministries of persecution.

C. THE FINAL TRIUMPH AT SMYRNA (2:10b-11)

The final triumph at Smyrna was to be twofold, for Satan is never allowed to win in the end.

1. SHARING IN CHRIST'S CROSS (2:10b)

The Lord reminded this church that He Himself was once dead. Now He says, *Be thou faithful unto death.* Ease and prosperity are nowhere promised the Christian as a reward for his faith. On the contrary, he is warned to expect persecution in this hostile world. Most of us have wondered if, faced with the prospect of a speedy or a lingering death as a reward for faithfulness to Christ, we would have the strength to endure to the end. We turn the pages of history and read of the terrible things that have been done to the saints. We wonder whether we should have the fortitude and the faith to hold out. We must live for Christ today. That is the only way to guarantee that we would be able to die for Christ tomorrow.

2. SHARING IN CHRIST'S CROWN (2:10b-11)

The victorious believer is promised *enduring supremacy.* The Lord says, *Be thou faithful unto death, and I will give thee a crown of life* (2:10b). The world offers the believer death by torture, death in a thousand fiendish ways. Christ crowns him with life, with a crown that will outlast the universe itself.

The victorious believer is promised *eternal security. He that hath an ear, let him hear what the Spirit saith unto the churches; He that overcometh shall not be hurt of the second death.* The text does not say that those who fail to overcome will be hurt of the second death. That is an inference unjustified by the text. The promise is that the overcomer will *not* be hurt of the second death. We must not read into Scripture something it does not say, nor build an argument on the silence of Scripture. The promise here has to do, not with the grounds of eternal security, but with the assurance of it. Those who unflinchingly face the fire and the foe will have the blessed assurance that the death they are facing is trivial; it is the second death that men must fear, and that terrible second death will never come near them. Peter provides us with an interesting example in Acts 12:1-6. He had been arrested by Herod and condemned to death, the sentence to be executed on the morrow. Already James had been slain. His turn was next. But what was Peter doing? Was he down on his knees praying for strength to go boldly to his execution? No! Was he pacing the floor gripping his hands and resolving to face his death like a man? No! He was asleep! He was not only conqueror, he was more than conqueror. He had the blessed assurance of eternal security. Death is the gateway to life!

IV. PERGAMOS: THE FALTERING CHURCH (2:12-17)

The letter to Pergamos was addressed to a church that was drifting into worldliness and carnality. There were some who were resisting the general flow of the tide, but the majority were being swept out to sea. The application of this message to our day must be obvious. Worldliness has swept into the church. There are some who still hold to the truth of separation, but the majority are content, like Lot, to seek the best of both this world and the one to come. Martin Luther, with his resounding "Here I stand!" would be a misfit in many Christian congregations today. It is more popular to seek a comfortable compromise with the world.

A. THE FAITHFUL CHRISTIANS IN THIS CHURCH (2:12-13)

As usual, the Lord begins the letter to Pergamos with a reference to Himself and with a word of commendation. He says, **To the angel of the church in Pergamos write; These things saith he which hath the sharp sword with two edges; I know thy works.** This expression "I know thy works" occurs in all seven letters.

1. THEIR LOYALTY TO THE LORD'S PERSON (2:13a)

Loyalty to the Lord's Person was being maintained in a most difficult and dangerous place. **I know... where thou dwellest, even where Satan's seat is: and thou holdest fast my name.** Satan's seat is, in reality, his throne.

Satan's ambition from the very beginning has been to exalt his throne above the stars. That ambition brought about his fall. Satan is a created being and is therefore possessed of none of the attributes of deity. He is not *omniscient*, though he does have at his disposal an efficient organization of fallen angels and demons united in a highly functional system of espionage and obstruction. When Daniel began to pray, for example, that organization went to work to hinder and obstruct the answer (Dan. 10:12-14, 20-21). Satan is not *omnipotent*, even though he is very powerful and exerts his power through a hierarchical structure made up of thrones, dominions, principalities, powers, the rulers of this world's darkness, and wicked spirits in high places (Eph. 6:12; Col. 1:16; 2:15). Nor is Satan *omnipresent*. As a created being, he can be in only one place at a time. He appeared before the Lord in the book of Job from his wanderings to and fro across the face of the earth. He is "the prince of the power of the air" (Eph. 2:2) and, as such, no doubt has a throne somewhere in the heavenlies. He is also "the prince of this world" (John 12:31) and, as such, maintains a throne somewhere on earth. In John's day, it was at Pergamos.

Commentators suggest that the expression "where Satan's seat is" refers to the fact that Pergamos had become the center of the Babylonian mystery cult. This seems to be an inadequate explanation of the phrase. There is no reason Satan, a created being, limited to being in one place at a time, should not also have had his earthly seat at Pergamos in John's day.

The faithful Christians at Pergamos were confessing the blessed name of Jesus in the very capital city of Satan's power structure on earth. It was an especially dangerous place in which to maintain a dynamic Christian testimony. *Thou holdest fast my name*, says the Lord. That glorious, saving, sovereign name rings the changes on all the dark and dreadful passions of the pit that rage in the twisted and tormented soul of Satan! He loathes and detests the name of Jesus, for it spells out his impotence and his doom. The believers at Pergamos were loyal to the Lord's Person.

2. *THEIR LOYALTY TO THE LORD'S PRECEPTS (2:13b)*

The Lord says, *Thou . . . hast not denied my faith, even those days wherein Antipas was my faithful martyr, who was slain among you, where Satan dwelleth.* The great precepts of the Christian faith were in good hands with the faithful ones at Pergamos. The great precepts of the Lord's virgin birth, His miraculous life, His atoning death, His bodily resurrection, His ascension into glory, His coming again, those were all doctrines loyally held by the believers there.

B. THE FALSE CREEDS IN THIS CHURCH (2:14-15)

There were two false creeds in the church. There was the doctrine of Balaam. That was an outward-looking heresy, a form of neoecumenicalism that might be summed up in the statement "Let's be more relaxed in our loyalties." There was *the doctrine of the Nicolaitanes*. That was an inward-looking error, a form of new ecclesiasticism that might be summed up in the statement "Let's be more restricted in our leadership."

1. *THE DOCTRINE OF BALAAM (2:14)*

There can be no doubt about the seriousness of this heresy. *I have a few things against thee, because thou hast there them that hold the doctrine of Balaam, who taught Balak to cast a stumblingblock before the children of Israel, to eat things sacrificed unto idols, and to commit fornication.* Balaam was a picturesque individual with a reputation as a prophet, hired by King Balak to curse the children of Israel, whose forward advance he feared. Balaam is mentioned a dozen times in Scripture. He was a Gentile prophet with a most remarkable grasp of truth, a thorough knowledge of the character of God, a deep insight into the future of Israel, and he possessed a laudable desire to die the death of the righteous. His two fatal lusts were for wealth and women. He is consistently held up to us in the New Testament as an outstanding example of an apostate. The cynical maxim "Every man has his price" was certainly true of Balaam. Although warned of God not to respond to Balak's invitation, Balaam went anyway. Four times he sought to curse Israel, and each time God changed the curse into a blessing. Faced with the rising wrath of King Balak, fearing loss of his remuneration and possibly loss of liberty and life, Balaam came up with the devilish suggestion which has earned him his opprobrium in Scripture. "My lord king," he apparently suggested, "If you cannot curse these people, then corrupt them" (see Num. 22–25).

The doctrine of Balaam, as summarized by the Lord in His letter to Pergamos, was in three parts. It was characterized first by *the wisdom of this world.* We are told that he taught Balak. "If you corrupt them," he intimated, "then God will have to correct them; and if God corrects them, King Balak, you can be sure that their numbers will diminish and their threat to your kingdom will decrease. Their God is a holy and a jealous God. He will not stand by and allow them to sin against Him with impunity." Balaam taught Balak how to use the holiness of God's character for his own evil ends. Just as many today abuse the grace of God, so Balaam taught Balak how to abuse the government of God.

His doctrine was characterized also by *the worship of this world.* He taught Balak *to cast a stumblingblock before the children of Israel, to eat things sacrificed unto idols.* His philosophy was simple: involve them in idolatry, and judgment will be swift and sure. The divine hatred of idolatry and anything connected with it blazes out again and again throughout Scripture. Balaam knew enough of the true and living God to realize that any deliberate entanglement by Israel in that which God consistently calls abomination would inevitably bring retribution upon them. The divine prohibitions against involvement in the idolatrous worship of this world are clear and plain.

The fact that a large segment of the professing church has espoused idolatry makes the judgment of Christendom certain and sure. Idolatry, however, can be more subtle than the brazen worship and adoration of graven images. The doctrine of Balaam, in its broadest aspect, is to bring some object between the soul and God. It is all too easy to set up some cherished thing, some idolized person, some secret ambition, and allow that to come between us and God so that God is robbed of both worship and service.

Balaam's doctrine was characterized moreover by *the wickedness of this world.* He taught Balak to persuade Israel to commit fornication. Many of the Canaanite cults employed sexual immorality as a part of religious worship. Balak seized on the idea and, so far as Israel was concerned, with a great measure of success. The doctrine of Balaam suggests simply that the wicked practices of the world are not really sinful and can be employed as a means of gaining an end.

So then, the doctrine of Balaam was really an attack upon the standards of separation and sanctification God expected Israel to maintain. But there was yet another form of false teaching in vogue at Pergamos.

2. THE DOCTRINE OF THE NICOLAITANES (2:15)

The Lord is emphatic in His repudiation of the doctrine of the Nicolaitanes. He says, *So hast thou also them that hold the doctrine of the Nicolaitanes, which thing I hate.* The deeds of the Nicolaitanes are mentioned in the letter to Ephesus. The deeds had by now become a doctrine. What was at first tolerated as an unscriptural practice was now accepted as an unscriptural principle. There is some dispute as to what the doctrine of the Nicolaitanes was. Some think it was an immoral teaching. C. I. Scofield, on the other hand, says that the word is derived from two roots, *nikao,* "to conquer" and *laos,* "the people" or "the laity." Maintaining that there is no real authority for a sect of the Nicolaitanes, he believes that the word is symbolic and refers to the earliest form of a priestly order or clergy, which later divided an equal brotherhood into priests and laity. If that is so, then the doctrine of the Nicolaitanes and the doctrine of Balaam were complementary errors. Denying the headship of Christ was the essence of the one; defiling the members of the body was the essence of the other.

C. THE FEARFUL CRISIS IN THIS CHURCH (2:16-17)

The Lord is seen standing in the midst of the congregation at Pergamos with a two-edged sword.

1. HOW THE LORD WARNED THE CHURCH (2:16)

He comes straight to the point. *Repent; or else I will come unto thee quickly, and will fight against them with the sword of my mouth.* Notice carefully the change in the pronouns. The Lord says, "I will come unto *thee;* I will fight against *them."* The church is still His, but those who are defiling it, He disowns. Against them, in fact, He declares war. Truly the Lord knows them that are His. He knows how to separate the wheat from the chaff, the sheep from the goats.

2. HOW THE LORD WOOED THE CHURCH (2:17)

Three things marked the heresy at Pergamos—idolatry, immorality, and infidelity. The overcomer in the church kept himself from all three, and his reward is commensurate with his conduct. He *kept Himself from idolatry* and refused to eat things sacrificed to idols. To him the Lord said, "He that hath an ear, let him hear what the Spirit saith unto the churches; To him that overcometh will I give to eat of the hidden manna." The manna was angel's food, poured down from heaven in miraculous provision for the children of Israel throughout their wilderness journey. A pot of that manna was hidden by Moses in the Ark of the Covenant in the Holy of Holies of the Tabernacle. To eat of the hidden manna is to express in a symbolic way that the overcomer may feast upon Christ in the hidden place. The wicked would prefer the luxurious banquet of the world, spread with all that would appeal to carnal appetite, and which is deliberately served to insult the living God. The saint of God would prefer to be alone with the Lord enjoying spiritual food.

The overcomer *kept himself from immorality* and refused to partake in the loose living of the cult. The Lord says, *I . . . will give him a white stone.* This, surely, if nothing else, is a symbol of changeless purity. Christ is that White Stone, the "stone cut without hands," the stone of dazzling purity. The overcomer is given evidence that he has entered into a knowledge of the Lord Jesus as the victor over every defiling thing.

The overcomer *kept himself from infidelity.* The Nicolaitanes were setting up the names of men in the place of His all-sufficient name. The overcomer refused to have any part of that. The Lord, in the stone bestowed, will give the overcomer *a new name written, which no man knoweth saving he that receiveth it.* The name is secret. The overcomer and the Lord are so close that the Lord can give him a knowledge of Himself no one else can share.

Not many experience that on earth. D. L. Moody did. He had been struggling with God's will for his life. God had been calling him to citywide, nationwide evangelism, and Moody did not want that. He fought and struggled with the will of God. Then one day, as he was walking the streets of New York, wrestling with God, he surrendered. He tells us exactly where it was—on Broadway and Fifth Avenue, one of the busiest thoroughfares in the world. Moody surrendered; every link in the chain of rebellion snapped. An overwhelming sense of the presence of God filled his soul. Said Moody, "God Almighty seemed to come very near me. I felt I must be alone."

He hurried to the house of a friend and, refusing all offers of food, asked for a room where he could be alone. He locked the door and sat down. The room seemed ablaze with God. Moody dropped to the floor, bathing his soul in the presence of God and experiencing the glory of the very mount of transfiguration itself. He wrote later that God revealed Himself to him, and he had such an experience of His love that he had to ask Him to stay His hand. The clock of a nearby church chimed away the hours, but Moody did not hear. He was alone with God in a nearness, an intimacy such as he had never known possible on earth. He says of that experience that he rarely spoke of it; it was too sacred.[2] In that blessed hour, God gave to D. L. Moody a taste of what was to come—a white stone, and a new name that no man would know but he himself.

V. THYATIRA: THE FALSE CHURCH (2:18-19)

It is within the bounds of possibility that the church at Thyatira was founded through the testimony of a woman. Paul's first convert in Europe was a woman from Asia Minor, from Thyatira (Acts 16:14-15). Thyatira was famous for the manufacture of purple cloth. Lydia, living in Philippi, was engaged in selling such cloth. Could it be that after her conversion she hurried home to Thyatira with the great news? Or did she perhaps make converts of the dye salesmen who called on her? Or might she have written long letters home telling of the coming of Paul, of the demon-possessed girl, of the jailor, and of her own wholehearted conversion to Christ? We cannot say. But at least there is a possibility that the testimony of Lydia might have played a part in the *founding* of the church at Thyatira.

Be that as it may, one thing is sure. A woman played a prominent part in the *foundering* of the church at Thyatira. This church made shipwreck over the preaching, the precepts, and the practices of a woman. Some versions render the phrase "that woman Jezebel" as "thy woman Jezebel." If that reading is correct, then we could infer that the woman was the wife of the presiding elder at Ephesus. Significantly, too, she is tarred with a particularly unpleasant and dirty brush. She is called Jezebel after the wickedest woman in Old Testament times. For a woman to be called a Jezebel is every bit as bad as for a man to be called a Judas.

So there she stood. She was probably a very attractive woman, no doubt possessed of a charming personality, a most persuasive tongue, forceful ideas, and great leadership qualities. She was, it would seem, a woman who put most men in the shade. Her husband and the board of elders ate out of her hand. "That woman Jezebel!" It may not have been her real name, but it fit her like a glove.

A. WHAT THE LORD DETECTED ABOUT THIS CHURCH (2:18-19)

The letter begins as usual with the Lord making pointed reference to Himself.

2. J. C. Pollock, *Moody: A Biographical Portrait* (New York: Macmillan, 1963), pp. 90-91.

1. WHAT HE EMPHASIZED ABOUT HIS PERSON (2:18)

The Lord says, *These things saith the Son of God, who hath his eyes like unto a flame of fire, and his feet are like fine brass.* We still speak of a person's eyes flashing. There was more than enough in this church to make the Lord's eyes blaze with indignation. When we remember that the church at Thyatira epitomizes the church in history between the age of Constantine and the dawning of the great Reformation we do not wonder at His wrath. In embryo form, all the sins and excesses of that age are present at Thyatira. The Lord's eyes kindle with wrath at what He sees.

His feet were like burnished bronze. Bronze, in the Scripture, is always a symbol of judgment. As the Lord looks at Thyatira and sees what a harvest of wickedness will grow from this Satanic seed being sown by the woman Jezebel, He shoes His feet with bronze. Judgment must begin in the house of God.

2. WHAT HE EMPHASIZED ABOUT HIS PEOPLE (2:19)

Notice the emphasis on works. *I know thy works, and charity, and service, and faith, and thy patience, and thy works; and the last to be more than the first.* The emphasis was on works. Works are well and good in their proper place, but they become a deadly peril when they come between the soul and Christ. Worship, in Scripture, comes before service. The Lord says "Come" before He says "Go." The classic New Testament example is that of Martha and Mary. The Lord had to say to Martha, upset because she seemingly was left with all the work while Mary just sat at Jesus' feet, "Martha, Martha, thou art careful and troubled about many things: But one thing is needful: and Mary hath chosen that good part, which shall not be taken away from her" (Luke 10:41-42).

The Lord is looking for worship from His people. The Lord Jesus made one of the most amazing statements about this, astonishingly enough, to a Samaritan woman. He said, "God is a Spirit; and they that worship him must worship him in spirit and in truth" (John 4:24). We must worship Him in spirit because of *what He is,* and in truth because of *what we are.* "The Father seeketh such," said Jesus, "to worship him" (John 4:23). He was pursuing this amazing quest in vain at Thyatira. All He could find was dead works.

B. WHAT THE LORD DETESTED ABOUT THIS CHURCH (2:20-23)

The church at Thyatira had become a hotbed of heresy. The Lord says four things about the false teaching and the false conduct at Thyatira.

1. THE SOURCE OF THE HERESY (2:20a)

First, there was, in this church, *an indulgent permissiveness.* He says, *Thou sufferest that woman Jezebel . . . to teach.* The church had in its midst a malignant heresy that struck at the very vitals of all that was good and holy, yet indulgently tolerated it. The application of this to our day is evident.

We are living in a most tolerant age. Everyone must be allowed to "do his thing." This is the age of relativism in morals and syncretism in religion. There are no absolutes. The spirit of the age has crept into the church. To denounce a belief as heresy is to be branded intolerant. Certainly there is no room for bigotry, but to accept anything in the name of Christian charity is a spirit foreign to Scripture. The strongest language in the Bible is reserved for those who depart from revealed truth.

There was in this church, moreover, *an influential personality.* There was "that woman Jezebel." The name speaks volumes to those who know their Bibles. Old Testament Jezebel was a colorful character in more ways than one. She would spend the first part of the day putting on her war paint and the rest of the day on the warpath! Woe betide her weakling husband, Ahab, or anyone else who stood in her way. The daughter of a pagan king, she imported into Israel the very worst type of heathenism. The worship of God was swept aside and idolatry put in its place. Purity became a thing of the past, as every form of lasciviousness was exalted as a ritual of religion. Jezebel's pagan priests came down on the land like a cloud of locusts. The saints were put to the sword.

Jezebel's spiritual heir and successor was in the church at Thyatira. She was the ultimate source of all the trouble.

2. THE SERIOUSNESS OF THE HERESY (2:20b)

In allowing this woman to assume leadership in their church, the believers at Thyatira exposed themselves to a threefold error. First, they were *wrong in principle.* The Lord said, **Thou sufferest that woman Jezebel, which calleth herself a prophetess, to teach.** The New Testament principle is clear on this matter. Paul says, "But I suffer not a woman to teach, nor to usurp authority over the man, but to be in silence. For Adam was first formed, then Eve. And Adam was not deceived, but the woman being deceived was in the transgression" (1 Tim. 2:12-14). The Scripture teaches the headship of the man over the woman, something that has its roots in the order of creation itself and that is mandatory for the church.

Second, the church at Thyatira was *wrong in precept.* The Lord said of this woman that she led His servants astray. The thought is that of deception. It is interesting to observe that many of the cults have been founded or promoted by women—Spiritism, Christian Science, and Theosophy, for example. That is not to say that men have not spawned false cults, because they have. But the Scripture teaches that a woman is susceptible to error in spiritual things, and for that reason the woman is refused permission to teach in the church.

Third, the church at Thyatira was *wrong in practice.* The Lord says of the followers of Jezebel that they **commit fornication, and . . . eat things** *sacrificed unto idols.* In other words, they were guilty of the gravest sins against man and God. Both of those sins are roundly condemned in Scripture, and both bring with them the direst penalties.

3. THE STUBBORNNESS OF THE HERESY *(2:21)*

I gave her space to repent of her fornication; and she repented not says the Lord. As so often happens, the Lord's longsuffering and patience was misconstrued. Because God does not strike down wickedness the moment it rears its head, men deceive themselves and imagine that He never will. "Not knowing that the goodness of God leadeth thee to repentance" is the way Paul puts it (Rom. 2:4). God stays His hand in government solely that men might have the opportunity to repent. Apparently the woman who was causing the trouble at Thyatira, far from seeing God's hand of mercy in the absence of judgment, simply congratulated herself on her apparent success. The wickedness she was spreading went on and on.

4. THE SUPPRESSION OF THE HERESY *(2:22-23)*

It is no wonder the Lord was outraged by this church and threatened the direst judgments. Three times He peals out His sovereign "I will" in warning the church of His intentions. Three things are revealed about the Lord's ways in judgment in the enunciation of these "I wills." It is evident that He is *patient in judgment.* He says, *Behold, I will cast her into a bed, and them that commit adultery with her into great tribulation, except they repent of their deeds* (2:22). The Lord still talks about the possibility of repentance. Prophecies of doom are usually uttered in hopes that they might never have to be fulfilled. The classic example of that in Scripture is the prophecy of Jonah. The Lord would much rather pardon than punish.

Furthermore, the Lord is *practical in judgment.* He says, *And I will kill her children with death; and all the churches shall know that I am he which searcheth the reins and hearts* (2:23a). Judgment is not only disciplinary; it is exemplary. "Them that sin rebuke before all, that others may fear" (1 Tim. 5:20). The same principle will be apparent when God finally deals with Russia and her satellites for their anti-Semitism and for their organized and massive invasion of Israel in a coming day. Again and again He says, "Thus will I magnify myself, and sanctify myself; and I will be known in the eyes of many nations, and they shall know that I am the Lord" (Ezek. 38:23). There are lessons to be learned from God's actions in judgment that have a salutary effect on those who see them. The judgment on Jezebel and her associates was to be such that others would know God had acted and would mend their own ways.

Finally, the Lord is *perfect in judgment.* He says, *And I will give unto every one of you according to your works* (2:23b). In Scripture, salvation is always according to faith; judgment is always according to works. The classic passage on this is Romans 2:1-16. The Lord who knows perfectly all that we do, the underlying motives and causes of our actions, their ultimate outcome, influence, and effect, is the only one able to give perfect judgment.[3] Hannah proclaimed it in her remarkable prayer of thanksgiving, "The Lord is a God of knowledge, and by him actions are weighed" (1 Sam. 2:3). Thus it was with Belshazzar. Daniel told this arrogant king, "Thou art weighed in the balances, and art found wanting" (Dan. 5:27).

C. WHAT THE LORD DETERMINED ABOUT THIS CHURCH (2:24-29)

Not all at Thyatira were party to the wicked precepts and practices of Jezebel. The Lord distinguishes between the false and the true.

1. THE OVERSEER AND HIS FELLOWS (2:24-25)

First the Lord addresses the rank and file of the believers who stood aloof from the cult. *But unto you I say, and unto the rest in Thyatira, as many as have not this doctrine, and which have not known the depths of Satan, as they speak; I will put upon you none other burden. But that which ye have already hold fast till I come.* Apparently, things at Thyatira were too far gone for the remnant to be able to cope with the matter. The Lord does not ask the impossible. He tells the faithful remnant to keep clear of the cult with its satanic doctrines and depths and to maintain their testimony until such time as He Himself steps in. Like righteous Lot in the midst of ancient Sodom, the faithful vexed their righteous souls from day to day because of the conduct and conversation of the wicked ones in their midst. They had not been able to stem the tide. Jezebel had been too deep, too dynamic, altogether too determined for them. But they had refused to follow the crowd. They held fast to the truth, although no doubt they were mocked, maligned, and misunderstood.

2. THE OVERCOMER AND HIS FUTURE (2:26-29)

The Lord promises the overcomer at Thyatira power on earth. *And he that overcometh, and keepeth my works unto the end, to him will I give power over the nations: And he shall rule them with a rod of iron; as the vessels of a potter shall they be broken to shivers: even as I received of my Father* (2:26-27). This is the language of Psalm 2, which anticipates the day when the Lord will return to smash His foes and to set up His righteous kingdom on earth. The saints are going to have their share in that.

It is evident that those who stand for God have power with men. It was Abraham, the Hebrew, the migrant, the separated man, who had power when the kings of the east invaded and smashed the Sodomite coalition, carrying Lot into captivity. Abraham's power was acknowledged later by the king of Sodom himself (Gen. 14). Still later, when he confessed himself to the sons of Heth to

3. See John Phillips, *Exploring Romans*, rev. ed. (Chicago: Moody, 1987).

be a stranger and a pilgrim, they replied, "Hear us, my lord: thou art a mighty prince among us" (Gen. 23:6). His reputation lingered on. It is not the natural man who makes the greatest impact on this world. It is the Martin Luther, the William Carey, the David Livingstone. The world itself acknowledges the authority of men like these.

The Lord promises the overcomer power in heaven. He says, *And I will give him the morning star. He that hath an ear, let him hear what the Spirit saith unto the churches* (2:28-29). Heaven itself owns the authority of the man who stands for God. Joseph's family had to learn that the twelve stars and the twelve sheaves would bow down before Joseph. The morning star, of course, is none other than the Lord Jesus Himself. Possessing Him, we possess all. We are reminded of the Roman patrician whose wealthy father had died, leaving all he possessed to Marcellus, a slave. In his will, he stipulated that his noble son could choose one thing and one thing only from his estate. "I'll take Marcellus," said the sharp-witted son.

VI. Sardis: The Fruitless Church (3:1-6)

Astronomers tell us that the light from the polar star takes thirty-three years to reach the earth. That star could have been plunged into darkness thirty years ago, and its light would still be pouring down to earth. It would be shining in the sky tonight as brightly as if nothing had happened. It could be a dead star, shining solely by the light of a brilliant past. The church at Sardis was like that. It had a name, but it was dead. It was shining solely by the light of a brilliant past.

A. THE NOTABLE REPUTATION OF THIS CHURCH (3:1-2)

God is the Judge of all the earth. He has various scales, all finely adjusted, into which He puts men, nations, and churches in order to weigh their actions. There is a careful adjustment, for example, between the moral and spiritual spheres and the material sphere. The book of Jonah makes it quite clear that the bad weather Jonah encountered was a direct result of his bad behavior. When Adam sinned in the Garden of Eden, he upset the entire ecology of the planet. In His great monologue with Job, God underlined Job's ignorance of God's ways in the material realm and his consequent greater ignorance of God's ways in the moral and spiritual realm. God has scales for weighing men, and their movements are amazingly precise. The church at Sardis was about to be put into one of those scales.

1. THE CHURCH IS FULLY WEIGHED BY THE LORD (3:1a)

The scene is solemn as Sardis is weighed against the background of time and space. *And unto the angel of the church in Sardis write; These things saith he that hath the seven Spirits of God, and the seven stars.* In one mighty hand, the Lord held the seven spirits of God; in the other, the seven stars. The church is to be weighed against all that is implied by the sevenfold Spirit of God. It is going to be weighed and measured to see if *its holy character* can stand the test. The church is to be weighed against all that is implied by the seven stars. Does it come up to *its heavenly calling?* This church with the resounding reputation is to be put to the test. What has she done with the Holy Spirit, with the *magnificent portion* that is hers? The church was born amid the mighty rushing wind and the cloven fiery tongues of Pentecost. Is the church living up to that? And what has this church done with the *magnificent position* that is hers? Christ has seated the church in heavenly places, far above all principalities and powers. Is Sardis living up to that? Has she traded heavenly things for earthly things? Has she sold her birthright for a mess of pottage?

The church at Sardis had forgotten the magnitude of its heavenly calling. It had forgotten the magnitude of its holy character. The finest gold had become dim; the spiritual worth was gone.

2. THE CHURCH IS FOUND WANTING BY THE LORD (3:1b-2)

The evaluation of this church is summed up in one terse statement. *I know thy works, that thou hast a name that thou livest, and art dead. Be watchful, and strengthen the things which remain, that are ready to die: for I have not found thy works perfect before God.* It would seem that this church was great for starting things but not for completing them. D. L. Moody used to remark, "I would rather say, 'This one thing I do' than say, 'These forty things I dabble with.' " The church at Sardis was dabbling instead of doing. It had a dozen programs, no doubt, launched with fanfare and flourish, none of which had come to anything.

When the Voice of the Andes radio station was founded, the men who had the vision for that work asked God to give them a great oak tree, the branches of which would reach all across Latin America. Instead, God gave them an acorn and told them to watch it grow. It is far better to begin small and grow than to begin with great plans, all of which dry up and come to nothing.

At Sardis, even the things that remained were in danger and needed strengthening. The Lord was very gentle in His admonition. "A bruised reed shall he not break, and smoking flax shall he not quench" (Matt. 12:20). The bruised reed represents things that have never been of any use; and the smoking flax, the smoking lamp, represent things that have been useful but are no longer so. From the bruised reed He can make a flute from which can flow the very harmony of heaven, and from the smoking flax He can make a lamp to light the world. So the Lord touches tenderly on the problem at Sardis. Yet without the restoration, little of good could be found in this church. It was like the little girl who, required to take her birth certificate to school, lost it on the way. The janitor saw her crying and asked her what was wrong. Said the tearful little girl, "I've lost my excuse for being born!" That was Sardis.

B. THE NEEDED REFORMATION IN THIS CHURCH (3:3-6)

1. THE CALL FOR A REMEMBRANCE BY THIS CHURCH (3:3)

The Lord called for a threefold remembrance. The Lord is ever calling our wandering thoughts and affections back to Himself. His last act before He went to Calvary was to institute a feast of remembrance to draw us back to Himself again and again during our pilgrimage on earth.

John Newton, author of some of our loveliest hymns, was plagued in his unconverted days by a very treacherous memory. On three separate occasions God spoke to him, and each time he forgot. He sank lower and lower until, living a wild and dissolute life on the high seas and in the far corners of the globe, he sank so low that he actually became for a while the slave of a slave. Two women prayed for John Newton, and their prayers never ceased. They pursued him down the Spanish Main, around the Horn of Africa, across the seven seas. In fair weather and in foul, through placid calm and howling hurricane, those prayers, like the hounds of God, kept hard upon his heels. Then, suddenly, in the midst of a fearful storm, with the deck heaving beneath his feet and death grasping his shoulder, John Newton was converted. He left the sea and went into the ministry. But over the mantelpiece in his peaceful study thereafter there stood guard a significant text: "Thou shalt remember that thou wast a bondman in the land of Egypt, and the Lord thy God redeemed thee" (Deut. 15:15).

John Newton says that, after his conversion, he never could forget again. On the deck of that sinking ship, the Lord seemed to look into his very soul. He wrote:

> Sure, never till my latest breath
> Can I forget that look;
> It seemed to charge me with His death
> Though not a word He spoke.

"Remember," says the Lord to Sardis. "Remember!" First, there was to be *a remembrance of the past.* The command is clear, **Remember therefore how thou hast received and heard.** Every church is born in a time of revival, in some time of the Spirit's moving. It is only when the first movings of God are forgotten that a church settles down and becomes institutionalized. The drive, the dynamic of the former years is replaced with a more formal, ritualistic, traditionalized, stereotyped, and complacent form of activity. The movement becomes a monument. God's demand at Sardis is that the church remember its heritage.

Furthermore, there must be *a recognition of the present.* The Lord says, **Hold fast and repent.** The dynamic of former years has to become again the norm for today. The demand is for self-examination and self-judgment. Alan Redpath was staying with some friends in England. There were two young boys in the home, full of life and energy, as boys usually are. One night the parents went out to the evening meeting with their guest, leaving the boys at home. When the family returned, a deathly stillness reigned supreme in the house. They unlocked the door with a feeling of apprehension and went inside. They called the boys, but there was no answer. They went into the living room, and there on the table, gathered together in a neat little pile, were the shattered fragments of a valuable vase, mother's pride and joy. Alongside the pathetic little heap of china fragments was a note: "Dear Mum and Dad. We're terribly sorry. We knocked over the vase, and it broke. We have put ourselves to bed without any supper." Says Alan Redpath, in telling the story, "What do you think that father did? Do you think he went upstairs and hauled those boys out of bed and gave them a beating? Not a bit of it! They had passed judgment on themselves and the parents were disarmed." Remember! Repent! Keep! That is all. Then the Lord will not have to judge.

There was also to be a *readiness for the future.* The Lord warns, **If therefore thou shalt not watch, I will come on thee as a thief, and thou shalt not know what hour I will come upon thee.** The second coming of the Lord is likened to the coming of a thief (Matt. 24:43), but that does not seem to be the thought here. Here the thought is that the Lord will come suddenly upon this church, which has nothing but an empty reputation, and will break it up. A thief comes to spoil and to remove everything of value. The Lord warns this local church that if there is not self-judgment, He will come suddenly and break up the testimony once and for all. It is a remarkable fact that western Asia Minor, now Turkey, was once the brightest spot on earth for gospel witness. Today it is one of the darkest.

2. THE CALL TO A REMNANT IN THIS CHURCH (3:4-6)

The church as a whole might not heed the Lord's call, but there would always be a remnant. The Lord ever has those who refuse to bow the knee to Baal. The first thing about the remnant at Sardis worthy of note is that they were *a virtuous remnant.* The Lord acknowledges, **Thou hast a few names even in Sardis which have not defiled their garments; and they shall walk with me in white: for they are worthy** (3:4). We are reminded of that stirring scene in heaven when God looks for a man worthy to take the book, open its seals, and rule the world (Rev. 4-5). Not a single one can be found until the Lord Himself steps forward, and then all heaven rings with praise. The slumbering echoes of the everlasting hills awake as the cry rings out, "Thou art worthy!" Here this worthy One is looking at the saints assembled at Sardis. He sees one here, one there, a faithful few, who are worthy. They are the aristocracy of heaven.

An old French count was reduced, by the spendthrift character of his ancestors, to living in a common lodging house in Paris. It was the haunt of nefarious notables of the underworld, of burglars, murderers, and the like. Many a time they tried to get the old gentleman to join them in their lawless enterprises. To all their temptations the old gentleman would reply, as he pulled himself up to his full height, "Excuse me, gentlemen, *noblesse oblige.* Privilege has its responsibilities. You see, I am a French count. If I were to join in your operations, why, my family name would be besmirched. I should bring disgrace upon the name I bear. No! No! Excuse me! *Noblesse oblige.*"

There were some at Sardis who had adopted that very attitude. They were a virtuous remnant. They had not defiled their garments. When tempted to do something wrong, they would say, "Excuse me, please. I am·a member of the royal family of heaven. God is my Father, His Son is my Savior, His Spirit is my comforter and guide, the Lord's people are my companions. If I did what you suggest, I should bring dishonor on the name I bear. Excuse me, please." How much temptation we could surmount if we adopted the attitude of that old French count and these Sardian overcomers!

This remnant, moreover, was *a victorious remnant.* The Lord concludes with the words, *He that overcometh, the same shall be clothed in white raiment; and I will not blot out his name out of the book of life, but I will confess his name before my Father, and before his angels. He that hath an ear, let him hear what the Spirit saith unto the churches* (3:5-6). Think of it! To be taken by the hand by the Lord Jesus, to be led up past the marshaled ranks of the angels, up along the golden boulevards of glory, up past the cherubim and the seraphim, up, up to the throne of God Himself and to hear the Lord Jesus call you by your name and present you in person as His well beloved! Then, to hear the Father say, "Bring the best robe and put it on him." Think of it, a robe of white, bright as the day, pure as the light! When the Lord Jesus was transfigured on the mount, something happened not only to His countenance, something happened also to his clothes. His raiment became white as the light. What a reward for faithfulness, to have a robe like that draped around the shoulders and to be invited to walk the shining ways of glory in light-transfigured clothes! Solomon in all his glory was not arrayed like one of these.

VII. PHILADELPHIA: THE FEEBLE CHURCH (3:7-13)

The church at Philadelphia was weak, but it was wonderful. There is not the slightest hint of rebuke from the Lord; nothing but praise is given. It was a revival church. It had experienced an *evangelical* revival; it had a world vision. It had experienced an *ecclesiastical* revival; the disruptive, deadening influence of those who would have snared the church with Judaistic ritualism and legalism had been overcome. It had experienced an *eschatological* revival; the truth of the Lord's imminent return was its beacon light. Thus the Lord stands before this church to offer not blame, but blessing; not the threat of a fearful vengeance, but the thrill of a fresh vision.

A. THE CALL TO BEHOLD (3:7-11)

He comes with the challenge of great opportunity. He says, *And to the angel of the church in Philadelphia write; These things saith he that is holy, he that is true, he that hath the key of David, he that openeth and no man shutteth; and shutteth and no man openeth.* Thus the saints at Philadelphia are given a fresh vision of the Lord, His attributes, His resources, and His prerogatives. They see the King in His beauty. The vision of the King always precedes the vision of the continents.

Thus it was with William Carey, the cobbler. In his little workshop could be found the tools of his trade, a book or two, a Bible, a Dutch grammar, and a copy of Captain Cook's voyages. But the thing that would hold the gaze of the visitor was the homemade, paper and leather map on the wall. As he cobbled shoes, Carey's thoughts were far away over the seven seas. He had seen the King in His beauty and the countries in their dark and crying need.

On May 31, 1792, William Carey preached his famous sermon in Nottingham in England. "Lengthen thy cords; and strengthen thy stakes," ran the text, Isaiah 54:2-3. The words poured forth like the waters of a fountain from the deep recesses of his soul. His message deeply impressed the delegates of the Northamptonshire Baptist Association, and thus was formed a mission society that awoke the church from the lethargy of a thousand years. Carey became the Association's first missionary.

He went to India and flung himself into the task. He started a factory; he learned a dozen languages; he became professor of Bengali, Sanskrit, and Mahratta. He sounded the gospel across the length and breadth of the land. He built the finest college in the country, produced a brilliant translation of the Bible, hired missionaries, and hammered at India's heart. The vision of the King had given birth to the vision of the crowds.

That is exactly where things begin at Philadelphia. The saints are given a vision of the *righteousness* of the King. He is holy and true. He is so dazzling in His holiness that the shining seraphim before Him hide their faces in their wings. He is so dependable that a man can stake everything on His word. The saints are given a vision of the *resources* of the King. He has the key of David.

The allusion is to Isaiah 22:22, where we are told that Eliakim, the son of Hilkiah, had "the key of the house of David," access to the treasures of the King. Moreover, the saints are given a vision of the *regality* of the King. He opens and no man shuts; shuts and no man opens. He is sovereign in all His ways.

1. ALL SAINTS ARE UNDER HIS CONTROL (3:7-8)

Three times the Lord calls upon the church at Philadelphia to "behold." First He shows that the saints are under His control. He says, *I know thy works: behold, I have set before thee an open door, and no man can shut it: for thou hast a little strength, and hast kept my word, and hast not denied my name.* The Lord saw their weakness, but He also saw their willingness. Because of this, He opened doors of opportunity that no power on earth could shut. We want the doors opened first, but often He says, "No! You be faithful and make the first move, and I will open the doors in time."

The story of Hugh Latimer's conversion shows what happens when feebleness is wedded to faithfulness. Hugh Latimer was known as the most honest man in England. He was the idol of the common people, bishop of the high church, and chaplain to the king. He was burned at the stake in Oxford for his refusal to bow to the whims of the court. On no account would he change his coat to suit the variations of the religious climate. He was burned along with Bishop Ridley. As his persecutors lighted the faggots beneath his feet, Latimer turned to the Bishop of London standing by, and said: "We shall this day, my Lord, light such a candle in England as shall never be extinguished."

Hugh Latimer was led to Christ by a nobody, a man of no account, known simply to his fellows as "Little Bilney." Bilney had found Christ through reading the writings of Erasmus. At that time, Hugh Latimer was preaching at Cambridge. Bilney went to hear him and was captivated by the man. He began to pray to the Lord for the privilege of leading Father Latimer to Christ. In those days, Latimer was the champion of Rome. Bilney, in his earnest prayers, urged that while he, Little Bilney, was a nobody, Father Latimer was really somebody. If Father Latimer were to be saved, the impact of his testimony would be felt far and wide. The Lord granted Little Bilney's request.

Little Bilney was not merely feeble; he was faithful. He went to the church where Latimer was preaching, waited until the popular prelate came striding down the aisle, then caught hold of his robe and gave it a tug. "Father Latimer," he said, "I want to confess my soul to you." Back they went to the confessional, and there Father Latimer had poured into his ears a confession the like of which he had never heard before. Bilney confessed to the astonished priest all the aching hunger of his heart, a hunger no priest or penance, no sacrifice or sacrament, no ritual or resolve was able to heal. He told of the coming of Erasmus, of the purchase of a book, and of how he found peace with God through the Lord Jesus Christ. "I went to the priests," he cried, "and they pointed me to broken cisterns which could hold no water. I found they only mocked my thirst. Then I came to Christ, and He saved me. Now I have peace with God." Father Latimer was assaulted on all fronts. He knew only too well what Little Bilney was saying. He had experienced the same aching void in his own soul. The most honest man in England had been confronted by the most faithful man in England. He rose from his seat in the confessional, came around to where Little Bilney was pouring out his heart, knelt down beside him, and accepted Christ for himself.[4]

Feebleness wedded to faithfulness! *I have set before thee an open door . . . for thou hast a little strength, and hast kept my word.* The saints are under His control. He can use the feeblest of them.

2. ALL SINNERS ARE UNDER HIS CONTROL (3:9)

In the Philadelphian church were some who were arrogant and proud and far from the truth. The Lord says to the feeble remnant, *Behold, I will make them of the synagogue of Satan, which say they are Jews, and are not, but do lie; behold I will make them to come and worship before thy feet, and to know that I have loved thee.* This dominant little clique of ungodly men in the church despised those who remained true to the Scriptures and to the Lord. "I will make them come and bow down at your feet," said the Lord. Joseph found it true in his day. There came a day when the sun and the moon and the eleven stars bowed down to him. Jephthah found it true. His brothers cast him out of the fellowship because they were able to pinpoint a flaw in his pedigree. They excommunicated him. Instead of becoming bitter, Jepththah used the time of his rejection to gather to himself a band of fighting men to whom he taught the secrets of victorious living. Then, in the hour of Israel's need, he was ready. He was God's man, and his brothers knew it. They came to him, inviting him back to the fellowship and to the seat of power.

3. ALL SITUATIONS ARE UNDER HIS CONTROL (3:10-11)

The Lord says, *Because thou hast kept the word of my patience, I also will keep thee from the hour of temptation, which shall come upon all the world, to try them that dwell upon the earth. Behold I come quickly: hold fast which thou hast, that no man take thy crown.* In its broader implication, this promise has reference to the Great Tribulation. The language of these verses indicates a trial of universal extent, not just a local outbreak of persecution in Philadelphia. It is an assurance to the church at large that it will be kept from that hour by the Lord's coming in the sky. This is

---

4. From F. W. Boreham, *A Bunch of Everlastings* (London: Epworth, 1920), pp. 48-57.

indeed a supreme example of all situations being under His control. The Scripture nowhere envisions a worse situation on earth than the one that will arise when the Beast reigns and the Great Tribulation begins. But even that situation will be under His control. Not only will the Lord seal a hundred and forty-four thousand Jews and place them beyond Satan's reach, not only will He save during that period an incalculable multitude of Gentiles, but here as elsewhere He guarantees that the church will not even see that trial!

Wicked men may come to power and defy God's throne, but He still has ultimate control over their actions. All situations are under His government. Yet His greatest desire is to find feeble ones, faithful ones, who will listen to His voice. To them He unveils the secrets of His heart, and He tells them what moves to make. He wants them to win! The King eternal, immortal, invisible, longs to bestow on His people the victor's crown. To that end He controls all situations, frustrates the moves of evil men, and reveals Himself to His own as the One who opens and no man shuts; shuts and no man opens.

B. THE CALL TO BEHAVE (3:12-13)

We are to behave as overcomers, as those who are on the victory side. We are to behave like sons and daughters of a King and be more than conquerors in view of the divine initiative and in view of the divine invitation.

1. THE DIVINE INITIATIVE (3:12)

Three times the Lord says, "I will." It is the divine initiative! This initiative guarantees that God will take the overcomer and *make* him. He will make him strong. He says, **Him that overcometh will I make a pillar in the temple of my God, and he shall go no more out.** The Philadelphia believers had but a little strength, but that is all God needs. He says, "My strength is made perfect in weakness" (2 Cor. 12:9). The Lord promises to make these feeble ones into temple pillars, the very symbol of solidarity, stability, and strength. God will use these feeble ones to support an aspect of His eternal purpose and will undergird them. They will help uphold the eternal worship of the ages in the lofty halls of heaven.

The divine initiative, moreover, guarantees that God will take the overcomer and *mark* him. He will mark him with a threefold identification. The overcomer will be forever identified with the Lord's *infinite greatness*. He says, "I will write upon him the name of my God." What could be greater than that? In the first place, Jesus Himself is God, yet He says, *I will write on him the name of* my *God,* the name, that is, of His own Father in heaven. What a distinguishing mark to bear for all eternity!

The overcomer will be identified forever with the Lord's *invincible gov-*

ernment. He says, *I will write upon him . . . the name of the city of my God, which is new Jerusalem, which cometh down out of heaven from my God.* The overcomer is to be eternally identified with the new Jerusalem. Wherever he goes, to the furthest outposts of God's vast empire in space, he will be instantly recognized as a member of the aristocracy of heaven. Paul could boast that he was a citizen "of no mean city" (Acts 21:39). But in a coming day it will not be necessary for these overcomers to say, "I am from the New Jerusalem." It will be written all over them.

The overcomer, moreover, will be identified with the Lord's *inherent glory.* He says, *And I will write upon him my new name.* There are mysteries of beauty, of brilliance, and of blessing in Jesus not yet revealed to a wondering universe, as when the Queen of Sheba came to Solomon and said, "Behold the half was not told me." But something of that unknown glory will be written into the shining countenances of the overcomers. His old name was *Jehovah.* How much that name unfolds! His present name is *Jesus,* and what a volume of revelation there is in that! As for His new name, "eye hath not seen, nor ear heard, neither hath entered into the heart of man the things which God hath prepared for them that love Him" (1 Cor. 2:9). We must be content with that.

2. THE DIVINE INVITATION *(3:13)*

It is the same invitation we meet repeatedly in these letters. The Lord, it would seem, cannot say it too often: *He that hath an ear, let him hear what the Spirit saith unto the churches.*

The Battle of Britain was at its height. Night and day the enemy bombers flew in across the English Channel to unload their cargoes of death and destruction on the cities and villages below. The Royal Air Force had put up a magnificent fight. Sir Winston Churchill, in recounting later what the world owed to that valiant group of men who flew their battered Hurricanes and Spitfires against incalculable odds, declared, "Never before in the field of human conflict have so many owed so much to so few." In one lonely RAF outpost, a group of fighter pilots was gathered in the mess hall. It was a scene often repeated in those days. The men were worn out with fatigue, they were dirty and disheveled, their eyes were bleary, and beards sprouted on their chins. They were snatching a moment's relaxation before climbing the skies again to fight off more of the Nazi airwolves. Suddenly a buzzer sounded, and a voice came over the intercom from the operations room. "Bandits at fifteen thousand feet over P25. Over!" At once the pilots were on their feet and racing for the runways. Pausing on his way, the squadron leader barked back into the intercom one short reply: "Message received and understood."

Message received and understood! *He that hath an ear, let him hear what the Spirit saith unto the churches.*

VIII. LAODICEA: THE FASHIONABLE CHURCH (3:14-22)

Imagine a doctor being lukewarm about disease. You feel sick, so you drag yourself along to his office. He feels your pulse, takes your temperature, and tells you to pay the nurse on the way out. You say, "Well, just a minute, what's wrong with me, doctor?" He looks up from the papers on his desk and says, "What's wrong with you? Oh, there's nothing to worry about. You've got a bad case of bubonic plague." You look at him in astonishment and say, "But aren't you going to give me an injection or put me in the hospital? People don't just walk around with bubonic plague, do they? It's catching, isn't it? What about my family? What about all those people in your waiting room? What about *me?* People die of bubonic plague, don't they?" The doctor just looks at you mildly and says, "That's all right, my friend. You have to die sometime. It might just as well be of bubonic plague as cancer or a coronary. Diseases don't interest me too much. Now, if you needed surgery, well, that's more my line." Imagine a doctor lukewarm about disease! Imagine a church lukewarm about Christ! It makes as much sense.

A fighter will take on any odds. A column is erected in London to the memory of Lord Nelson, one of England's greatest naval heroes. At the battle of Trafalgar, one of the great battles that turned the tide of history, Nelson's fleet was greatly outnumbered by the French. The enemy had more ships, heavier guns, and more men. But Nelson was neither fearful nor indifferent. He summoned his captains to his flagship to give them his orders. He described how the fleet would advance against the French and what signals he would use. Then looking at his men he said, "Gentlemen, in case these signals cannot be seen or clearly understood, no captain can do wrong if he places his ship alongside that of an enemy."

Imagine a fighter lukewarm about the foe! Imagine a church lukewarm about Christ! It makes as much sense. Yet such was Laodicea. It was lukewarm. There stands the Lord of glory, the altogether lovely One, the chiefest among ten thousand, the One whom angels worship. There He stands, the marks of the nails in His hands, a look of love upon His face. And this church shrugs its shoulders and offers Him a lukewarm interest at best. "Oh, that thou wert cold or hot," He says. In effect: "Give Me all your hate or all your heart, but do not offer Me lukewarm love. I will spue you out of My mouth!"

A. THE DYNAMIC CHRIST (3:14)

There is an interesting touch in the way the King James Version renders the Lord's introductory remarks: *And unto the angel of the church of the Laodiceans,* as if to say that the church at Laodicea was none of His, it was theirs; it was the church of the Laodiceans. The Lord stands before this church indignantly yet lovingly, to present the challenge of His Person and His presence.

1. HE IS THE ALL-CONQUERING ONE (3:14a)

He begins with the statement *These things saith the Amen.* The Lord Jesus is God's fullest Amen to all man's needs. Revelation begins and ends with a double amen. The first double amen has to do with the Lord Jesus as the final ruler of men (1:6-7); the last has to do with the Lord Jesus as the final revealer of God (22:20-21). With that first Amen, God begins this book and gives us a glimpse of the Lord Jesus as Prophet, Priest, and King, spanning the ages between His comings, meeting all the needs of men, able to subdue all things to Himself. With the last double Amen, God closes the book, once and for all. He has nothing more to say. In Christ, all has been said. From henceforth men are referred to Him and to Him alone. Both references refer us to His second coming. He is the all-conquering One.

2. HE IS THE ALL-CONVICTING ONE (3:14b)

He says, *These things saith . . . The faithful and true witness.* He is the faithful witness, which means He will not *dilute* the truth; He is the true witness, which means He will not *distort* the truth. He sees through all the sham, the shallowness, the outward show of our lives. He neither dilutes nor distorts what He sees. For those of us who spend our lives hiding behind little disguises and safe conventions, that can be a very disconcerting experience. The eyes of Jesus penetrate those disguises, strip away the conventions, and see us as we really are.

To English boys, Richmal Crompton's *William* books have a perennial appeal. One of the stories is called *William's Truthful Christmas.* It begins with William in church listening halfheartedly to the sermon, until his attention is caught and his imagination is fired by a challenge to "cast aside all deceit and hypocrisy and speak the truth in love." William determines to give it a try over Christmas. The Brown family are to spend Christmas with Uncle Frederick and Aunt Emma. On Christmas day, William opens his presents in his bedroom and is immediately disillusioned by the uninspiring presents he receives—a pen and pencil, a ruler, an (empty) purse, a tie, a brush and comb, and (the crowning insult) a book on church history.

William goes downstairs. Aunt Emma asks him if he likes the book on history. Determined to tell the truth at all costs, William, to the horror of his family, says, "No!" His family accuses him of rudeness and remains unimpressed by his efforts to speak the truth and to cast aside hypocrisy. The atmosphere brightens when William produces his presents for his aunt and uncle. Aunt Emma thanks William for being so kind. William says he is not being kind; he is giving her a present because his mother said he had to. His aunt somewhat coldly professes gratitude for the pin cushion he has given her.

William doggedly explains that he had not spent any money on the gift. It had been left over, he says, from a rummage sale, and his mother had said he might as well give it as a present since it was faded and would not be worth keeping for a later bazaar!

His uncle, in the meantime, holds up a leather purse. With an effort at joviality, he thanks William and says, "This is a really useful present." Treading the path of truth, William explains that it is not really useful. His Uncle Jim had sent it to William's father for his birthday, but since the catch would not work, William's father had given it to William to give to Uncle Frederick.

The denouement comes later in the day when William's uncle and aunt receive a visit from Lady Atkinson, a domineering and haughty member of the aristocracy. With great condescension she presents William's relatives with a picture of herself. Then, turning to William, she demands that he examine the picture. "Don't you think it's very like me?" she crows. William's final offering at the altar of truth is, "It's not as fat as you are!"

We could not stand being told the truth, the whole truth, and nothing but the truth. Society has invented a thousand ways of conveniently blunting the sharp edge of truth. The Lord Jesus is the faithful and true Witness. He sees a lukewarm church, and He tells it the truth about itself in a memorable and particularly undiluted form. Yet even that harsh truth is softened with His love.

3. HE IS THE ALL-CONTROLLING ONE (3:14c)

He introduces Himself to Laodicea as *the beginning of the creation of God,* or, as the margin of the *American Standard Version* puts it, "the origin of the creation of God." He it was who flung the stars into space, plowed out the basins of the sea, reared against the skyline of the world the mighty Himalayan range. Not a blade of grass grows without His permission; not a speck of dust moves. He is the origin of the creation of God, the all-controlling One, the dynamic Christ. He stands before this wretched church and penetrates its little disguises and sees it through and through. Thus this letter begins.

B. THE DELUDED CHURCH (3:15-17)

There was something actually nauseating about this church. Its lukewarmness was sickening to the Lord.

1. ITS SICKENING COMPROMISE (3:15-16)

Says the Lord, *I know thy works, that thou art neither cold nor hot: I would thou wert cold or hot. So then because thou art lukewarm, and neither cold nor hot, I will spue thee out of my mouth.* Laodicea had been reduced to room temperature. It was neither hot nor cold, neither one thing nor the other. It was marked by complete compromise.

This condition is illustrated in the story of Lot. The angels who visited this backslidden believer in Sodom could scarcely speak civilly to him, and only with the greatest reluctance did they accept his hospitality. They came as close to impatience as shining ones can. The citizens of Sodom detested Lot. They allowed him a high place in their councils, but they sneered at his religion and were contemptuous of his sermons. Lot lost his fortune in Sodom, he lost his family in Sodom, and he almost lost his faith in Sodom—all because he wanted the best out of both this world and the one to come. Thus it was with Laodicea. "I would thou wert cold or hot," said the Lord.

A little girl came home from Sunday school, and her mother asked her to recite the text she had learned: "Many are called but few are chosen." It came out like this: "Many are cold and a few are frozen!" There would have been some hope for Laodicea if it had been stone cold, but to be lukewarm, to be neither one thing nor the other, to be completely compromised, was a condition without hope.

2. *ITS SICKENING COMPLACENCY (3:17)*

The church at Laodicea was ignorant of its true condition. The Lord pinpoints this with the charge: *Because thou sayest, I am rich, and increased with goods, and have need of nothing; and knowest not that thou art wretched, and miserable, and poor, and blind, and naked.* The church at Laodicea would want the president of the bank as head deacon; as treasurer, a big industrialist; as secretary a member of the senate. Laodicea had everything a worldly church could desire. Influential men no doubt sat on its boards; large accounts gave it prestige at the bank. Doubtless it occupied the choicest location in town, had the best choir in Asia, summoned the most brilliant and eloquent of preachers to its pulpit, boasted a considerable membership, and had a well-oiled organization. Laodicea was a fashionable, worldly church, but it was powerless.

Thomas Aquinas once called upon Pope Innocent II. The pope was counting a large sum of money. "You see, Thomas," said the pope, "the church can no longer say, 'Silver and gold have I none.'" "True, holy Father," said Thomas, "and neither can it say to the lame any more, 'Arise and walk.'" The church at Laodicea was popular, prosperous, pragmatic, polished, and proud. But it was powerless.

It is the archetype of the present-day church. The church today is seeking escape from reality in a score of blind alleys. Some churches are seeking escape in *fundamentalism*. Correct in faith and doctrine, orthodox in teaching, they can say all the shibboleths of the faith, but they are cold as ice and hard as clay. Some are seeking escape in *exclusivism*. "We are the people; truth will die with us" is their creed. They think that separation means isolation; they retreat into a make-believe world and ban contact not only with the lost, but with other believers as well. "Come ye out from among them and be ye separate" is their watchword. Other churches are seeking escape in *ritualism*. They are satisfied with the external trappings of religion, with a stereotyped form of service in which a set and pre-arranged ritual and liturgy is followed from year to year. Others seek escape in *rationalism*. They have come to terms with the atheist, the evolutionist, and the Communist. The more extreme members of this group proclaim that God is dead. They deny every cardinal doctrine of the faith from the virgin birth to the second coming of Christ. Other churches seek escape in *socialism*. Theirs is a social gospel in which active participation in social and political issues becomes the beginning and end of God's way of salvation. Still other churches seek escape in *occultism*. They look for a new touch from the spirit world, for healings and tongues, and for voices and visions, with scant concern about their source. Others seek refuge in *ecumenicalism*. They plan a world superchurch as the answer to mankind's needs. They want a church in which doctrinal differences are submerged at the expense of truth and the endorsement of error. Other churches seek refuge from reality in *materialism*. Money is the solution to every problem. The solution to failure and loss of power is to pour in more money and to hire more efficient and better trained personnel.

"You say you are rich and have become wealthy and have need of nothing, and you do not know that you are wretched and miserable and poor and blind and naked." The Lord warns Laodicea that this state of affairs can have only one conclusion. He will spew this church out of His mouth. It would be hard to find a stronger or more expressive term of revulsion anywhere in the New Testament.

C. THE DEFINITE CHOICE (3:18-19)

The Lord sets the choice before this church. Will it elect God's dealings in grace or His dealings in judgment? He counsels *a restoration of spiritual values*. He says: *I counsel thee to buy of me gold tried in the fire, that thou mayest be rich*. The church was destitute of anything of spiritual worth. There must be a return to the gold standard, a return to Himself, for money cannot buy spiritual things. These can be purchased only by repentance and yieldedness to the Spirit of God.

Next, the Lord sets before this church *a restoration of spiritual virtues*. He says, *I counsel thee to buy of me . . . white raiment, that thou mayest be clothed, and that the shame of thy nakedness do not appear.* This church needed true righteousness. The world could see right through its materialistic finery. The church was actually naked. We have all chuckled over the childhood fairy story of the emperor's new clothes. The emperor could think of nothing but his wardrobe. One day two ingenious cheats calling themselves weavers appeared. They conned the king into purchasing, for a small fortune, some magnificent but invisible clothes. They set up their looms and pretended to weave the marvelous fabrics for the emperor's new robes. The king sent his agents to the weavers, but these, afraid of exposing themselves as fools, carried back glowing reports to the king of the wonderful garments which were being prepared. Presently the day came when the emperor donned his new robes and sallied forth in procession to show them off to his subjects. Nearly everyone pretended to admire them, until one little boy said: "But the emperor has nothing on at all!" The whisper began to grow and spread until even the emperor heard. But he kept up the pretense, and the lords of the bedchamber took greater pains than ever to appear to be holding up a train, although in reality, there was nothing to hold up at all! The church at Laodicea was like that foolish king. No wonder the Lord demanded that it buy white raiment from Him so its shame might be covered and it nakedness clothed.

The Lord then demands of this church *a restoration of spiritual vision.* He says, *I counsel thee to . . . anoint thine eyes with eyesalve, that thou mayest see.* Worldliness always clouds spiritual vision, and lack of spiritual vision is serious, for "where there is no vision the people perish" (Prov. 29:18). No wonder the Lord says to Laodicea, in essence, "Come out of your blind alleys, take your head out of the sand. Let Me give you a vision of heaven and of hell. Let Me give you a vision of the King."

How can a church recapture its spiritual values, its spiritual virtues, and its spiritual vision? The answer is in a single word—*repent! As many as I love, I rebuke, and chasten: be zealous therefore, and repent.* Repentance is the very last thing a sinner wants to do, and it is the very last thing a saint wants to do. We would rather do anything than repent.

D. THE DUAL CHALLENGE (3:20-22)
1. TO SINNERS IN THE CONGREGATION (3:20)

The Lord now makes a statement that has become one of the best known texts in the Bible. He says, *Behold, I stand at the door, and knock: if any man hear my voice, and open the door, I will come in to him, and will sup with him, and he with me.* The Lord is right outside the church at Laodicea, pleading for individuals to give Him His rightful place. That is the primary meaning of the verse. Yet it is with true evangelistic insight that preachers in all ages have seized upon this text and applied it to the unsaved. In such a materialistic church there must have been many unsaved members in the congregation. It is therefore quite legitimate to apply this text to sinners in the church.

What a tremendous view it gives us of the Lord Jesus, the patient, pleading, promising Savior of men. Holman Hunt has best captured the gospel appeal in the text. He painted a famous picture of Christ as the Light of the World, depicting the Lord, wearing a crown of thorns, standing outside the fast-bolted human heart, patiently knocking and calling for admittance. A copy of this painting now hangs in St. Paul's Cathedral in London. When it was first displayed, critics came to comment on the work. One of them turned to the painter and said, "Mr. Hunt, you have painted a masterpiece, but you have made one very serious mistake. You have painted a door without a handle." "That is no mistake," replied the artist. "The handle is on the *inside.*"

Christ makes three promises to those who open the door of their heart to Him. *I will come in to him,* He says. He enters the believer's heart and makes it His home. *I will sup with him.* He takes what we put at His disposal and, as He did with the loaves and fishes, blesses it, multiplies it, and makes it a blessing to others. *And He with me,* He says, thus promising that, if we open our hearts to Him, He will open heaven to us.

2. TO SAINTS IN THE CONGREGATION (3:21-22)

Again the last word is to the overcomer. *To him that overcometh will I grant to sit with me in my throne, even as I also overcame, and am set down with my Father in his throne. He that hath an ear, let him hear what the Spirit saith unto the churches.* Could there be a higher incentive than to have a place on His throne? The heart that remains unresponsive to a challenge like that must be cold and dead indeed!

Part Three:
Visions of Government (4:1–20:15)

I. THE SUPREME SOURCE OF DIVINE GOVERNMENT (4:1–5:14)

A. The Unforgettable Throne (4:1-6)
   1. The Mystery of the Throne (4:1-3*a*)
   2. The Majesty of the Throne (4:3*b*-6)
B. The Unforgettable Throng (4:7-11)
   1. The Cherubim Acknowledge Him as the Holiest One in the Universe (4:7-8)
   2. The Elders Acknowledge Him as the Highest One in the Universe (4:9-11)
C. The Unforgettable Thrill (5:1-14)
   1. The Challenge of God Is Proclaimed Throughout the Universe (5:1-4)
   2. The Christ of God Is Presented Throughout the Universe (5:5-7)
   3. The Choice of God Is Praised Throughout the Universe (5:8-14)

Part Three:

Visions of Government
(4:1–20:15)

Before studying in detail this third and largest section of the book of Revelation, it will be helpful to get a brief overview. The letters to the seven churches span the present age of grace. (The church is not mentioned again by name in the book until the postscript at the very end.) The visions of government that are before us now have to do with Israel and the nations—not the church. God judges the world that crucified His Son, precipitating those climactic events that usher in the end. The first scene is in heaven, where we are given a vision of the throne of God, a throne that is in absolute control throughout the entire period of judgment. Three series of judgments follow (seals, trumpets, vials), as the world becomes increasingly wicked and godless, and as lawlessness comes to a head. Then God steps in to make a full and final end to the problem of sin.

I. THE SUPREME SOURCE OF DIVINE GOVERNMENT (4:1–5:14)

The scene has changed from earth to heaven. John says, *After this I looked, and, behold, a door was opened in heaven: and the first voice which I heard was as it were of a trumpet talking with me; which said, Come up hither, and I will shew thee things which must be hereafter.* The apostle Paul was once caught up into the third heaven and saw things "not lawful for a man to utter" (2 Cor. 12:4). Now John is caught up and is shown things he has already been commanded to communicate to men (1:11). Three things are impressed indelibly upon his mind. He sees an unforgettable throne, an unforgettable throng, and experiences an unforgettable thrill.

A. THE UNFORGETTABLE THRONE (4:1-6)

The throne is mentioned seventeen times in chapters 4 and 5—twelve times in chapter 4, for there it is supremely a throne of government, and five times in chapter 5, for there it is preeminently a throne of grace.

1. THE MYSTERY OF THE THRONE (4:1-3a)

Everything connected with the throne, as it appears in Revelation 4, is awesome, strange, and unexpected. We instinctively feel out of our depth, for there is little or nothing to which we can relate. Everything described is outside the realm of normal experience. Who, for example, ever thinks of God as a stone? We can think of Him anthropomorphically and ascribe to Him physical parts. We can accept the symbolism that likens Jesus to a lion or to a lamb. The symbolism of Jesus as the vine is easily grasped. But the idea of God being like a stone is as startling as it is unexpected. Then, too, a rainbow is a familiar enough sight, but not an emerald rainbow, and certainly not a rainbow that completes a circle. And how familiar are we with the mysterious zoa, those strange beasts, the living creatures with the four faces? Then, too, who are the elders? And how remarkable is the symbol used for the Holy Spirit! We are in the realm of the unfamiliar. It is like being in a strange country where language, customs, and architecture are sufficiently like our own to be recognized, yet sufficiently exotic and strange to make us feel somewhat ill at ease.

John says, *And immediately I was in the spirit: and, behold, a throne was set in heaven, and one sat on the throne. And he that sat was to look upon like a jasper and a sardine stone.* The jasper emphasizes the *hardness* connected with the government of God, for jasper is hard and adamantine in nature. God's government is like that. His laws are fixed and firm, unyielding and unrelenting. All science is predicated on the rigidness of God's laws. If we put water on the stove to boil, we expect to see steam, not ice. A stone thrown from the top of a building will fall down, not up. God's moral laws are just as inflexible as His physical laws. One day the Lord Jesus will rule the earth with a rod of iron (Ps. 2:9), the very symbol of hardness and unyieldedness. The world in which we live desperately needs a firm hand, and God has pledged Himself to just such a government for mankind. Here, then, is a throne where the government is like jasper.

The sardine, or sardius stone, suggests the *holiness* connected with the government of God, for sardius is a deep, fiery, flashing red. It reminds us that "our God is a consuming fire" (Deut. 4:24). The fire on Israel's altars was a quenchless fire; its flames were never to die out. They were to burn on and on, day and night, year after year, throughout all generations. So long as sin exists in the universe, God's attitude toward it is one of burning holiness. The emasculated concepts of God popular with those who envision Him as a senile and indulgent old man or as a cosmic Santa Claus are far removed from the truth. God is holy, and His anger against sin burns and flashes like the glow of the sardius stone.

Put the jasper and the sardius stones together, and they suggest the *humanity* connected to the government of God. The high priest of Israel was commanded to wear a breastplate studded with twelve precious stones engraved with the names of the tribes of Israel (Ex. 28:17, 20). Thus, symbolically the people were ever to be upon his heart, the place of affection and love. The first and last of these stones was the jasper and the sardius. The mention of the jasper and the sardius in connection with the throne of God is a beautiful reminder that although there is an element of hardness and holiness inevitable in the judgment of God, those qualities, fearful in themselves, are not divorced from humanity. The One to whom all judgment will be given is Himself both God and man (John 5:22, 27).

2. THE MAJESTY OF THE THRONE (4:3b-6)

Statement after statement is now given to describe the throne of God and the things associated with it. The description is, at the same time, a description of the judgment that proceeds from the throne. It is *flawless judgment,* as intimated by the rainbow. John says, **And there was a rainbow round about the throne, in sight like unto an emerald.** The rainbow encircled the throne; it was not just an arc, but a complete circle. As a geometric figure, a circle symbolizes perfection. The rainbow was emerald in color emphasizing that the judgment has to do with the earth. The rainbow reminds us that judgment, when it comes, will be in keeping with God's covenant with the earth (Gen. 9:12-17). It is easy enough for unscrupulous men to subvert human justice and make a mockery of the courts, but God's judgment will be flawless.

It is also *formal judgment.* John says, **And round about the throne were four and twenty seats: and upon the seats I saw four and twenty elders sitting, clothed in white raiment; and they had on their heads crowns of gold.** At this point, the elders are introduced in their relationship to the throne of God. They themselves are enthroned and ranged in order around God's throne. They function as a jury, but their role is not to decide whether or not men are guilty, but to approve, by acts of deepest obeisance, the righteous acts of the Judge. In olden days, kings found it useful to surround their office with every form of pomp and ceremony to impress upon those brought before them the dignity and awesomeness of the throne. God likewise surrounds His throne with due formality. He insists that things be done decently and in order in His church, and He insists that things be done decently and in order in His court. There will be no contempt of court here. The terrible formality of things, the impressive dignity of the proceedings are calculated to strike a proper reverence in every heart.

God's judgment is *fearful judgment.* John says, **And out of the throne proceeded lightnings and thunderings and voices.** The proceedings are accompanied by terrifying sights and sounds. A full-scale tropical thunderstorm can be a frightening thing. How much more fearsome are the convulsions that emit from the throne of God! When God gave His law to men at Sinai, the mountain blazed with fire. We read, "And it came to pass on the third day in the morning, that there were thunderings and lightnings, and a thick cloud upon the mount, and the voice of a trumpet exceeding loud; so that all the people that was in the camp trembled. And mount Sinai was altogether on a smoke, because the Lord descended upon it in fire: and the smoke thereof ascended as the smoke of a furnace, and the whole mount quaked greatly" (Ex. 19:16, 18). "And so terrible was the sight that Moses said, I exceedingly fear and quake" (Heb. 12:21). The thunderings and lightnings proceeding from the throne remind us that God's judgment is something to be feared. "It is a fearful thing to fall into the hands of the living God" (Heb. 10:31).

It is also *factual judgment.* **There were seven lamps of fire burning before the throne, which are the seven Spirits of God.** The seven Spirits of God symbolize the Holy Spirit in His fullness. He will be there as the Prosecutor of the human race. The work of the Holy Spirit is to "reprove the world of sin, and of righteousness, and of judgment" (John 16:8). We are warned of the folly of doing "despite unto the Spirit of grace" (Heb. 10:29). The judgment will be factual, for the omniscient Spirit will be there with a full knowledge of every thought, word, and deed of every man, woman, and child. He knows the time, the place, the act, the motive, the deed, the result, the influence, and the consequences of every sin of omission and every sin of commission. No false evidence will be introduced, nor will cross-examination be necessary. The facts will be laid bare.

The judgment, furthermore, will be *final judgment*—final, that is, so far as its outcome is concerned. John says, **And before the throne there was a sea of glass like unto crystal.** There is nothing more fluctuating and changeable than the sea. It symbolizes the wicked in their restlessness. The sea is never the same for a moment, even in its most placid state. A sea of glass, however, suggests something no longer fluid, no longer capable of change. Glass is transparent and fixed. God's judgment will be transparent as crystal, and it will be fixed and beyond recall. There is no court of appeal from the verdicts of this throne, for this is the supreme court of the universe. A man might as well try to reverse the rotation of the earth upon its axis as try to reverse the decisions and decrees from the throne of God.

The judgment, moreover, is *fundamental judgment.* **In the midst of the throne, and round about the throne, were four beasts full of eyes before and behind.** John will have more to say about these living creatures. Probably they are the cherubim, the highest of all created intelligences from whose ranks Satan fell. The cherubim are first introduced in connection with man's expulsion from the Garden of Eden in Genesis 3, where they are associated with God's *creatorial* rights. They appear again in connection with the mercy seat in the Tabernacle, where they are associated with God's *redemptive* rights. In ways not fully revealed, God's rights in creation and redemption are upheld by these creatures. God has never surrendered His sovereignty to any of His creatures. The introduction of the cherubim here suggests that the issues being decided by the throne are the issues of God's creatorial and redemptive rights as those rights have to do with heaven and earth.

Finally, it is *fatal judgment.* We search the fourth chapter and the immediate context to these revelations in vain for any mention of the Lamb. Isaac's cry, "Where is the lamb?" might well be repeated here. Isaac could see in his father's hand the knife, speaking of death, and the fire, speaking of that which comes after death, but he could see no lamb (Gen. 22). How terrible is this throne! How fatal is the judgment where there is no Lamb to intervene.

B. the unforgettable throng (4:7-11)

Later on, John will tell us of the countless hosts that surround the throne. At this juncture, he details the two most important groups, both of whom are close to the throne, and both of whom respond magnificently to the judgment of God.

1. THE CHERUBIM ACKNOWLEDGE HIM AS THE HOLIEST ONE IN THE UNIVERSE (4:7-8)

John is impressed by two things about the cherubim. He is impressed by *the singularity of their form.* He says, **And the first beast was like a lion, and the second beast like a calf, and the third beast had a face as a man, and the fourth beast was like a flying eagle.** When Matthew drew his portrait of the Lord Jesus, he drew the picture of a *lion* and depicted the Lord as the Lion of the tribe of Judah. Matthew's is the sovereign gospel. It traces the ancestry of Jesus back to David, beginning with the cry of the wise men, "Where is He that is born King of the Jews?" Throughout, it keeps before the Jews the solemn fact that Jesus is the Messiah. Mark's portrait of the Christ is the portrait of a *calf.* The Lord Jesus is the One who came "not to be ministered unto, but to minister, and to give His life as a ransom for many" (Mark 10:45). Mark's objective is to show the Lord Jesus giving His life, first in service and then in sacrifice. It is essentially the portrait of an ox or a calf Luke draws the portrait of a *man,* tracing the ancestry of Jesus right back to Adam, and showing that Jesus is the last Adam. Luke's gospel is full of tender touches that emphasize the humanity of God's eternal Son. John's portrait of

Christ is the portrait of an *eagle.* Christ is the One who descended from on high and whose true sphere is in the highest vaults of heaven.

Now come back to the cherubim. One had the face of a lion, one the face of an ox, one the face of a man, and one the face of an eagle. In other words, each reflects an aspect of the likeness of the Lord. They are so much like Him because they are so much with Him. When Moses came down from the mount, unknown to him "the skin of his face shone" (Ex. 34:29) with the shining image of the Master. Those who spend time in the presence of God become like the Lord Jesus. "But we all, with open face beholding as in a glass the glory of the Lord, are changed into the same image from glory to glory, even as by the Spirit of the Lord" (2 Cor. 3:18). Anticipating the day when we shall be taken home to glory, John says, "We shall be like him; for we shall see him as he is" (1 John 3:2).

Looking at the cherubim, John is impressed not only with the singularity of their form, he is impressed also with *the singleness of their function.* It is this that explains why they are so much like Jesus. *And the four beasts had each of them six wings about him; and they were full of eyes within: and they rest not day and night, saying, Holy, holy, holy, Lord God Almighty, which was, and is, and is to come.* The cherubim are the highest of all created intelligences. They are full of eyes, implying clear insight into matters. These lofty ones employ the resources of their intellects, the deep emotions of their hearts, the ceaseless drive and dynamic of their powerful wills—and they worship! It is the one great, supreme, dominating activity of their lives. All else is counted worthless when compared to the supreme activity of worship. With all their heart and mind and soul and strength they worship Him that sits upon the throne. They acknowledge Him to be the holiest One in the universe. Holy! Holy! Holy! Thrice holy God! Holy Father, Holy Son, and Holy Ghost!

2. *THE ELDERS ACKNOWLEDGE HIM AS THE HIGHEST ONE IN THE UNIVERSE (4:9-11)*

A great deal of speculation centers on the elders. Some equate them with the church, or see them as representatives of the Old and New Testament saints—perhaps the patriarchs and the apostles. But there is another view. David organized the Old Testament priests into twenty-four courses (1 Chron. 24:3-4), and he did so by divine illumination. He says, "All this . . . the LORD made me to understand in writing by his hand upon me" (1 Chron. 28:19, see vv. 11-13). It was the same, long before David's day, with the Tabernacle. "See, saith he, that thou make all things according to the pattern showed to thee in the mount" (Heb. 8:5). Both the Tabernacle and the Temple were "patterns of things in the heavens" (Heb. 9:23). They were the types of the reality that is in heaven. The twenty-four elders seem to be angelic beings, crowned members of the aristocracy of heaven, possibly those alluded to by Paul in his reference to thrones (Col. 1:16). They distinguish themselves from men in Revelation 5:9-10 *(American Standard Version)*.

Two things are told us about the worship of these high ones. First, *their worship is instinctive.* John says, *And when those beasts give glory and honour and thanks to him that sat on the throne, who liveth for ever and ever, the four and twenty elders fall down before him that sat on the throne, and worship him that liveth for ever and ever, and cast their crowns before the throne.* They instinctively acknowledge Him to be the highest One in the universe. High and lofty as they are themselves, they abase themselves at His feet. They take off their crowns, which symbolize their own right to rule, and cast those crowns at His feet. They confess with joyful abandon that the right to rule is His alone.

Second, *their worship is instructive.* As they cast their crowns before God's throne they say, *Thou art worthy, O Lord, to receive glory and honour and power: for thou hast created all things, and for thy pleasure they are and were created.* Worship is the ascription of "worth-ship" to the Lord. It is the function of telling Him how absolutely worthy He is to receive our praise and our adoration. The elders worship Him as the Creator and instruct us in a basic truth of creation—all things were created by His power and for His pleasure. No creature has a right to existence apart from a willingness to accept that power and accord Him pleasure.

> All that I am and have, Thy gifts so free,
> In joy, in grief, through life, Dear Lord, for thee!
> And when thy face I see, My ransomed soul shall be,
> Through all eternity, Something for Thee.
>
> (Sylvanus D. Phelps)

C. THE UNFORGETTABLE THRILL (5:1-14)

To this point there has been no sign of the Lamb, but now He steps into the spotlight and fills the stage of the universe, drawing every eye and prompting endless applause.

1. THE CHALLENGE OF GOD IS PROCLAIMED THROUGHOUT THE UNIVERSE (5:1-4)

The gauntlet is now to be thrown down to men and angels, to principalities and powers, to thrones and dominions. Who, of all God's creatures, is fit to rule the world? Our attention is drawn to *the scroll.* John says, *And I saw in the right hand of him that sat on the throne a book written within and on the backside, sealed with seven seals.* The scroll is the title deed of earth. Two considerations lead to this conclusion. In the first place, the call having gone forth for an applicant to come and take the scroll, John wept because no *man* was found worthy to do so. The sphere of man is evidently in view. Furthermore, when the seals on the scroll are eventually broken, disasters overtake the *earth*. The right to rule the earth is now to be decided at the throne of God, once and for all.

Next comes *the silence*. John says, *And I saw a strong angel proclaiming with a loud voice, Who is worthy to open the book, and to loose the seals thereof? And no man in heaven, nor in earth, neither under the earth, was able to open the book, neither to look thereon.* Many would be willing to take the book and rule the earth—many an Alexander, Genghis Khan, Napoleon, or Hitler. But the question was not, Who is *willing?* but, Who is *worthy?* The ranks of the living and the dead, those on earth, those in heaven, and those in hell, are combed for a worthy king, but not a single one is found. Abraham is not worthy, neither Isaac nor Jacob, neither Enoch nor Elijah, neither David nor Solomon, neither Peter nor Paul nor James nor John nor Jude. A deep silence descends upon the scene, as every voice is hushed and the angels themselves cease to sing. Not a voice is raised to say, "Here am I, Lord, give that scroll to me!"

Suddenly the silence is broken. John tells us of *the sob*. He says, *And I wept much, because no man was found worthy to open and to read the book, neither to look thereon.* This is probably the first time a man had sobbed within the walls of heaven, for in that land of fadeless day there is no death, sorrow, crying, tears, or pain. There stood the aged apostle, amid scenes of grandeur that defy description, weeping with salt tears running down his weatherbeaten face, weeping in shame for all the sons of Adam's ruined race, not one of whom was worthy to take up the challenge from the throne. Think of it! Not a single man of all the billions who have lived on earth, not one fit to rule and reign!

2. *THE CHRIST OF GOD IS PRESENTED THROUGHOUT THE UNIVERSE*
   (5:5-7)

God never leaves Himself without a man, and in this hour of solemn crisis, He has One ready. Observe *the person of the Lord*. Says John, *One of the elders saith unto me, Weep not: behold, the Lion of the tribe of Judah, the Root of David, hath prevailed to open the book, and to loose the seven seals thereof.* As John stood there choked with sobs, one of the elders stepped down from his throne, walked over to where the weeping seer stood, and gently wiped away all tears from his eyes. "Weep not," he said. "Behold!" What a chord the mention of the Lion must have struck in John's soul, for that was the kind of Messiah the Jews had always wanted and expected. They had crucified Jesus because He was too tame for them. They had wanted a king who would smash the power of Rome and make Jerusalem capital of a new world empire. The last thing they wanted was One meek and lowly, gentle and kind. At last that longed-for militant Messiah is to be unveiled, David's Son and David's Lord.

Note *the position of the Lord.* John says, *And I beheld, and lo, in the midst of the throne and of the four beasts, and in the midst of the elders, stood a Lamb.* How could he ever have missed Him? There He was, in the midst all the time. John had been so taken up with the sights and sounds of glory, so occupied with the throne, the emerald rainbow, the thunderings and lightnings, the sea of glass, the elders, and the cherubim, that he had completely missed the Lamb! Yet the Lamb was in the midst of it all! How often we do the same. We come and go to meetings, we listen to the most stirring messages, read the most profound passages from God's Word, sing the most sublime hymns, harken to the noblest of prayers, and yet miss the Lord in the midst (Matt. 18:20).

John next becomes aware of *the passion of the Lord.* He says that there, in the midst, *stood a Lamb as it had been slain, having seven horns and seven eyes, which are the seven Spirits of God sent forth into all the earth.* John turned to behold a Lion. But instead of a shaggy mane and gaping jaws and dreadful teeth, he saw—a Lamb! Was there ever a more dramatic moment in the history of the universe? The Lion was none other than the Lamb! The Lord Jesus is referred to directly as the Lamb only twice in the Old Testament (Isa. 53:7; Jer. 11:19), only twice in the gospels (John 1:29, 36), only once in the book of Acts (Acts 8:32), and only once in the epistles (1 Pet. 1:19). But He is referred to as the Lamb twenty-eight times in the book of Revelation. It is His apocalyptical title. As Lamb, He came to save; as Lamb, He comes back to subdue. Nor is it the usual word for lamb that is used in the Apocalypse; it is a word that literally means *a little lamb.* Satan is a great red dragon in the Apocalypse; world power is concentrated in the hands of a fearful beast; the militant foes of God are massed on earth, in heaven, and in hell and numbered by the countless millions. Against all this God sets a little Lamb!

Surely this is what Paul meant when he said, "God hath chosen the foolish things of the world to confound the wise; and God hath chosen the weak things of the world to confound the things that are mighty; and the base things of the world, and things which are despised, hath God chosen, yea, and things which are not, to bring to nought the things that are" (1 Cor. 1:27-28). A little lamb! But this is no ordinary lamb, for this Lamb has the seven horns of omnipotence, and the seven eyes of omniscience. This Lamb is "Christ the power of God, and the wisdom of God" (1 Cor. 1:24).

And he came and took the book out of the right hand of him that sat upon the throne. Suppose the question had been asked Him, "What is the basis of Your claim to the title deed of earth?" His reply could have been threefold. He could have said, "That world is Mine by right of *creation,* for I made it; it is Mine by right of *Calvary,* for I redeemed it and bought it with My blood; it is Mine by right of *conquest* for, since the only language the unregenerate heart of man understands is the language of power, I'm going back to claim that world in war." The world is His, and His rights are not questioned at all. As He steps into the spotlight, His right is instantly owned. And notice this: from the moment the Lamb is put into the picture, John cannot take his eyes off Him. He mentions Him again and again—four times within the space of the rest of this chapter alone (5:6, 8, 12, 13).

3. *THE CHOICE OF GOD IS PRAISED THROUGHOUT THE UNIVERSE (5:8-14)*

The Lamb is introduced, and worship is immediately given to Him. He is worshiped at the *focal center* of the universe. The creatures at the throne worship Him. John says, ***And when he had taken the book, the four beasts and four and twenty elders fell down before the Lamb, having every one of them harps, and golden vials full of odours, which are the prayers of saints. And they sung a new song, saying, Thou are worthy to take the book, and to open the seals thereof: for thou wast slain, and hast redeemed us [NASB, men] to God by thy blood out of every kindred, and tongue, and people, and nation; and hast made us [NASB, them] unto our God kings and priests: and we [NASB, they] shall reign on the earth.*** These mighty creatures take the feeble prayers of God's people on earth and pour them out as a sweet fragrance before God. The worship of glory is now lifted an octave higher. In chapter four the theme was, "Thou art worthy for thou hast created." The theme here is, "Thou art worthy . . . for thou wast slain." Oh, the wonder of it all! That heaven's Beloved should beggar Himself, should be born in a barn, should be commonly called "the carpenter's son," should journey through time as a homeless Stranger in the very world His hands had made, should suffer unspeakable indignities and barbarities at the hands of His creatures, should be butchered on a cursed cross, and, above all, should be made sin! These are wonders that will never cease to draw out the awe and worship of those at the very focal center of things in glory.

In that bright scene of splendor, far beyond the skies, at the innermost heart of the universe, they worship Him. They see no man save Jesus only. They worship Him as the Lamb that was slain. It is Calvary that fills their vision and prompts their worship. Over yonder at this very moment they are doing what we do when we worship Him, when we spread the table and remember Him. For:

> When in scenes of glory
> I sing the new, new song;
> 'Twill be the same old story
> That I have loved so long.
>
> (A. Catherine Hanky)

"Worthy is the Lamb that was slain!" That is the theme of worship in heaven, and that is the theme of worship among the redeemed on earth.

The creatures at the throne worship Him. They praise God for putting the scroll of authority, of dominion, and of power into the hands of a man. And what a man He is! The countless angel throng worships Him. John says, *And I beheld, and I heard the voice of many angels round about the throne and the beasts and the elders: and the number of them was ten thousand times ten thousand, and thousands of thousands; Saying with a loud voice, Worthy is the Lamb that was slain to receive power, and riches, and wisdom, and strength, and honour, and glory, and blessing.* The triumphant anthems swell and roll and thunder out to the farthest reaches of space. They awaken the echoes of the everlasting hills. They reverberate and throb until all heaven is filled with praise. Just as a great crowd will pick up a slogan and beat it out in unison, so over yonder they thunder out the theme "Worthy is the Lamb! Worthy is the Lamb! Power! Riches! Wisdom! Strength! Honor! Glory! Blessing! Worthy is the Lamb!"

So then, at *the focal center* of the universe He is praised. But that is not all. He is worshiped also at *the furthest circumference* of the universe. John says, *And every creature which is in heaven, and on the earth, and under the earth, and such as are in the sea, and all that are in them, heard I saying, Blessing, and honour, and glory, and power, be unto him that sitteth upon the throne, and unto the Lamb for ever and ever. And the four beasts said, Amen. And the four and twenty elders fell down and worshipped him that liveth for ever and ever.* From every possible sphere and from every single tongue there rings out an acknowledgment at last that Jesus Christ is Lord. There will not be a single dissenting voice. The fallen angels, the angels imprisoned in the abyss, the angels bound near the Euphrates, the demon hordes, Satan himself, wicked, Christ-rejecting sinners of earth, one and all acknowledge Him as Lord. Deep in every heart will be the absolute conviction that the choice of Jesus is wise and just and blessed and honorable and glorious and irresistible. God has placed into the hands of men the decision as to whether or not they will accept Christ as Savior, but the decision as to whether or not they will acknowlege Him as Lord is not theirs to decide. The supreme tragedy of a lost eternity will be to know that there, shut out from the focal center, sentenced to the farthest, darkest, loneliest extreme of separation, His rejectors still have to acknowledge that Jesus is Lord. He will be praised at the focal center of things by the sinless sons of light and by the redeemed of all ages with joy unspeakable and full of glory. And He will be praised at the furthest circumference of things by every damned and outcast soul with sobs and tears and choking cries.

"God also hath highly exalted him, and given him a name which is above every name: that at the name of Jesus every knee should bow, of things in heaven, and things in earth, and things under the earth; and that every tongue should confess that Jesus Christ is Lord, to the glory of God the Father" (Phil. 2:9-11).

Part Three (Continued):
Visions of Government (4:1–20:15)

II. THE SUBLIME COURSE OF DIVINE GOVERNMENT (6:1–20:15)

A. The World Ruined by Man (6:1–7:17)

    1. What Is Recorded in Particular About the Seals (6:1-17)

        a. Seal One—The White Horse
           The Blasphemous Philosophies of the Last Days (6:1-2)

        b. Seal Two—The Red Horse
           The Belligerent Policies of the Last Days (6:3-4)

        c. Seal Three—The Black Horse
           The Blighted Prosperity of the Last Days (6:5-6)

        d. Seal Four—The Cadaverous Horse
           The Baneful Pestilences of the Last Days (9:7-8)

        e. Seal Five
           The Brutal Persecutions of the Last Days (6:9-11)

        f. Seal Six
           The Blind Panic of the Last Days (6:12-17)

    2. What Is Recorded in Parenthesis About the Seals (7:1-17)

        a. God's Providential Care for His Own (7:1-3)

        b. God's Personal Claim to His Own (7:4-12)

        c. God's Principal Concern for His Own (7:13-17)

Part Three (Continued):
Visions of Government (4:1–20:15)

II. THE SUBLIME COURSE OF DIVINE GOVERNMENT (6:1–20:15)

For two breathtaking, soul-inspiring chapters, we have been in heaven. The scroll has changed hands, and the right to judge and rule the world has been placed upon Jesus. Now we must come down from the mount and out of the ivory palaces. Down here, on the rebel planet of earth, the tempo is increasing, passions are rising. Evil men and seducers are waxing worse and worse. Disobedience to parents has grown up into brawling maturity, defying all authority. Men have become inventors of evil things, and their fearful inventions have become Frankenstein monsters, threatening to destroy the globe. The time has come for God to intervene in human affairs, so judgment is given to the Son. The seals on the scroll are to be broken.

There are three principal series of judgments in Revelation—the seal judgments, the trumpet judgments, and the vial judgments. The action of the book is carried forward, for the most part, by these series. The rest of the book is mainly parenthetical, either anticipating or reviewing a phase of that action.

Under the seal judgments, the world is *ruined by man*. Events recorded under the seals are extensions of things that are very evident in today's world. The chief difference is that the church will be gone, and to a great extent, restraint will be removed. The evil seeds men have sown will come to flower and fruit.

Under the trumpet judgments, the world is *ruled by Satan*. A vast and new dimension of the supernatural is introduced. Satan is cast down to earth; the planet is invaded by hordes of evil spirits; Satan's plans for this earth are matured.

Under the vial judgments, the world is *rescued by God*. The wrath of God is revealed from heaven. Satan's empire is dealt blow after blow by God

Himself, until at last the Lord, accompanied by His saints, returns from glory to put an end to this world's woes.

A. THE WORLD RUINED BY MAN (6:1–7:17)

1. WHAT IS RECORDED IN PARTICULAR ABOUT THE SEALS (6:1-17)

The seals are broken one by one, and restraint is increasingly removed from the earth. Vile human passions are given free rein, and the earth reaps the full harvest of man's sin.

      a. SEAL ONE—THE WHITE HORSE

         THE BLASPHEMOUS PHILOSOPHIES OF THE LAST DAYS

         (6:1-2)

The action begins at once as John says, *And I saw when the Lamb opened one of the seals, and I heard, as it were the noise of thunder, one of the four beasts saying, Come and see. And I saw, and behold a white horse: and he that sat on him had a bow; and a crown was given unto him: and he went forth conquering, and to conquer.* The mighty summons "Come!" rings out, and instantly the drumming of hoofs is heard as the first dread rider of the Apocalypse appears.

Who is this mysterious rider on the great white horse? In the Scripture, a horse is often used as a symbol for war. At the end of the Apocalypse, for example, the Lord Jesus Himself returns on a great white horse to settle the issues of Armageddon (Rev. 19:11-16). The white color of the horse suggests that the rider wins victories without bloodshed. Peaceful victory is implied— what we would call "cold war." The bow intimates that far-reaching objectives are in view, and the crown makes it clear that whatever is represented under the symbolism of this seal will be successful and victorious. At the command to come, the rider spurs forward both conquering, and to conquer.

But who is he? Some believe him to be the Antichrist. Others claim that he is Christ Himself. Some think he represents the gospel, its power, its goals, its peaceful conquest of the globe. Obviously he cannot be all of these. The context provides the needed clue, for the Holy Spirit Himself interprets the symbolism of the fourth horseman: he is Death, and Hades follows hard on his heels. The horsemen, therefore, are not persons, but personifications. More-over, they are personifications of things most unpleasant indeed.

Here, then, is a rider who personifies one of those factors, in the equation of the last days, that undermine the world and prepare it for God's final judgment. He is all-victorious and wins his victories relatively peacefully. He represents the blasphemous philosophies of the last days, those anti-Christian ideologies that prepare men's minds for the devil's gospel and the ultimate reception of the strong delusion, the great lie (2 Thess. 2:3-12).

Coming events always cast their shadows before them. That fact will become increasingly evident as the seals unfold. Things happen in the world that foreshadow and illustrate the eventual shape of things to come. It is not surprising that shadows can be discerned in today's world, shadows cast upon our times by soon-coming apocalyptic events. The days of the Apocalypse have not dawned yet, but enough is happening to enable us to clearly foresee what the judgment age will be like. The rider on the white horse is not yet abroad, for the great Restrainer is still here, and the book is still sealed. But we can surely see the shadow of this horse on every hand. We can see how radically and rapidly ideologies can change the world, and we can imagine what it will be like when restraints are removed and blasphemous propaganda is unleashed upon mankind, spurred on by permission from God's throne. The machinery for a major worldwide anti-God propaganda offensive already exists, and that machinery is being well oiled.

Take, for example, the rapid spread of communist ideology. The communist vision is simply the vision of man without God. With the Communists, propaganda comes first. It is ceaseless, tireless, ubiquitous. It acts as a stimulant or as a narcotic. It excites or soothes, proclaims a high ethic or undermines virtue; but it always deceives. It is spread by all communication media. It is written, spoken, sung, and danced. It reaches into all nations, speaks all languages and dialects, attracts all social levels. It uses front organizations; it employs slogans, demonstrations, parades; it incites sabotage and riot; it holds schools and seminars; it arranges trips behind the iron and bamboo curtains. It spends billions of dollars a year and employs hundreds of thousands of agents. It is hard at work undermining everything honorable and decent in the world.

Or take the spread of humanistic philosophy. Humanism has taken deep root in the Western world. It is a secular religion with many similarities to Communism. It emphasizes:

Evolution. There is no real evidence that God exists. The universe is the result of chance. Life forms gradually emerged over millions of years.

Situation ethics. Man is the final authority for his own actions. There are no absolute rules.

Moral freedom. Everyone (including children of any age) should be exposed to all viewpoints that are "realistic," including profanity, immorality, and perversion—all seen as acceptable methods of self expression. The Christian gospel is not realistic, so has no place in the system.

Self sufficiency. Man is not accountable to any higher power. He is responsible to himself.

Sexual permissiveness. All forms of sexual expression are acceptable and should be taught in schools free from biblical bias.

Anti-religious bias. Religion is harmful. It is either meaningless or irrelevant to the question of the survival and fulfillment of the human race.

Socialism. Government ownership or control of the economy should replace private enterprise and private ownership of property. There should be an all-pervasive welfare state.

One world government. "Global citizenship" should replace national self determination. There should be a system of world law, enforced by an international police force transcending national federal government.

Death education. There is no life beyond the grave. Euthanasia should be employed and suicide endorsed as acceptable ways to terminate life.

Human destiny. Man should take charge of his own future and realize that he has within himself the power to achieve the world of his dreams.

This creed is verbalized in the *Humanist Manifesto,* first drawn up in 1933 and updated in 1973. This creed is now being taught to millions in our public schools by teachers who perceive their roles in the classroom as that of missionaries of the humanist religion. The creed pervades our government, our courts, our educational institutions, our media, and our liberal churches. It is a creed tailor-made for the coming Antichrist. It is preparing the world for the breaking of the seals when all restraints will be removed and when global upheavals will prepare the final path for the world government of the Devil's Messiah.

And this is only the shadow of what is yet to come. When the first seal is broken and blasphemous philosophies are sent forth to subdue the earth, they will race around the world with unbelievable speed.

b. SEAL TWO—THE RED HORSE
THE BELLIGERENT POLICIES OF THE LAST DAYS (6:3-4)

John tells us, *And when he had opened the second seal, I heard the second beast say, Come and see. And there went out another horse that was red: and power was given unto him that sat thereon to take peace from the earth, and that they should kill one another: and there was given unto him a great sword.* This rider symbolizes the belligerent policies of the last days. He personifies world war on a scale never before known on earth, war that will make the conflicts of this century seem like scenes in a stilted play. Ever since Cain murdered Abel, man has been escalating war upon this earth. The end is not yet.

A book entitled *Report from Iron Mountain*[1] was published some time ago. It claimed to be a suppressed government report, the result of a high-

---

1. Leonard Levin, ed., *Report from Iron Mountain* (New York: Dial, 1967).

level study on the role played by war in the modern world. The book was highly controversial; some maintained it was a hoax, others claimed it was authentic. The study was allegedly conducted by fifteen scientists representing a wide range of disciplines. The group included a historian, a political theorist, a professor of international law, an economist, a sociologist, a cultural anthropologist, a physical chemist, a biochemist, a communications theorist, a systems analyst, a war planner, and an industrialist. The group was told to waste no time on "agonizing over cultural and religious values." It was to give the same kind of treatment to the hypothetical problems of peace as has been given to the hypothetical problems of nuclear war.

The first conclusion was that wars would cease if the will to make them cease were there. But since war itself is at the very root of mankind's social systems, it is not likely that peace will ever be a serious goal. No substitute is known that can better stabilize and control national economies. War, moreover, is the foundation of stable government; every governing body that has failed to sustain the continuing credibility of an external threat of war has lost control of its constituency. War provides a nation with a means of controlling its youth; it provides society with an effective means of dealing with overpopulation; it is probably the greatest single stimulant to scientific research; it has a high social value for dissipating boredom; and it gives the older generation an effective means for controlling a physically stronger and more vigorous younger generation.

The report found no satisfactory substitutes for war, although it explored a number of alternatives. Vast increases in social welfare expenditure would not be a sufficient countermeasure. Massive investments in space research would not be an adequate substitute for war for stimulating national economy. One startling conclusion was that, in the political realm, if war were to be abolished, some sort of slavery would need to be instituted as a means of controlling destabilizing social elements. Populations would need to be controlled by the compulsory introduction into water supplies of some sort of birth control chemical. The overall conclusion reached was that war is essential to society as now constituted, and it would be irresponsible to remove the war system until it was known exactly what would be put in its place.

No wonder God says of mankind that "the way of peace have they not known" (Rom. 3:17) and that the Lord Jesus declared, with characteristic incisive analysis, "Ye shall hear of wars and rumours of wars: see that ye be not troubled: for all these things must come to pass, but the end is not yet. For nation shall rise against nation, and kingdom against kingdom" (Matt. 24:6-7).

The human race finds the trappings of war fascinating. It loves the accoutrements that surround the military. Consider the words of Richard LaGallienne:

War
I abhor,
And yet how sweet
The sound along the marching street
Of drum and fife! And I forget
Wet eyes of widows, and forget
Broken old mothers, and the whole
Dark butchery without a soul.
Without a soul—save this bright drink
Of heady music, sweet as death;
And e'en my peace-abiding feet
Go marching with the marching street,
For yonder, yonder goes the fife
And what care I for human life?
The tears fill my astonished eyes,
And my full heart is like to break;
And yet 'tis all embannered lies,
A dream those little drummers make.
Oh, it is wickedness to clothe
Yon hideous, grinning thing that stalks
Hidden in music, like a queen
That in a garden of glory walks,
'Till good men love the thing they loathe!
Art! Thou hast many infamies,
But not an infamy like this!
Oh, snap the fife and still the drum
And show the monster as she is!

God once sent men a peace offer when the Prince of Peace was born, but men scorned and crucified Him. Until He comes back in power, war must go on until at last war itself is personified, mounted on a blood-red horse, and sent forth with a great red sword to summon men to the terrible wars of the Apocalypse.

c. SEAL THREE—THE BLACK HORSE
THE BLIGHTED PROSPERITY OF THE LAST DAYS (6:5-6)

Again the cry, Come! rings forth. John says, *And when he had opened the third seal, I heard the third beast say, Come and see. And I beheld, and lo a black horse; and he that sat on him had a pair of balances in his hand. And I heard a voice in the midst of the four beasts say, A measure of wheat for a penny, and three measures of barley for a penny; and see thou hurt not the oil and the wine.* The rider on the black horse is commanded to leave untouched the luxuries of the rich, but the staples, the wheat and barley of the poor, these are to be weighed out a pinch at a time. For this rider symbolizes the blighted prosperity of the last days; he represents famine and economic disaster. In Bible times, a man would work all day for a penny. In days to come, famine and inflation will play such havoc with the economies of the world that a working man's daily wage will buy only enough of the poorest food to satisfy his own immediate needs.

It has happened before. Charles Dickens described the want and privation, the hardship and hunger that gnawed at the vitals of Paris and produced one of the most terrible revolutions the world has ever known. Monseigneur, said Dickens in *The Tale of Two Cities*, "one of the great lords of the land must have his morning chocolate served up by four strong men besides the cook. One lacquey carried the chocolate pot into the sacred presence; a second, milled and frothed the chocolate; a third, presented the favoured napkin; a fourth poured the chocolate out. Monseigneur must have the luxuries of life and have them in magnificent style. But hunger stalked the streets and slums of the poor. Cold, dirt, sickness, ignorance and want were the lords in waiting in the streets and slums—nobles of great power all of them; but most especially the last. Hunger was prevalent everywhere. It was pushed out of the tall houses in the wretched clothing that hung upon poles and lines; Hunger stared down from the smokeless chimneys, and started up from the filthy street. Hunger was the inscription on the baker's shelves, written in every small loaf of his scanty stock of bad bread; at every sausage shop in every dead-dog preparation that was offered for sale."

It has happened before. It is with us today. Half the children of the world of preschool age are so undernourished that their physical and mental growth is retarded, and mortality among them is sixty times what it is in more fortunate societies. More than half the world goes to bed hungry. Even the magnificent bounty of the United States cannot stave off forever the mass starvation of the world. Malnutrition stalks the globe. It claims ten thousand lives every day. In the United States we throw into our garbage cans every day enough food to feed a family of six in India. Few Americans would admit to throwing away large quantities of food. One researcher, however, estimates that fifteen percent of all edible food in the United States ends up in the garbage—at a cost of $17.5 billion annually. (See William L. Rathje, "The Garbage Decade," in *American Behavioral Scientist,* Sept.-Oct. 1984). The average American dog has a higher protein diet than most peoples of the world. One-and-a-half million people are forever hungry on what Ghandi called "the eternal compulsory fast." While we sit down to dinner, four hundred people will starve to death. Each dawn finds 203,000 additional mouths to feed, each year 74,000,000 more—the net increase of births over deaths.

The stories that make the popular press are the horror stories, such as the famine in Ethiopia where millions face death by starvation. The situation is aggravated by Ethiopia's communist regime, which is more interested in putting down the freedom fighters in the north than in feeding its own people, and by the callous attitude of the Soviet Union, which supplies its client state with billions of dollars worth of armaments and barely a trickle of famine relief.

But the famine problem is global, and growing. The president's Council on Environmental Quality, after a three-year study released its findings in 1980 (findings considered on the conservative side by many experts) in *The Global 2000 Report to the President.* The picture it painted was apocalyptic.

By the year 2000 world population will have risen to 6.35 billion. Most of that population growth will be in the poorer, underdeveloped countries. The number of malnourished will rise to 1.3 *billion* people. Starvation will claim increasing numbers of babies, and many who survive will grow up physically and mentally stunted.

There will be other nightmares. On the fringes of the world's deserts there is a relentless search for firewood. In places like Africa's stricken Sahel and Asia's Himalayan foothills there is an *annual* loss of enough trees to cover half the state of California with forests. The commercial exploitation of the Amazon rain forest has had disasterous ecological results. As trees are cut down the ground becomes more arid and topsoil is lost. Ecologists predict the extinction of two million species of plants and animals in the next two decades alone— including rare plants needed for creating blight and pest-resistant hybrids. In more fertile areas, irrigation increases the soil's salinity, leading to smaller crops. All this points to worse famines ahead.

Each year the world consumes about 1.2 billion metric tons of grain alone (enough to build a highway—eighteen yards wide and six feet deep—around the world at the equator). And there is not much hope of increasing the supply. Almost all the world's land capable of economic cultivation (some 3.6 billion acres) is already in use.

And the deserts are spreading.

The Sahara, a naked empire of sand stretching across North Africa, covers more than 3,000,000 square miles in varying degrees of desolation—an area bigger than the continental United States (and much of it was productive land in Roman times). The once arable land on its southern edge is yielding to the unforgiving, relentless desert. Nations like Mauritania, Senegal, Mali, Upper Volta, Niger, and Chad, in a 2000-mile strip, are facing a losing battle. Dust storms prevail, and seas of sand surge south.

The reason? Trees are chopped down for fuel, marginal land is cleared and its fertility is cultivated away, grasslands are grazed to extinction. Governmental ineptitude and bureaucratic bungling make things worse. In some areas, denuding the land of trees has aptly been called "the other energy crisis."

The United Nations estimates that each year the process of erosion and desert expansion (not limited to Africa—much of the Tigris-Euphrates valley, where agriculture first took root, is salt desert today) claims an area the size of Maine. Areas totalling the combined land mass of the United States, the Soviet Union, and Australia are in danger. It estimates that it would take up to forty years and an investment of $20 billion just to reclaim land lost to deserts in the past twenty-five years. No wonder famines will be a large part of the end-time picture.

It has happened before. It is with us today. It will happen again. For this dread rider is not yet abroad; it is only his shadow we see. But when he comes, he will act as secretary of state for starving mankind, will wipe them out by the millions, and will dispose the survivors to listen to the buttered lies of the Beast.

d. SEAL FOUR—THE CADAVEROUS HORSE
THE BANEFUL PESTILENCES OF THE LAST DAYS (6:7-8)

For the last time the summons rings out. This time the horse is the color of death. John says, *And when he had opened the fourth seal, I heard the voice of the fourth beast say, Come and see, And I looked, and behold a pale horse: and his name that sat on him was Death, and Hell followed with him. And power was given unto them over the fourth part of the earth, to kill with sword, and with hunger, and with death [pestilence], and with the beasts of the earth.* War and famine will continue to plague mankind, breaking out on a local scale first here and then there, but a new horror is now added—pestilence. War and famine invariably give rise to pestilence. Twenty million people died in the influenza epidemics of World War I, and six million more died of typhus.

The new wonder drugs have not eliminated the possibility of mass death by pestilence. Prominent medical men warn that antibiotics and sulfa drugs, when used with routine frequency, may defeat their germ-killing purpose and lead to more resistent germs. Drug-resistant bacteria that can foil several antibiotics at once have already appeared. Unless drastic measures are taken, physicians may find themselves back in the pre-antibiotic Middle Ages in the treatment of infectious diseases. And the deadly AIDS virus is a harbinger of things to come.

Modern man has crowned all his other insanities by adding pestilence to his arsenals. We have enough bacteria stockpiled today to infect people with scores of diseases, and we have chemical agents that can destroy entire populations with terrifying ease. Such weapons can be ground into fine powders and sprayed into favorable winds; many can be introduced into a nation's water supply. Some can be dropped into enemy territory in infected rodents, ticks, and lice. Many biological weapons carry a death menace that cannot be detected and that can stay alive and potent for years. The leading world powers have pledged themselves not to use such weapons, but pragmatism rules most warring nations, not sentiment. Given a favorable opportunity and a big enough incentive, most nations would resort to bacteriological war.

It was not until 1975 that the United States signed an international treaty banning the first use of biological and chemical weapons and ratified, along with the USSR, the production and stockpiling of biological weapons for defensive purposes. The period since 1975 has not been an easy one. Indeed it has been called a period of "benign neglect" on the part of the U.S.A. since it has become increasingly evident that the Soviet Union has ignored the treaty. Their use of chemical weapons in Afghanistan, allegations that they supplied "yellow rain" for use in Laos and Kampuchea, rumors of a mysterious 1979 epidemic killing considerable numbers of people in the Soviet city of Sverdlovsk, caused by organisms released during an explosion in a nearby military laboratory, and similar indications of Soviet cynicism have given the United States second thoughts.

The U.S. Army has quietly proceeded with plans of its own, including a sophisticated biological laboratory in Utah. One goal is to test defenses against aerosols containing deadly organisms including thorax (believed to be behind the Sverdlovsk disaster), or microbes for spreading pneumonic plague, typhus, and equine encephalitis. In order to test defenses against such microbes the Army, of course, will have to stock them.

On the horizon are organisms created by recombinant DNA technology. Recombinant DNA promises to raise new nightmares because it can be used to create large amounts of pure vaccines and if a country has a vaccine against its own biological weapons it can protect itself—which means it has offensive capability. Not that new microbes are needed to accommodate the wickedness of men. The Mongols are said to have catapulted the bodies of plague victims into the Crimean town of Kaffa in order to bring an end to resistance.

So far the Russians have taken biological and chemical warfare much more seriously than has the United States. Evidence is piling up that they have supplied the client state of Ethiopia with deadly nerve gas to use against the Eritreans. U.S. military intelligence estimates that a third of the USSR's tactical missiles are equipped with chemical warheads and that a chemical-defense company is assigned to every line regiment.

Quite apart from the exotic DNA experiments, weapons already available are truly apocalyptical. Nerve gases, for instance, are horrifying. A few drops of the most potent nerve poisons in the U.S. arsenal can kill just by being brushed on the skin. A quart of the deadly stuff could theoretically kill a million people. Some forms are "persistent" because they remain deadly after settling on the ground. One form of the nerve poison, spread in mist form, sticks to everything it touches. It can penetrate clothing and skin. Unprotected people can pick up a lethal dose later just by touching a contaminated object.

The shadow of the rider on the pale horse lies black across the world. Associated with pestilence are "the beasts of the earth." Is this a literal or a symbolic reference? It seems inconceivable that, in an age of napalm and atomic bombs, mankind could be imperiled by lions and tigers and bears. Since the Greek word translated "beasts" occurs thirty-eight times in the Revelation, and in all other references has to do with the Beast—the coming superman— the beasts referred to here might well be bestial men who rise to power to plague mankind. Such an idea is certainly consistent with the book of Revelation and with the book of Daniel.

But another thought demands consideration. The beasts are closely linked with the pestilence, and that might be a clue. The most destructive creature on earth, so far as mankind is concerned, is not the lion or the bear, but the rat. The rat is clever, adaptable, and destructive. If ninety-five percent of the rat population is exterminated in a given area, the rat population will replace itself within a year. It has killed more people than all the wars of history, and it makes its home wherever man is found. Rats carry as many as thirty-five different diseases. Their fleas carry bubonic plague, which killed a third of the population of Europe in the fourteenth century. Their fleas also carry typhus, which in four centuries has killed an estimated 200 million people. Beasts, in this passage, are linked not only with pestilence, but with famine, Rats menace human food supplies, which they both devour and contaminate, especially in the more underdeveloped countries that can least afford to suffer loss.

So then, the breaking of the fourth seal unleashes pestilence upon the earth. The ingredients for this visitation of judgment are already present, and it needs just the right mix of circumstances to touch off the disasters described.

e. SEAL FIVE
THE BRUTAL PERSECUTIONS OF THE LAST DAYS (6:9-11)

The seals are divided into four and three, a common division of the various sevens of the Apocalypse. Our attention is now drawn to the brazen altar. John says, *And when he had opened the fifth seal, I saw under the altar the souls of them that were slain for the word of God, and for the testimony which they held: And they cried with a loud voice, saying, How long, O Lord, holy and true, dost thou not judge and avenge our blood on them that dwell on the earth? And white robes were given unto every one of them; and it was said unto them, that they should rest yet for a little season, until their fellowservants also and their brethren, that should be killed as they were, should be fulfilled.* This gives a glimpse of the brutal persecutions of the last days.

We are living already in an age of mass persecution. The horror camps of the Nazis have provided a terrible illustration of what lies ahead for the world. After World War II, the Nazi war criminals were put on trial at Nuremberg, and their unbelievable atrocities were put on public display. Justice Jackson, in his opening speech for the prosecution, described the crimes committed against the Jews. First there was discrimination; then the ghettos, used as laboratories for testing repressive measures; then came the concentration camps and the mass extermination camps. As a result, nearly 6 million Jews, 60 percent of the Jews in Nazi-dominated Europe, were killed. Justice Jackson described the sadistic cruelty, the torture, the starvation, the mass murder, the diabolical experiments on live human guinea pigs. "History," he said, "does not record a crime perpetuated against so many victims or ever carried out with such calculated cruelty."

When the evidence was all in, Sir Hartley Shawcross summed up for the British delegation. He rehearsed the barbarous deeds that had been done. He told how lampshades had been made from tatooed human skin, how human hair had been baled for commercial purposes, how gold teeth had been extracted from victims and shipped in ingots to the Reichbank. "Mass murder," he said, "was becoming a State industry, with byproducts."[2] That is only one page from the sordid story of modern persecution. There are many pages more. The world is getting ready for the breaking of this seal.

The slaughter continues today. Indeed, the atrocities committed by the Communists in Indochina alone make the Nazi holocaust look almost mild.

In Cambodia, for instance, after the Communist take-over in April, 1975, the greatest forced mass evacuation of a nation's cities in all of history took place. The forced exodus of some 3.5 million people, half the country's population, was part of a plan to destroy a society's past and present.

Hours after the communist troops entered Phnom Penh the residents were being ordered to leave. It made no difference that there was no food or water, that temperatures exceeded 100 degrees, that people were in hospital beds or that women were pregnant. Those who couldn't keep up were left by the road to die or were shot. And long after the forced evacuations ended, the Communists continued systematically killing off anyone with even so much as a high school education.

And it was not only Phnom Penh. The Communists systematically emptied all the cities. Some 4 million men, women, and children were driven into the countryside. The capital, which had once contained 3 million people, was reduced to 15,000. Cambodia was transformed into a vast slave camp. Men, women, and children were segregated from each other and forced to toil up to fourteen hours a day, seven days a week, breaking only to watch executions.

Similar atrocities were committed by the Vietnamese Communists. The Hanoi government, for instance, decided that its Chinese population was a

2. G. M. Gilbert, *Nuremberg Diary* (New York: New American Lib., 1971).

potential threat. It began the systematic elimination of the million ethnic Chinese, giving them the choice of leaving the country or being moved to rural labor camps.

The refugees began to flee the country. They became known as "the boat people" because so many were callously turned loose on the high seas with nowhere to go. The Hanoi government discovered that it could extract enormous sums of money from its victims in the process of getting rid of them. Hong Kong government officials have said that the trade in human lives actually replaced coal as Hanoi's principal source of gold and hard currency. The Viet Nam government aimed to collect up to $3 billion by the time all its Chinese population would be expelled. Hanoi maintained its heartless policy with the certain knowledge that many of the refugees would perish at sea. Most were set adrift in vessels which were hopelessly overcrowded, with insufficient food and water, and sent forth to face the added perils of storms at sea, pirates, and ports closed to them in country after country.

Dramatic and terrible as the plight of the boat people may be, they represent only a small percentage of the world's unwanted, people. It has been estimated that between 10 million and 13 million people are at present permanently unsettled, many living in refugee camps in overcrowded, insanitary conditions, malnourished, unemployed, unwanted, and hopeless.

The cry that ascends to God from the brazen altar is not a Christian cry. It is a cry for vengeance, a cry that will be quite appropriate once the age of grace is over and conditions revert back to a pre-Christian era. What is shown here, under the breaking of the fifth seal, is elaborated further in chapter 7, where the Great Tribulation is introduced. Here only a preview is given of the terrible persecutions that will engulf the globe in a coming day.

f. SEAL SIX
THE BLIND PANIC OF THE LAST DAYS (6:12-17)

There follows now a description of total chaos on earth. Men are absolutely horrified at what they see. John says, *And I beheld when he had opened the sixth seal, and, lo, there was a great earthquake; and the sun became black as sackcloth of hair, and the moon became as blood; and the stars of heaven fell unto the earth, even as a fig tree casteth her untimely figs, when she is shaken of a mighty wind. And the heaven departed as a scroll when it is rolled together; and every mountain and island were moved out of their places. And the kings of the earth, and the great men, and the rich men, and the chief captains, and the mighty men, and every bondman, and every free man, hid themselves in the dens and in the rocks of the mountains, and said to the mountains and rocks, Fall on us, and hide us from the face of him that sitteth on the throne, and from the wrath of the Lamb: for the great day of his wrath is come; and who shall be able to stand?* This is a picture of the blind panic of the last days. Men's hearts are now failing with fear as they look at what is coming on the earth. They feel that the day of wrath has come. In this they are wrong, for these things are only "the beginning of sorrows" (Matt. 24:8).

The *cause of the panic* is first described. The disasters described here can, of course, be taken as literal. Drastic changes in the heavens could result in earthquakes and drastic changes in the topography of the planet. It is also possible that the description is symbolic and depicts total collapse of the establishment. The earthquake suggests that everything stable in society will be shaken. The disasters to the sun, the moon, and the stars suggest the downfall or the plunging into confusion of all governing bodies. The moving of the islands and the mountains indicates tremendous changes in constituted government.

The *completeness of the panic* is described next. It affects every class of society from the meanest slave to the greatest king. Men lose all hope and can find no place to hide from the anarchy that grips the globe.

Forces of anarchy are already active in the world. Lawlessness is evident in every country on earth, in the mighty nations that control international affairs and in the newly emerging nations that are but a step removed from the jungle. Lawlessness will be an important factor in making possible the eventual power play of the beast. He is called "the lawless one" in 2 Thessalonians 2:8, NASB. He profits from lawlessness and uses it for his own advancement. The hundreds of radical groups, dedicated to the overthrow of society as it is now constituted, preaching the death of the establishment are, at present, divinely restrained. One day the seal of restraint will be broken and, as during the days of the French and Russian revolutions, the old order will be swept away. A new society will emerge, with its constitution drawn up in hell.

So then, six of the seven seals are broken. The seventh is not described until later (8:1-6) and relates to the believing prayers of the last days. As the seals are broken, the forces of destruction, latent in human society, are allowed to develop apace, and under the trumpets they precipitate the crisis that makes it possible for the Beast to take over. First, however, demon forces must be hurled into the maelstrom of human affairs, to the utter woe of mankind. That happens when the trumpets are blown.

2. WHAT IS RECORDED IN PARENTHESIS ABOUT THE SEALS *(7:1-17)*

Revelation 7 explains and expands the horror unleashed at the breaking of the fifth seal. Persecution develops into the full-blown horrors of the Great Tribulation. This chapter is parenthetical. The events described do not take place until later in the book, when the beast comes to power and puts down all that stands in his way. Once the seals are broken and the restraints removed, it can only be a matter of time before such wickedness comes to a head. Here the ultimate, inevitable collision between holiness and iniquity is described. God wants us to know what lies ahead for His people in the terrible period of trial that follows the rapture of the church.

The multitudes of sealed and saved persons who come into view in this chapter are probably the fruit of the ministry of those two mysterious witnesses whom God will raise up during the first part of the Beast's career. It will be his murder of these two witnesses that will give the Beast much of his rapport with godless humanity. The converts of these two men will face the rage and fury of the Beast and will be called upon to seal their testimony with their blood. This chapter focuses on that testing and triumph. The world, exasperated by the hardening judgments of the seals and trumpets, will look for a scapegoat on which to vent its rage. As Nero singled out the Christians for persecution, so the beast will turn in fury on those who believe in God in his day. Long before the dreadful time comes, God tells in advance how He will love and care for His own, sealing some and strengthening others for the dreadful hour of trial.

a. GOD'S PROVIDENTIAL CARE FOR HIS OWN (7:1-3)

First there is given a magnificent revelation of God's absolute control over all the factors of time and space. John says, *And after these things I saw four angels standing on the four corners of the earth, holding the four winds of the earth, that the wind should not blow on the earth, nor on the sea, nor on any tree. And I saw another angel ascending from the east, having the seal of the living God: and he cried with a loud voice to the four angels, to whom it was given to hurt the earth and the sea, Saying Hurt not the earth, neither the sea, nor the trees, till we have sealed the servants of our God in their foreheads.* There is a calm in the midst of the storm. Four angels, who are active in the judgments and who hold in their hands further tempests of fury, are restrained by a decree of God. Some of God's people must be sealed before anything else can transpire.

A stillness will descend on human affairs. The world's politicians no doubt will pride themselves that their diplomacy and astuteness have brought about this tranquility. The sudden peace, however, will be none of man's doing, but God's. It is, in reality, just a lull between storms. Man consistently ignores the biblical truth that the heavens do rule. To man, every phenomenon, especially of a political nature, must have a natural explanation. It would never do to admit that there is a higher hand than man's controlling human affairs.

This sudden stillness is so that the 144,000 can be sealed. God said to delinquent Lot, "I cannot do anything till thou be come thither" (Gen. 19:22). Just so, God will not allow the Great Tribulation to develop until He has secured and sealed a remnant of believing Jews. The angel with the seal comes from the east. The final disaster comes from the east when the time for

Armageddon is ripe. The Lord also comes from the east when He comes in His glory. "For as the lightning cometh out of the east, and shineth even unto the west; so shall also the coming of the Son of man be" (Matt. 24:27).

b. GOD'S PERSONAL CLAIM TO HIS OWN (7:4-12)

God always lays claim to His own. When Abimelech tampered with Abraham's affairs, God warned, "Restore the man his wife; for he is a prophet, and he shall pray for thee" (Gen. 20:7). To Elijah He said, "Yet I have left me seven thousand in Israel, all the knees which have not bowed unto Baal" (1 Kings 19:18). God lays claim to His own, but that does not mean they necessarily escape the common disasters of earth. It means that God watches over them and takes careful note of their affairs. There are two very different companies of people in this section. One company is Jewish; the other is Gentile. One passes unscathed through the fiery furnace of the Tribulation; the other is martyred to the very last man.

There are those who are *sealed to defy the totality of Satan's secular dominion.* They are drawn from the various tribes of Israel. John says, *And I heard the number of them which were sealed: and there were sealed an hundred and forty and four thousand of all the tribes of the children of Israel.* There were 12,000 from the tribes of Judah, Reuben, Gad, Asher, Naphtali, Manasseh, Simeon, Levi, Issachar, Zebulon, Joseph, and Benjamin. Dan and Ephraim are missing from the list. In Old Testament history, both of those tribes were prominent for their connection with idolatry. Perhaps in a coming day they take the lead in hailing the Beast as Messiah. Israel's tribal divisions are no longer known. But God knows them, and in a coming day he will see to it that each of the appropriate tribes is equally represented in the sealing. Joseph provides us with an illustration. He could seat his brethren in proper order around the festive board and select his full brother, Benjamin, for a worthy portion. It was no problem to him, although it greatly astonished them (Gen. 43:33-34). The Lord knows what Israel's tribal divisions are.

Those sealed will go unscathed through the Great Tribulation. They will be a perpetual thorn in the side of the Beast and a constant reminder to the devil that, while millions may bow to his will, God still has him on a leash and says to him, "Thus far and no farther." The mobilized armies of the earth will not be able to touch a hair of the heads of these sealed ones. The concentration camps and torture chambers of the Beast's fearful inquisition will leave them unscathed. The fire will not kindle upon them, nor will the smell of smoke be on their garments. The floods will not be able to drown them. The secret police will have dossiers as thick as prison walls, but they will be unable to harm them. The seal of God rests upon them, and they are saved and secured, come what may. They will be a living proof to the devil that not only is his secular power strictly limited by divine decree, but in the end he cannot win. If he cannot conquer these, then he cannot possibly win in the end. No matter how many millions he liquidates in his insane rage, he is obviously under the control of God.

So then, the 144,000 are sealed to defy the totality of Satan's secular dominion. They are a reminder to him that every knee does not bow to him and that God is sovereign and in invincible control.

But there is another company to be considered. There is a great multitude of Gentiles who will be saved during the tribulation period and who will seal their testimony with their blood. They are *saved to deny the totality of Satan's spiritual dominion.* Notice, first, *where they are standing.* John says, *After this I beheld, and, lo, a great multitude, which no man could number, of all nations, and kindreds, and people, and tongues, stood before the throne, and before the Lamb, clothed with white robes, and palms in their hands.*

They were standing before the throne and before the Lamb. The throne carries us back in thought to chapters 4 and 5. It reminds us that God is still sovereign, even in earth's darkest and most dreadful hour, during the diabolical reign of the Beast. The thought of the Lamb reminds us that Jesus is still Savior, even during the Tribulation period. Millions upon millions will be saved during this time, to the glory of God's grace. These saved ones are standing before the throne.

As to their *number,* they are countless. The day of Pentecost was magnificent, with about three thousand being saved on the church's birthday alone. It was a great victory, but in terms of numbers it was nothing like this visitation of the latter rain that will come after the church has gone. Nineveh repented at the preaching of Jonah, and it is estimated that about a million souls were saved. It was a great victory, but it is not to be compared with this. Some 3 million people followed Moses out of Egypt, having responded to the way of redemption through the shed blood of the lamb. It was a great victory, but this surpasses it by far. Here is a multitude no man can number!

As to their *nationalities,* we observe that not a single tribe or tongue is missing. There was a roll call of the nations at Pentecost, but it was nothing like this! The persecuted saints during the Tribulation, fleeing from country to country, will carry with them a veritable epidemic of revival. The more the Beast fans the flames of repression, the more the Holy Ghost fans the flames of revival! The church may not reach to every kindred and every tongue, but the Tribulation saints will.

As to their *nature,* we are told that they stand before the Lord, clothed with white robes and with palms in their hands. This is a picturesque way of telling us that they are both virtuous and victorious. Together the facts add up to a resounding defeat of the devil at the hands of these majestic martyrs of the faith. So when it is all over, they are seen standing, highly exalted by God, at a place near His throne.

We note also *what they were saying.* John tells us that they **cried with a loud voice, saying, Salvation to our God which sitteth upon the throne, and unto the Lamb.** They were praising God *for His grace.* They were saying, "Praise God for our salvation." Every one of them, it seems, pays the price of martyrdom for his faith, yet they thank God for their salvation. They leave life through the terrifying gates of the most horrible deaths that Satan can devise. The faggot and the fires, the rack, the thumbscrew and the wheel, the scalpel and the sword are their means of exodus. But it is all over now! They are saved! They thank God for His grace.

They thank God also *for His government.* They say, "Salvation to our God which sitteth upon the throne." Their days on earth are dark and dreadful, and no doubt they cry again and again, "Why, O God, why? O Lord, how long?" God is silent, the heavens are as brass as evil triumphs everywhere, and the heathen rage. They are often tempted to believe that God has abdicated His throne, but now they see Him sitting there.

They thank God, moreover, *for His gift.* "Salvation," they say, "unto the Lamb." They are in heaven, not because they were willing to be martyred, not because they gave their bodies to be burned, not because they were counted as sheep for the slaughter, not because they endured to the end, not because they took joyfully the despoiling of their goods, not because they came through Great Tribulation, but because of the Lamb. And they know it!

We notice also *who they were stimulating.* John says, **And all the angels stood round about the throne, and about the elders and the four beasts, and fell before the throne on their faces, and worshipped God. Saying, Amen: Blessing, and glory, and wisdom, and thanksgiving, and honour, and power, and might, be unto our God for ever and ever. Amen.** It is a great thing when something we say or do stimulates another person to worship. Imagine stimulating to adoring worship those high and lofty ones, who abide ever in the immediate presence of God! Worship is their deathless delight, their ceaseless function. Yet when they see these victorious martyrs standing before the throne, see them in their white robes of virtue and with their green palms of victory, and when they hear these conquerors lift up their voices in worship, the elders and the living creatures cannot contain themselves! They too burst out into an unrehearsed paean of praise. "Blessing!" they cry. "And glory, and wisdom, and thanksgiving, and honour, and power, and might, be unto our God for ever and ever. Amen." They worship God because out of the fire and fury of the Great Tribulation has come such a multitude of martyrs. His strength has been made perfect in weakness. We are prone to weep because of trial and tribulation, but on the other side of death we shall worship God for it. What a challenge these Tribulation saints should be to us. We should see to it that we act in such a way that God is praised by those who surround His throne.

c. GOD'S PRINCIPAL CONCERN FOR HIS OWN (7:13-17)

God has two principal concerns for His own beloved ones who have so triumphantly honored Him in the face of the fiercest persecution ever to be known on earth. He is concerned that they be *properly recognized.* To ensure that, one of the elders is moved to approach the seer with a question. John tells us what happened. *And one of the elders answered, saying unto me, What are these which are arrayed in white robes? and whence came they? And I said unto him, Sir, thou knowest. And he said to me, These are they which came out of great tribulation, and have washed their robes, and made them white in the blood of the Lamb.* The elder knew all along who they were, but God wanted John to know, and He wants us to know. These glorious martyrs have not died as yet; they may not even have been born, but God wants the saints of all ages to know about them. He wants them properly recognized. He wants their glorious victory to be eternally recorded on the deathless page of Holy Writ so that the record may be read long after the stars have ceased to shine!

God is concerned not only that His own be properly recognized, but that they also be *properly rewarded.* He is going to bestow upon them the *highest possible dignity.* John is told *Therefore are they before the throne of God, and serve him day and night in his temple.* They are in the innermost court; they are at His instant command. They are in the holiest place of the sanctuary. They have the very front seats in heaven! They are before the throne of God, not behind it, not off to one side, but right there where they can look into the face of God and watch every expression on His glorious countenance. They have a place no money can buy, reserved seats in His innermost court.

They are there not only to see, but also to serve. "They serve him day and night in his temple." It is a fitting role for those who can prompt worship from angels. And remember, they are Gentiles! These are not Jews, nor are they members of the church. These are the Gentile victors from the Tribulation. They have an access and an activity in heaven that must cause the evil one to gnash his teeth in rage. To think that the very worst he could do to these he hated most turns out to be the very best he could do for them! Truly, God makes the wrath of man—and the wrath of the devil, too—to praise Him.

These victors are marked out for the highest possible dignity. They are also marked out for *the happiest possible destiny.* In fact, three things are in store for them. They are to enjoy eternally *God's broadest protection.* John says, *He that sitteth on the throne shall dwell among them,* or, as it is rendered in the revised text, "He who sits on the throne shall spread His tabernacle over them" (NASB). When the Israelites marched out of Egypt, God spread over them a cloudy, fiery pillar, a vast canopy of protection against all that might harm them. No foe could daunt them, no fear could haunt them. Just so with these victorious martyrs. On earth they had known nothing but insecurity. They had been hunted like the partridge on the mountain. But no more! The living God spreads His tabernacle over them. They enjoy His broadest protection. Eternal security is theirs.

They enjoy, moreover, *God's boundless provision.* John tells us, *They shall hunger no more, neither thirst any more; neither shall the sun light on them, nor any heat.* All their blessings are stated in the negative. They had done without so much for the cause of Christ. They have given up father and mother, sister and brother, houses and land, home and hearth, fame and fortune. Now there are other things for them to do without—hunger and thirst, torment and pain! Never again will such things be their portion. God's boundless provision will see to that.

Last of all, they will enjoy eternally *God's blessed presence.* John concludes, *For the Lamb which is in the midst of the throne shall feed them, and shall lead them unto living fountains of waters; and God shall wipe away all tears from their eyes.* Their reward is to be close to the Lamb. He will be their Shepherd, dedicated to their welfare, their happiness, and their undying bliss. No reward could be greater than that!

Part Three (Continued):
Visions of Government
(4:1–20:15)

The World Ruled by Satan (8:1–13:18)
1. What Is Recorded in Preparation About the Trumpets (8:1-6)
   a. The Postponing of the Judgment (8:1-4)
   b. The Precipitating of the Judgment (8:5-6)
2. What Is Recorded in Particular About the Trumpets (8:7–9:21)
   a. War Intensified on Earth (8:7-13)
      (1) The First Trumpet—The Brewing Storm (8:7)
      (2) The Second Trumpet—The Boiling Sea (8:8-9)
      (3) The Third Trumpet—The Banished Star (8:10-11)
      (4) The Fourth Trumpet—The Blackened Sky (8:12-13)
   b. Woe Intensified on Earth (9:1-21)
      (1) The Fifth Trumpet (Woe 1)—A Satanically Energized Belief
          that Affects Humanity (9:1-12)
      (2) The Sixth Trumpet (Woe 2)—A Satanically Energized Battle
          that Alters History (9:13-21)
3. What Is Recorded in Parenthesis About the Trumpets (10:1–13:18)
   a. The Purposes of Heaven Revealed (10:1–11:19)
      (1) The Completion of the Mystery (10:1-11)
          (a) We Turn Our Eyes upon Jesus (10:1-3)
          (b) We Turn Our Eyes upon John (10:4-11)
      (2) The Coming of the Messengers (11:1-13)
          (a) The Mandate of the Messengers (11:1-5)
          (b) The Miracles of the Messengers (11:6)
          (c) The Martyrdom of the Messengers (11:7-10)
          (d) The Might of the Messengers (11:11-13)
      (3) The Crowning of the Messiah (11:14-19)
          (a) The Third Woe on the Earth (11:14-15)
          (b) The Thankful Worship in Heaven (11:16-19)

116

Part Three (Continued):
Visions of Government
(4:1–20:15)

B. THE WORLD RULED BY SATAN (8:1–13:18)

The world is now to be presented with Satan's man, the devil's messiah. The seals have been broken, the cries have rung out, the riders have appeared, and conditions on earth have grown rapidly worse. Men have become horrified, and imagining that the day of wrath has dawned, have called on the mountains and rocks to fall upon them and hide them from the Lamb. But worse is to come. Seven trumpets have yet to be blown, and wars worse than anything history records have yet to be fought. The war and famines, persecutions and pestilences unleashed under the seals are, after all, but the beginning of sorrows.

During the trumpet judgments, Satan is cast out of heaven and produces his trump card on earth—a superman. Men, no longer concerned about the Lamb, will be ready for the Beast.

1. WHAT IS RECORDED IN PREPARATION ABOUT THE TRUMPETS (8:1-6)

Before the trumpets are blown, one of the seals remains to be broken. The breaking of this seal produces a deep silence in heaven, a silence that is caused by the prayers of God's beleagured saints on earth. Two items of great interest are to be noted about these prayers.

a. THE POSTPONING OF THE JUDGMENT (8:1-4)

God holds up the entire process of judgment while He receives and weighs the prayers of His own. John says, *And when he had opened the seventh seal, there was silence in heaven about the space of half an hour. And I saw the seven angels which stood before God; and to them were given seven trumpets. And another angel came and stood at the altar, having a golden censer; and there was given unto him much incense, that he should offer it with the prayers of all saints upon the golden altar which was before the throne. And the smoke of the incense, which came with the prayers of the saints, ascended up before God out of the angel's hand.* These prayers result in judgment before long, so evidently they were prayers for vengeance, the kind of prayers already heard ascending from the brazen altar at the breaking of the fifth seal. In a coming age, the imprecatory psalms (e.g., 35:4-6; 59:13-15; 83:14-17; and 109:6-20) will come into their own. Such prayers as these, wholly unfit for an age of grace, will be most fitting for the persecuted martyrs of the Tribulation age. So then, God waits while His tormented and terrified people on earth pray.

What a potent force is prayer! The saints go into their bedrooms, close the doors, kneel down, and pray. They spread out before God their petitions, and God hears. The prayers are placed in the scales of judgment. In some mysterious way not explained to us, prayer changes things. This is true in every age. In a coming day, as the saints pray, "the angel of the Lord" (surely the Lord Himself) will come forward and add to the groans and cries the perfume and the fragrance of His finished work. For prayer never reaches God in the clumsy, inept, feeble way it leaves our lips. The Holy Spirit's energizing of our prayers and the risen Lord's endorsement of our prayers make them a force to be reckoned with in the universe. So then, there is silence in heaven for half an hour (of heaven's time) while God graciously takes into consideration the prayers of His own.

b. THE PRECIPITATING OF THE JUDGMENT (8:5-6)

In direct answer to prayer, God acts by setting in motion the trumpet judgments. John tells us, *And the angel took the censer, and filled it with fire of the altar, and cast it into the earth: and there were voices, and thunderings, and lightnings, and an earthquake. And the seven angels which had the seven trumpets prepared themselves to sound.* Preliminary rumblings are heard, presaging the great upheavals soon to take place. Voices! Thunderings! Lightnings! Earthquakes! In its essence, this formula, sometimes called a formula for catastrophe, is repeated four times in the Apocalypse (4:5; 8:5; 11:19; 16:18). Prayer that can precipitate such things truly must be potent indeed! So the silence ends. The prayers of God's people have been flung into the scales and have tipped the balance in favor of an immediate resumption of hostilities by heaven.

2. *WHAT IS RECORDED IN PARTICULAR ABOUT THE TRUMPETS (8:7-9:21)*

Just as the seals were divided into four and three, so are the trumpets. The first four trumpets are war trumpets, the last three are woe trumpets; woes are added to the continuing wars.

a. WAR INTENSIFIED ON EARTH (8:7-13)

The correlation among Revelation, Daniel, and other prophetic Scriptures is not always clear. Room must therefore be left, in presenting any interpretation, for dissenting opinion. The best the expositor can do, when treading on controversial ground, is to proceed with caution and honesty and state matters as they appear to him. With that in mind, the position is now taken that the Great Tribulation proper, really begins with the later trumpets. During the earlier trumpets, conditions on earth are made ripe for the coming of the Beast. Also, it would seem that the Beast has two comings. He appears first as the "beast . . . out of the sea" (13:1), and later, after his assassination, as the "beast . . . out of the abyss" (17:8).

Trumpets are connected with war in the Old Testament (Num. 10:9; Josh. 6:4-20; Judg. 7:8, 16-18). Particularly interesting is the overthrow of Jericho with its series of seven trumpet blowings.

(1) THE FIRST TRUMPET—THE BREWING STORM (8:7)

John says, *The first angel sounded, and there followed hail and fire mingled with blood, and they were cast upon the earth: and the third part of the trees was burnt up, and all green grass was burnt up.* This can be interpreted symbolically or literally, or the interpretation might include both symbolic and literal elements. Looked upon as a literal occurrence, an ecological disaster without parallel in historic times is described. The planet is denuded of a third of its trees and all of its grass. The consequences of this are bound to be terrible. The United States, for example, has already proceeded with deforestation to such an extent that the country contains only enough vegetation to produce 60 percent of the oxygen it consumes. Modern warfare now includes the deliberate defoliating of large areas of forest to deprive the enemy of cover. A literal fulfillment of this judgment is certainly credible.

On the other hand, the verse can just as easily be symbolic. In this case the grass could represent the masses of mankind and the trees could represent prominent leaders and rulers (Ps. 103:15; Judg. 9:7-15; Dan. 4:4-27). What is symbolized is a major upheaveal among the nations that results in the downfall of many people in high places and a mass depopulation of the globe. But this event, terrible as it will be, is but the beginning of the disasters described under the trumpets.

(2) THE SECOND TRUMPET—THE BOILING SEA (8:8-9)

Attention is now directed from the land to the sea. John says, *And the second angel sounded, and as it were a great mountain burning with fire was cast into the sea: and the third part of the sea became blood: and the third part of the creatures which were in the sea, and had life, died; and the third part of the ships were destroyed.* Is this a literal or a symbolic event? Ships are literal enough, but the casting of a mountain into the sea surely has to be symbolic. The sea in Scripture is a well-known symbol of godless mankind (Isa. 57:20). A mountain is frequently used to symbolize a great nation. Babylon, for example, is called a destroying mountain (Jer. 51:25), and the Lord's coming worldwide empire is likened to a mountain (Dan.

2:35). The mountain mentioned here in the Apocalypse is a volcano, a burning mountain.

Recent history vividly illustrates what is likely to happen. In the early part of the twentieth century, a half-mad tyrant emerged as head of state of one of the greatest, most gifted, enlightened, and cultured industrial nations of Europe. He was convinced that he was a man of destiny and that the Germans were a super race. His philosophy was a patchwork quilt of ideas gleaned from here and there and woven into an ideology of hate. His ideologies, seething like the fires of a volcano, became white hot and gave ominous rumblings of what was to come. This evil genius saw life as a struggle and the world as a jungle in which only the fittest survive or even deserve to survive, and where only the strongest should rule. He had drunk deep of Darwin and Nietzsche. His ideal man was Nietzsche's "magnificent blond brute, avidly rampant for spoil and victory." This tyrant regimented his "magnificent blond brutes," clothed them in armor and steel, and taught them to trample the weak and inherit the earth.

In 1939, the hour came, and the Nazi volcano erupted. Burning and blazing with fierce energy for war, it was cast into the sea of the nations. For six long years "the sea" boiled and foamed as it sought to extinguish the fires that burned in the heart of that terrible mountain. It is a picture of what is to come.

Another great nation is to erupt on earth one day and make the nations seethe and roar as they seek to subdue its struggle for power. Mention of the sea suggests that it is this upheaval that throws the Beast up as a power to be reckoned with in the affairs of Europe and the world, for he is "the beast out of the sea" in Revelation 13:1. The outcome of this struggle, possibly European, puts the Beast into power in at least one nation of a coming European federation. At first he will not be recognized for who he really is. He has yet to be energized by Satan and have his power satanically confirmed. That comes next.

(3) THE THIRD TRUMPET—THE BANISHED STAR (8:10-11)

The third trumpet is blown, and a giant step forward is taken in the process of judgment. John tells us, *And the third angel sounded, and there fell a great star from heaven, burning as it were a lamp, and it fell upon the third part of the rivers, and upon the fountains of waters; and the name of the star is called Wormwood: and the third part of the waters became wormwood; and many men died of the waters, because they were made bitter.* If this is taken literally, then a third ecological disaster is depicted. The trees, the grass, the sea have all been devastated; now the rivers and fountains are spoiled.

But a disaster affecting the water supply of mankind hardly seems a sufficient explanation of what happens under this trumpet. The events described must probably be taken symbolically, even though interpreters have varied widely in seeking to identify the fallen star. Simon Magus; Attila, "the scourge of God"; Muhammad; and even the Jewish historian Josephus have been suggested. Some have identified the fallen star with the Antichrist. Others identify the star as Satan.

The clue to the interpretation is in Revelation 12:12, where we read, *Woe to the inhabiters of the earth and of the sea! for the devil is come down unto you, having great wrath, because he knoweth that he hath but a short time.* The earlier part of the chapter tells how, in his original fall, the devil, the great red dragon, cast a third part of the stars (i.e., his angels) out of heaven.[1] With Satan's fall from heaven, recorded parenthetically in Revelation 13, a new woe is to be added to the horrors taking place on earth. Michael warns mankind that Satan's expulsion from heaven causes woe on earth. It is significant that the last three trumpets are specifically called *woe* trumpets. Revelation 13 lends strong support to the view that the fallen star is Satan himself.

He is given the symbolic name of Wormwood (absinth, a bitter and deleterious plant), and he poisons the third part of "the waters," which become bitter and result in the death of many men. The symbolism of the waters is explained in Revelation 17:15: "the waters . . . are peoples, and multitudes, and nations, and tongues." In other words, Satan's fall to earth results in the immediate poisoning of human life and society. The peoples of the earth take on the character of the evil one and become "wormwood" too. Satan is bitter because he has been cast out of heaven. Men become bitter, and many people die.

When God's Son descended from heaven to earth at the incarnation, God put a new star in the sky. It is possible that, when Satan is cast down from heaven to earth, his fall will be heralded by the fall of a giant comet. The fall of Satan adds a new dimension to the disasters which now overtake the globe. The Beast will already be here, benign as yet; and now Satan arrives, knowing that his time is short. It will take only a step or two for Satan's plans for the planet to mature.

(4) THE FOURTH TRUMPET—THE BLACKENED SKY (8:12-13)

The blowing of the fourth trumpet brings great changes everywhere. John says, *And the fourth angel sounded, and the third part of the sun was smitten, and the third part of the moon, and the third part of the stars; so as the third part of them was darkened, and the day shone not for a third part of it, and the night likewise. And I beheld, and heard an angel flying*

---

1. This, incidentally, sheds light on the frequently-repeated formula "a third part" so characteristic of the trumpets. The expression seems to refer to the sphere of satanic influence.

through the midst of heaven, saying with a loud voice, Woe, woe, woe, to the inhabiters of the earth by reason of the other voices of the trumpet of the three angels, which are yet to sound! This verse is probably to be taken symbolically. The sun, the moon, and the stars are well-established symbols in the Bible for ruling authorities. Under this trumpet the old order is broken up. The establishment is swept away as convulsions break out everywhere. The true church has gone; restraints have been removed; and Satan is on earth, black rage boiling in his heart. The stage is now set for the final plunge into midnight darkness for mankind. All the traditional guiding lights are gone.

The great upheaval depicted here gives the Beast his chance to seize control of Western Europe. We know from Daniel's prophecies that "the little horn," as the Beast is called there, takes advantage of conditions on earth to overthrow three contemporary kings in order to seize complete control of the revived Roman Empire. That will possibly take place under this trumpet, leaving the Beast in supreme power in Western Europe and commanding immense potential resources.

At first, Satan's messiah will not be known as the Beast. He will appear as a wonderful person, who knows how to act decisively when need be and who seemingly has the answer to the world's enormous problems. He will fascinate and awe the masses of mankind. He will surface in troubled times and will seem a veritable messiah, able to deal dramatically and effectively with the world's political, economic, cultural, and technological ills. He will still the storm, on the crest of which he will ride to power. The shaken nations of Europe will be glad that an authoritative person is at last in firm control of affairs. He will act swiftly in the Middle East by making a pact with Israel under the terms of which he will unconditionally guarantee the security of Israel and Jerusalem. He will over-awe the Arabs, warn off Russia and China, and give the nations a much-needed breathing spell from the disasters that have overtaken them since the rapture of the church. Men will be thankful for this man of genius and will exalt him in their minds and hearts.

These times may be much nearer than we think. Forces are already at work in society that presage the overthrow of the existing order of things. Forces of subversion are hard at work in every country of the world. Every known vice and all forms of social and family indiscipline are encouraged. Religion, the home, family life, everything in society that is normal and stabilizing is under attack. Agents of subversion leave no stone unturned as they pursue their goals. Sabotage, guerrilla warfare, street violence, anarchy, and insurrection are common. Lawlessness is an accepted part of modern society and is being subtly inculcated into the minds of the young.

Terrorism has become a worldwide phenomenon. In 1984 alone, for instance, according to one who has made an in-depth study of the subject, there were 2.679 attacks committed by 126 of the world's 174 existing terrorist groups.

Favorite targets for terrorists are the United States and Europe. There is increasing evidence that terrorist groups in West Germany, France, Italy, Belgium, and Portugal are beginning to coordinate their efforts. Not long ago the Italian defense minister stated that "a terrorist multinational" has already been formed in France capable of striking throughout Europe.

The Iranian hostage crisis and the crisis caused by the abduction of American tourists to Beirut on board a flight from Athens, both by Shi'ite Muslims, have helped underline the seeming paralysis of the Western powers in the face of terrorism. Former CIA Director William Casey declared in the midst of the Beirut crisis, "We are in the middle of an undeclared war." But no one had any practical suggestions on how to effectively retaliate.

The dilemma is real enough. There are some 3 million U.S. citizens dispersed around the world at any given time. There are American businesses and institutions in all of the world's 169 countries. Some days as many as 570 international flights of U.S. airlines take off using more than 80 foreign airports. No U.S. president can unconditionally guarantee to protect them all. They are all vulnerable.

The rabble rousers, the demonstrators, the subverters of modern society have little concern about what will replace the establishment once they succeed in pulling it down. But Satan knows. These disruptive forces are tools, ready-made for his purpose, being forged in the fires of today for the crisis of tomorrow. They will be at hand when he is flung from the sky. He will pick himself up, snarling with rage. He will look around for a weapon. He will pick up these anarchist forces and lash out with them at every vestige of established power in Europe, striking down with shrewd, calculating blows the few remaining rulers who stand in his way. With all his fury and rage he will stir up the seething cauldron of the nations. His actions will not be without order or plan. His mind is cunning, sharpened, and honed through countless millennia, and he has a plan predetermined from ages past. He will build a new order, a "brave new world," a society headed by his own messiah, the Beast, the man of sin. Satan is determined to be cheered, hailed, and worshiped on earth even if God has denied him further place in the sky.

So then, the war trumpets are blown, and from the turmoil they cause, a dazzling, charming, bewitching, splendid man emerges, a solver of earth's problems, a defender of its gods, a man hand-in-glove with every source of political, religious, and economic power, a well-masked man; the man the world awaits.

b. WOE INTENSIFIED ON EARTH (9:1-21)

The trumpets continue to bring war, but war to which woe is added. The war to be described next is probably one of the most important in the Bible. Trumpets five and six move matters on earth along to the point where Satan's man is left undisputed master of the globe—for a season. First, men are brainwashed by the Beast and are psychologically prepared to embrace the ultimate lie. Then the Beast consolidates his position in the west, deals decisively with the great foe to the north, brings to heel for a while the awakened millions of the east, throws off all pretense, and sets himself up as this world's god. First comes the strong delusion, that dark satanic lie, that ultimate horror of blasphemy, for the acceptance of which no place of repentance can be found. Men, like fated Esau, will barter their birthrights for a mess of Satan's pottage and will find no place of repentance, though they seek it with bitterest tears.

There are three woe trumpets. The third precipitates the end and is described only after a lengthy parenthesis. At this point a description is given of just the first two. The first of these describes a satanically energized belief that afflicts humanity. The second describes a satanically energized battle that alters history.

(1) THE FIFTH TRUMPET (WOE 1)—A SATANICALLY ENERGIZED BELIEF THAT AFFLICTS HUMANITY (9:1-12)

The description that follows is highly symbolic. It tells of a fearful demon host that is to be unleashed by divine permission. The terrible demons loosed thus from the pit will seize upon men and prepare them for the strong delusion and for the exaltation of the Beast to complete and universal power.

The world is already being prepared for what is to come. It is one of the ironies of the age in which we live that, at a time when scientific enlightenment is at its zenith and men are educated, pragmatic, and materialistic in the extreme, millions are turning to the occult for entertainment, enlightenment, and eventual enslavement. Every year, hundreds of new books are published dealing with demonism, witchcraft, magic, spiritism, ghosts, and prophecy. Every season brings its quota of television shows featuring similar themes. Soothsayers, prophets, astrologers, fortune tellers are given avid hearing by millions. The groundwork is being laid for an enormous increase in demon activity soon to burst upon the world. What will happen under the blowing of the fifth trumpet will be made all the easier because men have been preconditioned to reject biblical truth and to accept the doctrines of demons.

The uncanny creatures released upon the blowing of the fifth trumpet are evil spirits. The description given of their *appearance* is, at the same time, a description of their *character*. We are told thirteen things about them.

One, they are *incarcerated*. John says, **And the fifth angel sounded, and I saw a star fall from heaven unto the earth: and to him was given** *the key of the bottomless pit. And he opened the bottomless pit; and there arose a smoke out of the pit, as the smoke of a great furnace; and the sun and the air were darkened by reason of the smoke of the pit.* The *New American Standard Bible* renders the phrase "I saw a star fall from heaven" as "I saw a star from heaven which had fallen to the earth." That helps identify the star here with the fallen star of the third trumpet. In other words, the fallen star is Satan, who is now given authority to open the abyss and unleash the terrible beings incarcerated there. The imagination cannot picture what the earth will be like when the church is removed from the scene, when society, having completely corrupted itself, is handed over to the malignant attention of the most horrible fiends of hell. Those wicked spirits, long mercifully chained by God, are now let loose upon the earth.

From now on, their prison house becomes increasingly prominent in the Apocalypse. It is an ancient penitentiary for evil spirits, or at least for those of them who are so vile that God keeps them "reserved in chains" (2 Pet. 2:4). The demons mentioned in Luke 8:31 knew of this prison house and besought the Lord not to send them there. "The deep" referred to is really "the abyss." That is where Satan himself will be chained throughout the millennium age. It is from this same terrible pit that the soul of the Beast will be summoned when, after his assassination, he re-emerges as this world's final Gentile ruler.

Picture what the world would be like if we were to open the doors of all the penitentiaries of earth and set free the world's most vicious and violent criminals, giving them full reign to practice their infamies upon mankind. Something worse than that lies in store for the world. Satan, cast out of heaven, is now permitted to summon to his aid the most diabolical fiends in the abyss to act as his agents in bringing mankind to the footstool of the Beast.

Two, these demons are *infernal.* John says, *And there came out of the smoke locusts upon the earth: and unto them was given power.* Anticipating for a moment the full description of the dreadful beings that follows, they appear to be a form of satanic cherubim. The horse, the man, the locust, the lion, and the scorpion all combine in their appearance. They are not ordinary locusts, for they are supernatural and are incapable of being killed.

Three, they are *insatiable.* John says, *And it was commanded them that they should not hurt the grass of the earth, neither any green thing, neither any tree; but only those men which have not the seal of God in their foreheads.* The ordinary locust descends upon the earth in dense clouds and devours every green thing in sight. The worst locust plague in modern times struck the Middle East in 1951-52 when in Iran, Iraq, Jordan, and Saudi Arabia every green and growing thing was devoured across hundreds of thousands of square miles. Locusts eat grain, leaf, and stalk, right down to the bare ground. When a swarm arises and flies on its way, the green field is left a desert; barrenness and desolation stretches as far as eye can see.

These demons are so locust-like in their voracious appetites that they have to be divinely restrained and are forbidden to touch those whom God has sealed. Their hunger is for men, and unregenerate, godless, Christ-rejecting men are given to them as their prey.

Four, they are *intolerable*. We are told, **And to them it was given that they should not kill them, but that they should be tormented five months: and their torment was as the torment of a scorpion, when he striketh a man. And in those days shall men seek death, and shall not find it; and shall desire to die, and death shall flee from them.** Five months, from May to September, is the natural life of a locust. These demon locusts inflict a sting that produces the most intolerable anguish. The sting of a natural scorpion is not generally fatal, but it produces the most intense pain that any creature can inflict on the human body. The sting of these demon locusts produces anguish of mind and spirit almost beyond endurance. The word used to describe the effect of their sting is "torment," a word generally associated with demons. The agony they produce is so great that men who normally flee from death will scream for death to come and end their miseries. Imagine a world in which men court death, attempt suicide, expose themselves to the reaper's scythe, chase after him with all their might, only to find that, for once, he cannot be found! These tormented men cannot die yet they are in anguish beyond words to describe. It is hell on earth.

Five, they are *intrepid*. John says, **And the shapes of the locusts were like unto horses prepared unto battle.** Throughout the book of Revelation the horse is the war horse, a symbol of defiance. These terrible creatures from the abyss are like high-mettled steeds, seemingly straining at the leash and pawing the ground in their eagerness to fling themselves forward on their mission of doom.

Six, they are *invincible*. John saw that **on their heads were, as it were, crowns like gold.** They conquer all in their path. Man has no weapon against them; no medicine, no psychiatry, no incantation, no discovery of science will avail. The medical associations of earth will confess themselves baffled. Scientists will work around the clock seeking some wonder drug that will restore some semblance of sanity to men who are screaming in their agonies and delirious with torment. Everything will fail. These horrible demons are crowned with gold.

Seven, they are *intelligent*. John says, **And their faces were as the faces of men.** A man's face is the index of his soul. It is mobile and expressive and gives countenance to his emotions and intelligence. No beast has a face so expressive of the hidden life within. Faces like men! It is a symbolic way of telling us that these fiends are highly intelligent. Their onslaught against the human race is the result not of blind instinct, but of rational thought.

Modern man professes not to believe in demons, but they exist just the same. Moreover, they are clever with a diabolical cunning. Man's attitude toward the demon world may well be likened to man's attitude in the Dark Ages toward bacteria. If we could be transported back to London in the year 1666, we would find ourselves in a nightmare world. The great bubonic plague was at its height. The sights and sounds of the city were like the terrible climax of a horror movie. It was generally believed that fresh air was the culprit. The College of Physicians recommended the frequent firing of guns to blow away the deadly air. People sealed themselves in their rooms and burned foul-smelling messes to ward off the fresh air. Chimneys were sealed, rooms were gray with smoke, and people choked in the suffocating stench. Outside, palls of black smoke hung over the city. People sat in the tightly sealed chambers, grimly determined to endure the smarting smoke, convinced they were thus immune to the plague. We could tell them they were wrong, that the plague is not caused by fresh air but by germs—microscopic organisms spread by fleas—and they would laugh us to scorn.

Modern man has adopted a similar attitude toward the demon world. We tell them that the world is in the grip of Satan and that he has countless hosts of invisible demons to aid him in his dark designs against mankind. We say that these unseen beings are intelligent, and that before long, they are to be joined by countless more of their kind worse even than themselves. People look at us with pitying scorn and suggest we peddle our theories to the publishers of science fiction. But it is true all the same. Once the pit is opened, the world of men will be invaded by a virus far more dreadful than the bubonic plague, a virus all the more deadly because it is able to think and because it directs its attack against the soul rather than the body.

Eight, they are *insidious.* John says that **they had hair as the hair of women.** A woman's hair is her glory (1 Cor. 11:6-7); it is beautiful and attractive to the eye of the beholder. The long hair of these demon locusts suggests that there is something horribly and seductively attractive about them. The occult world has always exerted a fascination to men—even to those who profess to be enlightened and delivered from such "superstitions." It may be that when these fearful beings are released from the pit, they will at first employ arts and wiles that will make their advent attractive to men. They are insidious, however, and they use their attractions to lure men on to their doom.

Nine, they are *inexorable.* We are told that **their teeth were as the teeth of lions.** Woe betide those who become their prey! They will rend and tear and destroy. The teeth of a lion inflict a terrible wound, and even when its bite does not kill, its teeth are so filled with infection that the wound rarely heals completely. From time to time it breaks wide open again. Nor can anyone rob a lion of its prey once it has sunk its teeth into its victim. Just so, these fearful demons will fasten onto their human victims, and nothing will pry them loose.

Ten, they are *insensitive*. John says that **they had breastplates, as it were breastplates of iron.** They are completely insensitive to the suffering they cause, and the cries and agonies of their victims leave them unmoved. They are without heart, at least without a heart that can be touched by mankind. They know no mercy. Even the most insensitive person has some tender spot, some chord that can be touched, but these alien creatures are merciless. They feast on human pain as on a tasty morsel. The shriller the shriek of pain, the sharper, the tangier the taste!

Eleven, they are *inescapable*. John says, **And the sound of their wings was as the sound of chariots of many horses running to battle.** They travel like the wind, flying swiftly and surely toward their prey. The picture John paints is graphic enough. The scene is that of a defenseless city. Coming up over the hill is a highly mobile force of fierce warriors, lusting for the kill and eager for the sack of the city. Where can the frightened citizens flee? How can they escape? Already the thundering hoofs of the cavalry sound in their ears. Already the sky is black with dust. Now the city is surrounded, and the encircling cordon grows tighter, cutting off all hope of escape, until nothing remains but the imminent prospect of torment, ravishment, and pain. When these demon hordes are let loose out of hell, they will be inescapable. There will be no place to hide. Mankind has no refuge from them, none at all.

Twelve, they are *injurious*. John says, **And they had tails like unto scorpions, and there were stings in their tails: and their power was to hurt men five months.** Reference has already been made to their scorpion-like tails. When the Holy Spirit repeats a detail, and that within a score of lines, it is because that detail is important. Here the fact is emphasized that these loathsome spirits have but a single aim—to injure men. For long years men have spurned the Holy Spirit of God, so they will be given over by a righteous God to the voracious appetites, the satanic hungers of evil spirits, the foulest and fiercest in the universe.

Thirteen, they are *indivisible*. John tells us, **They had a king over them, which is the angel of the bottomless pit, whose name in the Hebrew tongue is Abaddon, but in the Greek tongue hath his name Apollyon.** Solomon, that shrewd observer of nature wrote, "The locusts have no king" (Prov. 30:27). These demon locusts do. As though it were not bad enough for them to be intelligent in themselves, they are capably and ably led by the satanic angel who reigns over the abyss itself. This angel is obviously not Satan—he does not come up from the abyss; he opens it. Even God's prison houses are run in an orderly way; the bottomless pit has its king. His name is given in two languages, Hebrew and Greek, for Jew and Gentile alike will fall prey to this dark angel and his minions. His name means "destroyer," and destroy he will. The locust fiends who follow him are no blind swarm, descending at the whim of the wind. They are an organized host. Rank after rank they come to add another dimension of terror to an age already insane with folly and fear. And then, as though even this were not enough, the Holy Spirit adds, *One woe is past; and, behold, there come two woes more hereafter.*

The first woe trumpet causes men to be afflicted with a satanically-inspired belief, propagated by demons from the pit. This doctrine of demons leads to anguish of soul like a scorpion's sting, like an adder's bite. Man is now in the hands of demons who drive the human race from one insanity to another.

(2) THE SIXTH TRUMPET (WOE 2)—A SATANICALLY ENERGIZED BATTLE THAT ALTERS HISTORY (9:13-21)

Another of God's prison houses is now to be unlocked, and more evil spirits are unchained and sent forth on an errand of terror for mankind. Satan's plans for putting the Beast into firm control of things on earth take another giant step forward. John sets before us three aspects of this hateful visitation of satanic emissaries.

There is *the divine outlook* (9:13-15). This particular judgment has been anticipated by God for a very long time. That is evident from verse 15. God has foreordained that, in this judgment, there are to be spirit powers involved, a special place involved, and a specific period involved.

First we are told of *the spirit powers involved.* John says, *And the sixth angel sounded, and I heard a voice from the four horns of the golden altar which is before God, saying to the sixth angel which had the trumpet, Loose the four angels which are bound in the great river Euphrates.* The voice came from the golden altar. It will be remembered that the trumpet judgments are introduced by prayer ascending to God from the beleaguered martyrs on earth by way of this very altar. The prayers of the saints on earth are still being answered—answered in an unexpected way, perhaps, but answered just the same.

Peter and Jude both tell of certain angels who sinned beyond the measure of their fellows and who are, at present, kept imprisoned by God (2 Pet. 2:4; Jude 6). We do not know how many there are, but we know there are some. Four of those fallen angels are now loosed to carry out a predetermined plan. These angels are called "the four," as though to intimate that they are a special four. Doubtless they are of great influence and power because they are able to marshal their armies by the millions the moment they are released. The mention of the river Euphrates gives a clue as to who these angels might be. All the world powers of Scripture are associated with the Euphrates and Babylon. These four angels then might be the very ones who in times past controlled the

Babylonian, the Medo-Persian, the Grecian, and the Roman empires on Satan's behalf. Daniel 10:13, 20-21 makes quite clear that such angelic princes exist. Or perhaps these angels are the four angels of world empire who control the nations of the earth to the four points of the compass on Satan's behalf.

Next we are told about *the special place involved.* John heard the voice say, *Release the four angels which are bound in the great river Euphrates.* This river is prominent in Scripture. It is the dividing line between east and west, between what we call the Near East and the Far East. It is to be the eastern boundary of the Promised Land in a coming day. It was included in the territory given to the four great world powers of Scripture. It was in the region of the Euphrates that man first saw the light of day. This river was one of the four that flowed out of Eden's garden paradise. Here Satan first alighted on the planet and made his successful attack upon the human race; here all earth's miseries were introduced; here the first murder was committed and the first martyr was slain; here the Jews dragged out their bitter exile; here Babylon arose; and here four special angels of Satan rage in bonds.

We are told of *the special period* involved. John says, *And the four angels were loosed, which were prepared for an hour, and a day, and a month, and a year, for to slay the third part of men.* This rendering of the text suggests that the ministry of these four angels will extend over a period of thirteen months and one day. The *New American Standard* rendering suggests that these angels are loosed "for *the* hour and the day and the year." That is, the exact moment of the terrible visitation is foreknown to God and appointed by Him. "Known unto God are all his works from the beginning of the world" (Acts 15:18).

In any case, attention is drawn to a specific period. All events are under God's control, and nothing happens without His approval. Not a speck of dust moves, not a blade of grass stirs, not an army can move, not a shot can be fired without His knowing all about it and granting His permission. He weaves all things into the overall pattern of His will.

There is, further, *the satanic outreach* (9:16-19) involved. What follows is a description of one of the most important battles in the Bible. John tells us of the number and of the nature of the combatants. As to *the number* of the combatants he says, *And the number of the army of the horsemen were two hundred thousand thousand: and I heard the number of them.* Evidently John gave up all thought of counting this seemingly endless host. He was told how many troops were involved—200 million. Commentators, at this point, usually leap over to Revelation 16:12-16, where a second reference is made to the Euphrates, and where "the kings of the east" are mentioned. This military campaign here is arbitrarily equated with that one, whereas the two are actually distinct. The campaign in chapter 16 is the Battle of Armageddon, as is plainly stated. The chief feature of that battle is the involvement of the hordes of the Far East. Here in chapter nine, there is no reference to "the kings of the east," nor to Armageddon. This is another battle altogether, but one that is only slightly less important.

John looks with awe at the millions summoned to war by the four angels from the Euphrates prison. Rank after endless rank they come, their feet beating out the time like the rhythmic rolling of drums. The sun glints on their weapons, dense as corn stalks bowing before a prairie wind. The swing of their arms and the stride of their marching feet holds his gaze, and the thunder of their transportation fills his ears. Here they come, 200 million men, marching to their doom to forward Satan's plans for the Beast.

John next draws our attention to *the nature* of the combatants. He says, *And thus I saw the horses in the vision, and them that sat on them, having breastplates of fire, and of jacinth, and brimstone: and the heads of the horses were as the heads of lions; and out of their mouths issued fire and smoke and brimstone.* Is this an army of men or of demons? Probably the description is that of an army of men driven by demons. Certainly the language has to be symbolic. Just as the shapes of the "locusts" released under the previous trumpet depicted the characteristics of the demons they symbolized, so the shapes of the "horses" here indicate the warlike, ferocious nature of the demons they represent. So then, the four angels from the Euphrates conjure up spirit legions who madden men and drive them forth to battle. The mention of the fire, smoke, and brimstone might also be a symbolic reference to modern warfare with its emphasis on fire and flame.

The carnage resulting from this outbreak of war is staggering. John says, *By these three was the third part of men killed, by the fire, and by the smoke, and by the brimstone, which issued out of their mouths. For their power is in their mouth, and in their tails: for their tails were like unto serpents, and had heads, and with them they do hurt.* The battle is terrible, both in its beginning and in its end. The world, to this point in its history, will never have seen such carnage before. If the figure is to be taken literally, then a third part of the earth's population is killed in this war. The earth becomes the graveyard for a billion people, indicating that far more are affected than the number enrolled in the actual army, vast as that is.

The expression "a third part" has been used now a total of thirteen times in connection with the trumpets. It has been used in connection with the earth and the trees, the fishes, the sea and the ships, the rivers and the waters, the sun, the moon and the stars, and now in relation to men.

A number of questions arise at this point. Is there any hint of a war like this elsewhere in the Bible? What is the outcome of this war on the kingdom of the Beast? (We know from Rev. 11:14 that the Beast is now in power and rapidly stepping forward to assume his role as this world's god.) How does Satan use this war to further his plans in connection with the Beast?

There *is* such a war mentioned in Scripture—that described by Ezekiel (38-39) when Russia invades Israel. Some have equated the Russian invasion of Israel with Armageddon. But a careful study of the battle Ezekiel describes (Ezek. 38-39) and the Battle of Armageddon (Rev. 16:12-16; 19:11-21) will soon highlight the differences and show that conclusion to be untenable.

1. The Russian invasion is preceded by the rebirth of the state of Israel (Ezek. 37); Armageddon takes place much later at a time when the Beast tears up his treaty obligations with Israel and at a time when a world-wide persecution and dispersal of the Jewish people is in force (Rev. 12:13-17).

2. The Russian invasion involves certain other nations—especially those in the Soviet sphere of influence such as Libya, Persia, Ethiopia, Gomer, Togarmah. The Russian invasion is opposed only by certain Western nations (Tarshish, Sheba, and Dedan). Armageddon involves all nations.

3. Ezekiel 38 and 39 envisions an invasion of Israel from "the uttermost parts of the north." Armageddon is precipitated by an invasion of nations from beyond the Euphrates and is headed by "the kings of the east."

4. The Russian coalition falls apart as various members of the alliance turn against each other. The Battle of Armageddon is terminated by the personal return of the Lord Himself from glory.

5. The Russian war will be promoted by four of Satan's subordinates released from incarceration in or near the Euphrates River. Armageddon is precipitated by three frog demons sent on their mission by Satan, the Beast, and the False Prophet.

6. When Russia invades Israel there are those in the West who still have a vested interest in the preservation of Israel as a state. When Armageddon is fought Israel will be alone and friendless and in her final extremity. Indeed, a coalition comprising contingents from "all nations" will be actively engaged in attacking Jerusalem at the time of the Lord's return. Russia's armies never get that far.

7. At the time of the Russian invasion, Israel will be dwelling in safety, secure in her treaty alliance with the Antichrist. When the Battle of Armageddon is staged the Great Tribulation will be reaching its peak and the Jews will have no safe place to flee except, perhaps, to Petra.

8. The overthrow of Russia will leave Israel with a seven-year supply of captured fuel. It will take the Jews seven months to bury all the dead bodies of the invaders. The dead, after the Battle of Armageddon, will be "buried" by carrion birds.

9. The fall of Russia will leave a deep impression on the nations of the world. Armageddon will be followed by the judgment of the nations by Christ Himself.

10. A number of factors will unite to bring a swift end to the Russian invasion of Israel. The West will protest the invasion and will doubtless make the necessary moves to ensure its own strategic interests in the Middle East. There will be wholesale war between the various members of the Russian invasion force themselves, few of whom have any reason to love the Russians. There will be earthquakes and other similar disasters as God unleashes His own arsenal. And, possibly, there will be a nuclear holocaust that will devastate the Russian mainland. Armageddon, on the other hand, is terminated by the return of Christ and His heavenly throng and is followed by the judgment of Satan and his agents and their dupes.

In view of these differences it is hard to see how the Russian invasion can be the same as Armageddon. If, however, we equate the Russian invasion with what we have here in Revelation 9, things fall easily into place. Here is a suggested sequence of events.

1. The Antichrist (generally called the beast in the Apocalypse) will arise in western Europe. He is called "the beast out of the sea" so doubtless he emerges in one of the lands bordering the Mediterranean (the "great sea" of Bible geography). His personal appearing will coincide with the formal federation of the nations of Western Europe into a revived Roman Empire.

2. Called "the little horn" by Daniel (7:7-8, 19-25), the Antichrist will be one of the more insignificant members of the emerging revived Roman Empire. He will probably be a Roman. In a swift move he will overthrow three of the newly confederated states and will then rule all ten.

3. He will use the religious system centered at Rome in his opening bid for power (Rev. 17) but, once it has served its purpose, he will hand it over to the members of the European Alliance to be dismembered and its wealth seized.

4. Since the Beast eventually is to rule the world, something will have to be done to force the Western Hemisphere into compliance with his plans. The most likely tool he will use will be economic. The American international debt, for instance, might give him the stranglehold he needs. The bankruptcy of many Latin American countries will quickly force them into line. Most Americans underestimate the size and the seriousness of the American deficit and the power of the European bankers. When President Carter seized Iranian assets, during the hostage crisis, the European bankers sent him a curt warning: "We'll let you get away with it this time—but don't do it again." One way or

another the Western Hemisphere will be forced into subservience to the Beast and will take ultimate orders from Rome, no matter how many face-saving formulas will be devised to disguise the fact.

5. Once the Beast commands the enormous political, industrial, economic, and military might of the West he will feel strong enough to deal with Russia. Russia alone stands in the way of his assuming absolute world power, so he will set in motion plans to get rid of this colossus. One move, doubtless, will be to turn Russia's international terrorism against herself. The Soviet Union is not the monolithic giant she would like the rest of the world to believe. Russia is made up of some hundred different nationalities, many of them potentially dangerous to the union, especially the large Muslim bloc. There are almost as many languages spoken within the Soviet Union. Most Westerners do not know that the Russians themselves are a permanent minority in the Soviet Union. And they are hated by millions. What is true of the Soviet Union itself is even more true of the satellite nations of Eastern Europe. More than once Russia has had to send her tanks into Warsaw Pact countries to keep them in line. East Germany, Czechoslovakia, Hungary, and Poland are all potential trouble spots. The Beast will know that quite well. He will not be restrained by the factors that inhibit the West today. He will command an overwhelming preponderance of power, and he will know it and not hesitate to use it. The Soviets will have their hands full putting down insurrections all across their vast empire.

6. Then, too, the Beast might well encourage China to embark on some military venture against the Soviet Union. The nightmare of a billion Chinese camped along a 4,500-mile frontier haunts the Kremlin and accounts for much of the Soviet Union's activities in the world today.[2]

7. As part of his plan for destroying the Soviet Union, the Beast will sign a seven-year treaty with Israel. This, incidentally, is what signals the commencement of the final "seventieth week" of Daniel (Dan. 9:24-27). Under the terms of this treaty the Beast will unconditionally guarantee the security of the state of Israel. Under this umbrella the Jews will take full possession of the Temple Mount and will rebuild their temple, possibly destroying the Muslim structures on the site. The rebuilding of the Temple in Jerusalem is a top-secret and high-priority matter with the Beast. He has plans to use that temple for his most daring act of blasphemy.

8. The infuriated Muslim and Arab states, helpless in the face of Western power, now fully mobilized and on a war-time footing, and not daring to try another oil embargo for fear of simply being occupied by the Beast's armies and

2. See John Phillips, *Exploring the Future* (Nashville: Thomas Nelson, 1983).

summarily dealt with, will turn to the Soviet Union. The Kremlin, seeing its entire international position being undermined by a determined and expansionist and evermore powerful Western dictator will be forced to make a desperate gamble in the Middle East.

9. Russia will call up her reserves and summon her allies and will make a massive and lightning attack against Israel. The mobilization of Russia's millions will be matched by a mobilization of the millions dominated by the Beast in the West. The figure of 200 million men involved in this battle need not necessarily be taken as a literal number, but even if it is, it will be no exaggeration. The text does not say that this enormous number of men under arms all belong to the same side.

10. God will allow the Soviet forces to cross the borders of Israel. Then He will settle the long account with the godless nation that has done so much to infuriate Him for so long. "I will put hooks in thy jaws," He warned through the pen of Ezekiel many centuries ago. In the last analysis, Russian foreign policy is not being decided by the men in the Kremlin, Machiavellian as they are in their cunning and ruthlessness; it is being decided in heaven. Once the invaders cross into Israel, with certain doom awaiting the Jewish state, God will act.

11. Russia's huge invading army will then be completely destroyed in what has to be the most devastating and costly defeat in all of history. It is uncertain whether that collapse is to be brought about by an atomic war or whether it will be caused solely by supernatural means. In any case, the collapse of Russia is to be a divine judgment and will fulfill a long-standing prophecy. An aghast and appalled world, even in that satanic era of human history, will attribute Russia's demise to God.

12. At some point in his career, the Beast, prior to the conclusion of events under the sixth trumpet, is to be killed, only to return from the abyss in such a way that all nations will fall down and worship him (11:7). Possibly this astounding event will take the edge off the impact made on the nations by Russia's collapse. The two witnesses (chap. 11) will be concluding their ministry in Jerusalem at this time and will be slain by the Beast, confirming him in the minds of men as a superman (11:3-12). The earthquake mentioned in connection with the killing of the two witnesses may be part of a general series of disasters, in the vortex of which the Russian armies might well be trapped.

13. The removal of Russia as a major world power will create an enormous geopolitical vacuum on earth, and two powers will rush in to fill that vacuum. The Western powers headed by the Beast will move to take over the vast Russian hinterland and empire; and China, now to emerge as the leader of an Eastern coalition (styled in Revelation "the kings of the east"), will also

move to seize what she can of Siberia. In this power play, the Beast will win, and his position and authority will be assured. He will be too strong then to be opposed by any nation on earth.

14. He will convene a world conference at which God will be officially ruled out of His universe so far as men are concerned (Ps. 2). He will rebuild the city of Babylon and make it the world's capital. He will set himself up as this world's God and will launch a worldwide persecution of all those who refuse to bow to his image and wear his mark. Eventually the Eastern powers will break away and mobilize against him, thus precipitating the Battle of Armageddon. Color is added to the above suggested sequence of events by the fact that Russia today is the paramount world power in the Middle East and dominates the countries which border on the Euphrates.[3]

John has set before us the divine outlook and the satanic outreach of the events under the sixth trumpet. Now he shows us *the human outcome* (9:20-21). At the end of the first series of judgments, those under the seals, men were horrified. At the end of the second series of judgments, under the trumpets, men are merely hardened. The world is now ready to embrace the ultimate and final lie in all its length and breadth, height, and depth. God's reminder to men that He is still on the throne, so evident in the collapse of Russia, is soon forgotten. The fascinating Beast erases all traces of any impression left by that event. The most terrible things take place on earth and men could not care less—except to blaspheme.

There is *a lack of repentance Godward.* John says, **And the rest of the**

---

3. No less an authority than Walter Scott, writing *Palestine Restored* (London: Pickering & Inglis, n.d.) back in the mid nineteenth century before Russia had any real hopes of becoming a power in the Middle East, made these prophetic statements about Russia and her future:

> Russia is evidently destined to become the master in Asia. Her frontier line across Asia is 5,000 miles in length. . . . It is well known that the Russian policy is one of steady aggression, not chiefly in Europe but in Asia [pp. 27-28].

> Russia is the most ambitious and grasping of modern kingdoms, . . . most faithless in public honour and treaty engagements. . . . The character ascribed to her in the prophetic Scriptures, coupled with her frequent outbreaks of undisguised hostility to her Jewish subjects, exhibit Russia in a most unfavourable light [p. 29].

> We judge that the tide of Muscovite conquest will flow on to the very frontiers of China. . . . The ascendency of Russia in the east, and the revival of the old Roman Empire in the west, necessitate . . . political changes of vast importance. . . . The great Jewish Question . . . must be settled at Jerusalem, "the city of the Great King," and in the millennial triumph of Israel, and of her headship over the nations and countries of the world [p. 32].

> We believe, from the place assigned to Russia in the Word of God, that her legions will yet sweep over the plains and mountains of Asia and become the dominant power all over the East till she falls ingloriously and for ever on the mountains of Judea (Ezek. 39). Thus she will command for a time the powers north of Palestine (Lebanon mountains) and those bordering on the river Euphrates [p. 34].

men which were not killed by these plagues yet repented not of the works of their hands, that they should not worship devils, and idols of gold, and silver, and brass, and stone, and of wood: which neither can see, nor hear, nor walk. Demon worship and idolatry are twins and have been the prevalent form of worship among men since the days of Nimrod. Under the reign of the Beast, idolatry will become the only legitimate form of worship, since the various forms of idolatry practiced around the globe will fit hand in glove with the worship of the image of the Beast.

There is *a lack of repentance manward.* John tells us, *Neither repented they of their murders, nor of their sorceries, nor of their fornication, nor of their thefts.* What a picture of a crime-oriented culture! Man has finally arrived at his goal—a government and culture in which permissiveness is the accepted norm and where all kinds of deviation and misbehavior are applauded and encouraged, a government presided over by a fascinating but foul individual called the man of sin (2 Thess. 2:3).

The word rendered "sorceries," incidentally, literally means "use of drugs" and is derived from the Greek word from which we get our English word "pharmacy." The word is primarily used to signify medicine, drugs, spells, then poisoning and sorcery. Drugs were used in sorcery, generally accompanied by incantations and the use of various charms. Today's world is fast becoming a drug- and demon-oriented world.

Thus the trumpet judgments have delivered the world over to Satan and the Beast. Men remain unrepentant so that still further judgments are necessary—the judgment of the vials. Under the vials, God's wrath will be outpoured, and the world will be given a taste of all that means.

3. *WHAT IS RECORDED IN PARENTHESIS ABOUT THE TRUMPETS (10:1–13:18)*

a. THE PURPOSES OF HEAVEN REVEALED (10:1–11:19)

There now follows a long parenthesis in the prophecy. The four chapters it embraces give us a description of what God has been doing and what Satan has been doing during the blowing of the trumpets. The mystery of iniquity comes to a swift and fateful head in the worship of the Beast; the mystery of godliness comes to a head in the anticipated crowning of the Messiah. The next two chapters of Revelation review the completion of the mystery, the coming of the messengers, and the crowning of the Messiah. They assure us that not for a single moment has God abandoned this beleagured planet to His foes.

(1) THE COMPLETION OF THE MYSTERY (10:1-11)

Like the shining through of the sun in the midst of an earth-shaking storm, this chapter brings us relief and hope. It is one of those chapters in the Apocalypse that bisects the book from time to time in order to turn our eyes upon Jesus. Actually the chapter is in two parts: first we turn our eyes upon Jesus, and then we turn our eyes upon John. Both exercises are refreshing indeed.

(a) WE TURN OUR EYES UPON JESUS (10:1-3)

All the troubles in the world stem from the fact that men have lost sight of Him. At this point in the Apocalypse, men have ruled out Christ as a factor in world affairs, and the devil has provided them with a more exciting messiah. The world today is hastening in this direction. Men are leaving the Lord out of their calculations, and the result is that little if anything makes sense. An illustration will help us see this.

For centuries men believed the theories of astronomy as propounded by Greek philosophers. The writings of Aristotle and Ptolemy were scientific gospels, and to challenge them was the worst of heresies. Men were expected to believe without debate that the earth was the center of the universe, for example, and that the heavenly bodies moved in perfect circles. Ingenious theories were invented to explain the seeming retrograde motion of Mars, the alternation of day and night on earth, and various inconsistencies not account-ed for by the astronomy of the Greeks. But astronomy was in a hopeless muddle. Men simply did not have the key for they ignored the centrality of the sun.

Then came Nicholas Copernicus and Johannes Kepler. The sun was put in its proper place as the center of the solar system. It was established that the earth and the planets revolve around the sun and that the true path of the planets is an ellipse, not a circle. Then everything fell into place. Copernicus and his followers won lasting fame simply by giving the sun its rightful place.

Thus it is in the affairs of men. The world has forgotten the centrality of the Son and that He is the center of everything. It is no wonder that human affairs are in such a muddle. Men have postulated, in the place of Jesus as Creator, a fortuitous concourse of atoms, the blind workings of chance or evolution. Behind the working of history, men see some form of dialectic. The Prince of Peace has been banished from men's minds, and a grandiose United Nations organization has been put in His place. The world has lost sight of the Lord Jesus, and since everything revolves around Him, the resulting chaos is evident everywhere. So John begins by turning our eyes upon Jesus.

He first draws attention to *His character.* He says, *And I saw another angel come down from heaven, clothed with a cloud: and a rainbow was upon his head, and his face was as it were the sun, and his feet as pillars of fire.* This is no ordinary angel, for no created being, however, lofty, however high, has prerogatives, powers, and attributes like these. This is the Lord! Once, long years ago, He trod the trackless desert sands clothed in a cloud— out of Egypt across the Red Sea, and on to Kadesh, with Israel marching in ranks behind. Now again He is clothed in swirling banks of cloud. Once He hung the rainbow in the sky. There it remained with its bow bent toward the heart of heaven, a bow without an arrow as if to say that the arrow has been discharged into the very heart of God Himself. Now He wears the rainbow on His brow, a diadem of light. Once He put out the sun. His enemies tempted Him, saying, "Give us a sign from heaven." And so He did! When He was born, He put a new star in the sky; when He died, He put out the sun. Now His face is as the sun. He gazes out across the world with light-eclipsing splendor flashing from His countenance. And His feet are pillars of fire. Fire burns! Fire spreads! Fire purifies! Those fiery feet of His are about to kindle such a conflagration on earth as has never been known before.

This, then, is His character. Once He sojourned on this rebel orb with all His glory veiled—a babe! a boy! a carpenter! a traveling preacher! He was insulted, ridiculed, and scorned. From generation to generation He has watched men persecute His saints, squander the wealth of His world, abuse His hospitality on a planet that belongs to Him alone. But He is coming back, and here in this chapter of the Apocalypse we have the intimation that His return is to be soon.

John next draws our attention to *His claims*. He says that *he had in his hand a little book open: and he set his right foot upon the sea, and his left foot on the earth.* This is not His final coming, for other things must take place first. What we have here is the formal assertion by Him of His right to reign. This claim has already been acknowledged in heaven (Rev. 5); now it is asserted on earth. He claims dominion over all the world—river, sea, and shore; the Gentile nations and Israel: the settled, civilized world, and the surging, restless tribes of earth—all belong to Him. There is an open book in His hand. What Daniel was told to "seal . . . to the time of the end" (Dan. 12:4) is now to be opened up to full view, for the end time has come. The Lord is about to act, but He will act in compliance with the mind and will of God. All unfulfilled prophecies and promises will now come to pass.

So He asserts His right to rule. Moses said to Israel, "Every place whereon the soles of your feet shall tread shall be yours" (Deut. 11:24). So with grand assurance, the Lord Jesus plants His feet upon the sea and upon the earth. Capitalist lands, communist lands, colonial lands, He claims them all from pole to pole and from sea to sea, from the river to the ends of the earth. He puts down His foot with unshakable resolve—which is exactly what this world needs. No dissent will be allowed. People will either be right in, or they will be out forever.

Next, John draws our attention to *His cry*. He says that the Angel *cried with a loud voice, as when a lion roareth: and when he had cried, seven thunders uttered their voices.* There are few sounds to compare with the roar of an angry lion in its own unfettered domain. The lion's roar is calculated to chill the stoutest heart, give pause to its most dauntless foe, and petrify its prey. Thus, the Lord, the mighty Lion of the tribe of Judah, sounds forth His cry, a cry that brooks defiance from none.

So we turn our eyes upon the Lord Jesus and see Him taking giant strides toward His goal. Having gazed on so much in this book that offends the mind and heart, we feast our eyes upon this glorious sight. But then, dramatically, startlingly, John intrudes himself into the scene. *I was about to write*, he says, *I heard . . . I saw. . . . I heard again . . . I went . . . I said . . . I took . . . I ate.* How practical is the Word of God! It is all very well to be taken up with the King in His beauty, to have one's head in the clouds, but we must never forget that our feet are still on earth. We may be "in Christ," as Paul puts it in writing to the Colossian believers, but we are still "at Colosse." We see the Lord asserting His royal rights, but on earth there remains much land to be possessed. John has to prophesy before many peoples, nations, tongues, and kings.

(b) WE TURN OUR EYES UPON JOHN (10:4-11)

The remainder of the chapter is occupied with the seer and his response to the Word and will of God. We notice first *how attentive he was to the Word of God.* John is brought to the forefront of the chapter to demonstrate the practical effect the visions of the Apocalypse should have upon our daily lives.

We observe that John paid strict attention to *the voices he heard.* He tells us, *And when the seven thunders had uttered their voices, I was about to write: and I heard a voice from heaven saying unto me, Seal up those things which the seven thunders uttered, and write them not.* Some feel that when the seven thunders pealed forth their message, they gave utterance to great, mysterious truths, hidden from men and sealed away with other mysteries for the enlightenment of a future age. God does not reveal His secrets to everyone, nor are all His mysteries unveiled to all His saints. That view, of course, assumes that the thunders John heard were thunders of divine revelation. Another view is suggested here.

The Lord has just asserted His royal rights and roared out His claims to the earth. John says, *And when he had cried, seven thunders uttered their voices.* It seems more in keeping with the passage to envision Satan giving vent to his rage in answer to the Lord's roar. The nations, too, give vent to their wrath. The seven thunders would thus symbolize the response of the rebels to the Lord's announced intention of taking over the earth and the sea. It is like Pharaoh's response to Moses, "I know not the LORD, neither will I let Israel go" (Exod. 5:2). John is about to record what the seven thunders had uttered but is told to "write them not," to disregard what the seven thunders have to say. With majestic disdain, the Lord simply sweeps aside the united thunderings of His foes. What they have to say is not important, and His servant is to ignore them. He is not to waste paper, ink, and energy on them.

John not only paid strict attention to the voices he heard, he paid attention to *the vow he heard.* He says, *And the angel which I saw upon the sea and upon the earth lifted up his hand to heaven, And sware by him that liveth for ever and ever, who created heaven, and the things that therein are, and the earth, and the things that therein are, and the sea, and the things which are therein, that there should be time no longer: But in the days of the voice of the seventh angel, when he shall begin to sound, the mystery of God should be finished, as he hath declared to his servants the prophets.* When He lived on earth, the Lord Jesus said, "Swear not at all; neither by heaven; for it is God's throne: Nor by earth; for it is his footstool" (Matt. 5:34-35). But there is One whose right it is to sit upon that throne and whose right it is to rule the earth. He can swear, and so He does. He takes a solemn vow that matters will now be hastened to their full and final end. There shall be delay no longer.

The mystery is the secret of His allowing Satan to have his own way, and man too. A very great mystery it is indeed. You will remember what a mystery it was to Robinson Crusoe, the lonely castaway on a cannibal isle. He had rescued, not long before, a man-eating savage, and having taught him sufficient English for simple conversation, Robinson Crusoe began to teach Friday the knowledge of the one true God. He impressed upon his servant the fact that God was all-powerful, and he found the savage easily able to comprehend that. "But," says Crusoe, "I found it was not easy to imprint right thoughts in his mind about the devil." Finally Friday floored his teacher, who was just a fledgling theologian himself. Says Crusoe, "I had been talking a great deal to him of the power of God, of His omnipotence, His dread aversion to sin, His being a consuming fire to the workers of iniquity . . . He listened with great seriousness to me all the while. After this, I had been telling him how the devil was God's enemy in the hearts of men, and used all his malice and skill to defeat the good designs of Providence, and to ruin the kingdom of Christ in the world." Then Friday came out with the question. "Well, but you say God is so strong, so great, is He not much strong, much might as the devil?" "Yes, yes," said Robinson Crusoe, "God is much stronger than the devil." Said Friday, "But, if God much strong, much might as the devil, why God not kill the devil?" Robinson Crusoe pretended not to hear the question and hastily found some excuse to send Friday on an errand to the other end of the island![4]

That mystery has puzzled more people than Robinson Crusoe. But not for much longer! The Lord has taken His vow that this mystery will be finished.

4. Daniel Defoe, *Robinson Crusoe* (Chicago: Moody Press, 1965). pp. 192-95.

There will be no more delay. The days will be shortened. As we read on through the Apocalypse, we discover that what has yet to come is to be very sharp, but it is also to be very short. "For he will finish the work, and cut it short in righteousness: because a short work will the Lord make upon the earth" (Rom. 9:28).

So then we see how attentive John was to the Word of God. Next we see *how attuned he was to the will of God.* There is now set before us a tremendous lesson in obedience. *And the voice which I heard from heaven spake unto me again, and said, Go and take the little book which is open in the hand of the angel which standeth upon the sea and upon the earth.* At the commencement of all these revelations, John had fallen at the foot of this One as dead, only to feel His hand upon him and hear His gracious word, "Fear not!" Henceforth John feared nothing. We see him unafraid amid the cherubim, unafraid in the presence of the twenty-four elders. He is plagued by none of that self-consciousness, that sense of personal inferiority that holds us back so often from doing the will of God. He is told to go up to that glorious One who holds the book in His hand and boldly ask that the book be given to him! What an astonishing demand to make of the mighty Conqueror! Think of the audacity of it, the holy boldness of it! The Lord has been waiting for centuries to open that book and to proceed with the closing chapters of God's divine purposes for the end of the age. Now John is told to go up to Him and say, "Please give that book to me!" One would need to be well-attuned to the will of God to do a thing like that; yet that is exactly what John did! Oh, for such prompt, unquestioning obedience to the revealed will of God! Oh, to be so attuned to that will! God does not have many servants like John. Is it any wonder that our eyes are turned upon him?

Because of his prompt obedience to God's will, John is given a fresh comprehension of God's Word. He learns how that Word is to be *personally experienced in his life.* He tells us, *And I went unto the angel, and said unto him, Give me the little book. And he said unto me, Take it, and eat it up; and it shall make thy belly bitter, but it shall be in thy mouth sweet as honey. And I took the little book out of the angel's hand, and ate it up; and it was in my mouth sweet as honey: and as soon as I had eaten it, my belly was bitter.* Eating is an easily recognized symbol for receiving knowledge. For example, we ourselves speak of digesting a piece of information. What John savored of the mind and will of God in that little book was sweet to the taste, for the prayers of God's people were to be fully answered at last, and the coming of the Lord was at hand. But oh, the bitterness of what lay ahead first! How bitter it was to have it revealed that things had to get worse before they could get better! How bitter was the further revelation of beasts and bowls and battles before the final breaking of the day! John could not take a merely academic interest in these revelations. They upset him. Perhaps that is one reason God cannot reveal much to us of His plans. We would be too content, perhaps, with a head knowledge of the facts; the deep significance of them would not affect us in the inner man.

Having learned how the Word of God must be experienced in the life, John next is taught that it must be *publicly expressed to the lost.* He records what he was told, *And he said unto me, Thou must prophesy again before many peoples, and nations, and tongues, and kings.* John's prompt obedience to God's will and his personal appropriation of God's Word fitted him for a new and larger ministry.

(2) THE COMING OF THE MESSENGERS (11:1-13)

In describing the days that immediately preceded the coming of the French Revolution, Charles Dickens, in his *Tale of Two Cities,* at the very beginning of the story, tells us, "It was the best of times, it was the worst of times, it was the age of wisdom, it was the age of foolishness, it was the epoch of belief, it was the epoch of incredulity, it was the season of Light, it was the season of Darkness, it was the spring of hope, it was the winter of despair, we had everything before us, we had nothing before us, we were all going direct to Heaven, we were all going direct the other way." The same superlatives can be used to describe the age about to be opened in this portion of the Apocalypse. It is to be the worst of times, an age of foolishness, an epoch of incredulity, a season of darkness, the winter of despair, with nothing except judgment before those deluded by the Beast. It is to be the best of times, an age of wisdom, a season of light, the spring of hope, with everything before those who are going to heaven.

In the long parenthesis we are considering, we are looking on the bright side of a very dark picture. Mention has already been made of the completion of the mystery. Now we see the coming of the messengers, for God never leaves Himself without a witness. The more degenerate the times, the more definite the testimony. In the days before the Flood, God raised up Enoch and Noah. In the days of Israel's darkest apostasy, He raised up Elijah and Elisha. He will do the same again. God is now about to unleash His wrath, for nothing considered so far in the book can properly be described as "the wrath of God." Judgment, yes! The beginning of sorrows, yes! But wrath? No! That still lies ahead. The cup of human iniquity is almost full, but not quite. A few more drops need to be added. The lie must be consummated, blasphemy must be crowned, and then God will act in wrath.

Revelation 11 anticipates Revelation 13 and has its roots in Revelation 9. In Revelation 13, the Beast's coming is described. It is helpful to see how some of the major parenthetical passages of the Apocalypse relate to each other and especially to the crucial eighth and ninth chapters and the sounding of two key trumpets:

Chapter 8: The war trumpets. The Beast emerges from the sea (trumpet 2); Satan falls from heaven (trumpet 3); upheavals put the Beast at the head of the revived Roman Empire (trumpet 4).

Chapter 13 (parenthetical). Details are given about the Beast (the Antichrist) and the false prophet; one is a Gentile, coming from the sea, symbol of the nations; the other is a Jew, coming from the earth, symbol of Israel.

Chapter 17 (parenthetical). Mystery Babylon is discussed giving further details of the Beast's rise to power. He uses the religious system symbolized by the scarlet woman. Details are also given of his death and resurrection as "the eighth" Roman dictator. From this point on he is a supernatural being—no longer the Beast from the sea (as in chapter 13) but the Beast from the abyss.

Chapter 9: The woe trumpets. The two trumpets in this chapter give details of the Beast's assumption of absolute power over the earth. There is a world-wide demonic seduction of mankind, millions of people being drawn into a vast delusion (trumpet 5); a great war is fought in which some 200 million people are involved. This war is inspired by "the four," a reference to angels presently incarcerated in or at the Euphrates—probably a reference to the satanic principalities who ruled the four world empires of prophecy as Satan's regents (Babylon, Persia, Greece, and Rome), and now united to bring world rule to the Beast. This war removes Russia from the scene and clears the world stage for a one-world empire dominated by the Beast.

Chapter 11 (parenthetical). This chapter tells of the coming of God's two witnesses. They center their activities in Jerusalem and enforce their preaching with judgment miracles. They are opposed by the Beast and the false prophet. Thus God has two men here and Satan has two men here. They all perform miracles. As Jannes and Jambres withstood Moses and Aaron and their miracles with counterfeit, satanic miracles, so Satan's two men oppose God's two men.

While the text does not actually say so, it is not at all unlikely that God's two witnesses execute the Beast who is promptly brought back to life again by the false prophet. (The Beast is called "the beast whose deadly wound was healed"). The Beast, now no longer simply a human, demon-taught, Satan-filled genius, but now a supernatural being, executes the two witnesses and wins the gratitude as well as the awe of mankind. The triumph is short-lived. God raises His two men, takes them to glory, and pours out a judgment on the earth. The text fixes these events as being part of the second woe, which, in turn, is part of the sixth trumpet.

Chapter 7 (parenthetical). Here we have recorded the sealing of the 144,000 witnesses. These men, all drawn from the tribes of Israel, seem to be the fruit of the ministry of the two witnesses, whose spiritual heirs they become. Satan has no power over them. Having rid himself of the two witnesses, the Beast is now confronted with 144,000 witnesses. These Hebrew evangelists preach the gospel of the kingdom to all mankind and reap an enormous harvest of souls. Those saved through their ministry will not be in the church, long since raptured to heaven, but they will be in the kingdom. The majority of these converts will pay a high price for their faith. They will be persecuted and will suffer martyrdom at the hands of the enraged Beast.

Chapter 12 (parenthetical). This chapter describes the Great Tribulation. It shows that it results from Satan's fall from heaven and his confinement to the environs of the earth. The focus of the Tribulation is pre-eminently the nation of Israel.

Chapter 18 (parenthetical). This chapter deals with the city of Babylon. Evidently this city is rebuilt by the Beast. He has three capital cities—Rome, which is his political capital; Jerusalem, which is his religious capital; and Babylon, which is his financial capital. The overthrow of this great vanity fair of tomorrow's world causes great consternation in the financial centers of the world.

In studying the book of Revelation it is important to keep these parenthetical passages in mind. Their purpose is to shed light on the rise and fall of the devil's messiah.

The chapter we are now considering anticipates one of the important crises of the Beast's reign, for God has sent to earth two miraculous witnesses, armed with credentials of supernatural power, and able to defy all might and all authority on earth, even that of the Beast himself. The fame of these two witnesses will be universal, and their names will be household words. In this chapter, the mystery of iniquity and the mystery of godliness come into a head-on collision.

(a) THE MANDATE OF THE MESSENGERS (11:1-5)

We are left in no doubt as to the sphere, the scope, and the strength of their witness. Two things stand out in the background. First, a careful description is given of *the special place involved.* John says, *And there was given me a reed like unto a rod: and the angel stood, saying, Rise, and measure the temple of God, and the altar, and them that worship therein. But the court which is without the temple leave out, and measure it not; for it is given unto the Gentiles: and the holy city shall they tread under foot.*

This part of the parenthesis shows how the sixth trumpet affects the Jewish world. The scene is Jerusalem and the rebuilt Temple. John, who was a passive onlooker and reporter during the previous judgments, is now spurred to action. He is told to measure the Temple and its courts.

Evidently the Jews have by now regained possession not only of the Temple site, but of the right to do something with it. The Mosque of Omar has been reduced to rubble, and a glorious new Temple to Jehovah has been built in its place. Mention of the Temple presupposes a number of things not specifically mentioned in the Apocalypse, but well known from other prophetic Scriptures. The Jews will have entered into a seven-year pact with the Beast and, under his patronage, will have defied the Arabs and rebuilt their temple. Isaiah calls this covenant a covenant with death, and an agreement with hell (28:15). The Jews have made lies their refuge. They are completely deceived by both the character and the intentions of the Beast. They are prepared to accept him as the Messiah, a fact that suggests he has some Jewish blood in his veins. No doubt the secularized Israelis will hail the Beast because he endorses the political aspirations of their state; and the orthodox religious Jews will accept him because he enables them to build their temple and revive the Mosaic ritual law. But although Israel will have won such sweeping concessions and will be enjoying such unprecedented guarantees of security, the fact remains that they still hold Jerusalem on sufferance. The Lord Jesus Himself declared that "Jerusalem shall be trodden down of the Gentiles, until the times of the Gentiles be fulfilled" (Luke 21:24). The "times of the Gentiles" began with Nebuchadnezzar and the captivity of Judah; it has continued until this day and will not be consummated until the downfall of the Beast, the last Gentile ruler on earth. So much, then, for the place. It is Jerusalem and the rebuilt Temple.

Second, a careful description is also given of *the specific period involved.* John was told not to measure the outer court of the Temple because this, together with the holy city, was given over to the Gentiles who will tread it under foot "forty and two months." This period is exactly three-and-a-half years and refers to the second half of Daniel's seventieth "week" (Dan. 9:27). It is common in Scripture to reckon judgment in months. The beginning and duration of the Flood was given in months. The plague of locusts was to be for five months. The blasphemies and persecutions of the Beast are to continue for certain months.

Daniel's seventieth week coincides with the seven-year pact between the Beast and Israel. During the first half of the period, the Beast will honor his treaty commitments, no doubt because it is in his interest to do so. But halfway through the period there will be a change of policy, possibly connected with the downfall of Russia and possibly connected, too, with the emergence of the Beast in his new character as "the beast that ascendeth out of the bottomless pit" (11:7). The persecutions of Revelation 7 relate to this period, commonly called the Great Tribulation. The Beast has already moved his armies into Jerusalem, presumably under the terms of the pact that promises protection for Israel against the Arabs and the Russians. With the Russian threat gone and the Arab states in complete disarray, the Beast now plans to rule the world and to weld it into a single political, cultural, religious, and economic entity. Israel is now only of minor importance to him, and the fact that resistance to his religious program is centered there only enrages him. That resistance is focused in the dramatic ministry of the two witnesses, which has already been of considerable duration.

We are told that their witness will last 1,260 days, or three-and-a-half years using the biblical 360-day calendar as the basis for calculation. God, who numbers the very hairs of our heads, is much more specific, detailed, and minute in recording the ministry of His two faithful witnesses than He is in mentioning the duration of the Beast's rage. He describes the ministry of His two witnesses as a day-by-day ministry and counts up the exact number of those days.

There are two periods of three-and-a-half years involved here, and while they are the same in length, they do not run concurrently. The end of the three-and-a-half year period connected with the two witnesses is marked by their martyrdom and by the outbreak of the Great Tribulation. The end of the three-and-a-half year period connected with the Beast is marked by the return of Christ to set up His kingdom on earth. In other words, the ministry of the two witnesses would seem to be during the first half of Daniel's seventieth week, while the Beast is still merely a superman and not yet a resurrected man. The death of the prophets triggers the Great Tribulation. Thus the period covered by their ministry runs through much of the period covered by the trumpet judgments. They are slain during the period of the second woe, the sixth trumpet.

Their mandate is remarkable for *the supernatural power involved.* John tells us of these two men that they performed great signs in executing their mandate. God says of them, *These are the two olive trees, and the two candlesticks standing before the God of the earth. And if any man will hurt them, fire proceedeth out of their mouth, and devoureth their enemies: and if any man will hurt them, he must in this manner be killed.* There has been much speculation about the identity of these two men. One of them is probably Elijah. Fire was characteristic of his ministry, and his miracles were frequently those of judgment. Some think the other witness might be Moses, for he, like Elijah, was a representative man. Between them they stood for the Old Testament ministry, "the law and the prophets." Together they stood with the Lord on the mount of transfiguration. But since both these witnesses are to be executed by the Beast, the case for Moses is weakened. Moses has already died, and "it is appointed unto men once to die" (Heb. 9:27). Some think the second witness is Enoch. Enoch, like Elijah, was a lonely voice for God in an apostate age, and again like Elijah, he was caught up living into heaven without passing through the article of death.

So much, then, for the mandate of these messengers. It was a mandate of supernatural power, entrusted to them for a specific period and centered in a special place. When their voices are silenced, the last woe comes and the earth is soon thereafter wrested from Satan's grasp.

(b) THE MIRACLES OF THE MESSENGERS (11:6)

Three supernatural weapons are given to these outstanding servants of God. They are armed with *drought*. John says, ***These have power to shut heaven, that it rain not in the days of their prophecy.*** This was one of Elijah's great miracles. In fact, the drought caused by Elijah's prayers lasted three-and-a-half years in the days of Ahab. When the two witnesses close the heavens, the rainmakers of earth will seed the clouds in vain. No invention of science, no incantation to Satan will help. The two witnesses are armed also with *death*. John says that they ***have power over waters to turn them to blood.*** Moses did that, and though the magicians of Egypt were able to mimic that particular miracle of his, they were unable to reverse his actions. The Beast is a man of blood. It is fitting that he and his subjects be given blood to drink, if indeed, this miracle is to be interpreted literally rather than symbolically.

The two witnesses are armed also with *disease*. John says that they have power ***to smite the earth with all plagues, as often as they will.*** Moses did that too. He called for murrain upon cattle and for boils and blains upon men. Terrible new viruses and revitalized plagues that long have cursed mankind will seize upon the world at a word from these two men. No wonder they will be detested and feared around the world.

(c) THE MARTYRDOM OF THE MESSENGERS (11:7-10)

The two messengers are immortal until their work is done. Then, like John the Baptist, they will fall before their foes. As to *the purpose of their martyrdom,* John says, ***And when they shall have finished their testimony, the beast that ascendeth out of the bottomless pit shall make war against them, and shall overcome them, and kill them.*** Nobody else had been able to touch them, but the Beast does, and in so doing he establishes his final bridgehead in the hearts and minds of unregenerate men. There can no longer be any doubt. This wonderful man is the false messiah, the kind of savior the world has always wanted. He has dazzled men time and again before. His own resurrection awed the world, but his conquest over these two miracle workers, his ridding the earth of these detested holy men, will be the capstone of success. Now nothing will be denied him, for he will not only have won the minds of men, but their hearts as well.

Mention is made also of *the place of their martyrdom.* John says, **And their dead bodies shall lie in the street of the great city, which spiritually is called Sodom and Egypt, where also our Lord was crucified.** Jerusalem was called the holy city so long as it was the center of the ministry of the two witnesses. Now it is simply "Sodom and Egypt." The name Sodom emphasizes *vice,* and Egypt points up the *vanity* that has now enthroned itself in this city. It is the place "where also our Lord was crucified," adding the thought that *violence* also is enthroned in this city. Jerusalem, one of the cities of the Beast, has become the center of all that is degrading and defiling. Thus Satan treats the city, which is to be the Lord's capital for a thousand years, with utter contempt.

Mention is made, furthermore, of *the publicity of this martyrdom.* Satan will see to it that the killing of these two detested enemies of his will be blazed abroad. In fact, the Beast's triumph will be *shown to the world.* John says, **And they of the people and kindreds and tongues and nations shall see their dead bodies three days and a half, and shall not suffer their dead bodies to be put in graves.** The television cameras of the world will be focused on this event. It will be the gossip of the globe. News of it will filter into every nook and cranny of the earth. And as in olden times when the bodies of criminals were hung up to rot in public view, so the bodies of these two witnesses will be left on public display in scornful ignominy for half a week. "By this time he stinketh," said Martha to Jesus when the Lord commanded the opening of the tomb of Lazarus after a lapse of four days. The horrible sight of two dead bodies will delight a world insensate to all but its own lusts.

The Beast's triumph will not only be shown to the world, it will be *shared by the world.* John says, **And they that dwell upon the earth shall rejoice over them, and make merry, and shall send gifts one to another; because these two prophets tormented them that dwelt on the earth.** God calls their witness a testimony (11:7); the world will call it a torment. But now, thanks to the Beast, the torment is over! By this time, Christmas Day will have become a mere anachronism on earth. A new festival will be provided, one much more meaningful and relevant for a pagan world. Instead of commemorating the birth of the Messiah, the world will commemorate the death of the messengers and will spontaneously, making a holiday of the event, send gifts one to another, congratulating one another that the earth is finally rid of its chief tormentors. But the celebrations are too hasty! In the midst of the fun and feasting comes startling, sobering news. God has vindicated His own.

(d) THE MIGHT OF THE MESSENGERS (11:11-13)

Death cannot hold them, and they arise from the grave. John tells us that they have *a triumphant resurrection.* He says, *And after three days and a half the spirit of life from God entered into them, and they stood upon their feet; and great fear fell upon them which saw them.* Picture the scene—the sun-drenched streets of Jerusalem, the holiday crowds flown in from the ends of the earth for a firsthand look at the corpses of these detested men, the troops in the Beast's uniform, the temple police. There they are, devilish men from every kingdom under heaven, come to dance and feast at the triumph of the Beast. And then it happens! As the crowds strain at the police cordon to peer curiously at the two dead bodies, there comes a sudden change. Their color changes from cadaverous hue to the blooming, rosy glow of youth. Those stiff, stark limbs—they bend, they move! Oh, what a sight! They rise! The crowds fall back, break, and form again.

They also have *a trimphant rapture.* John says, *And they heard a great voice from heaven saying unto them, Come up hither. And they ascended up to heaven in a cloud; and their enemies beheld them.* But will these evil men repent when faced with this, the greatest of all miracles? Not a bit of it! "Father Abraham" cried the rich man from the flames of a lost eternity, "Father Abraham . . . if one went unto them from the dead, they will repent." Back came the solemn reply, "If they hear not Moses and the prophets, neither will they be persuaded though one rose from the dead" (Luke 16:30-31). And here not just one, but two arise, and repentance is the furthest thing from the minds of men.

Then also, they have *a trimphant revenge.* We read, *And the same hour was there a great earthquake, and the tenth part of the city fell, and in the earthquake were slain of men seven thousand: and the remnant were affrighted, and gave glory to the God of heaven.* A few, a remnant of men, give grudging acknowledgment that there is indeed a living God, but the impression does not last. The last woe that ushers in the end of the age follows fast.

(3) THE CROWNING OF THE MESSIAH (11:14-19)

The last trump is about to sound, precipitating the outpouring of the vials of God's wrath. But first we are given a glimpse of the crowning in heaven of God's rightful king. It seems as though they never get tired of crowning Him in heaven! David was anointed king three times, once when he was a mere youth; once in Hebron over the tribe of Judah; and once again over all Israel. Thus, too, the Lord! The title deeds of earth were given to Him in chapter five, and the elders cast their crowns at His feet. Here He is acknowledged as earth's rightful King. Later, in chapter 19, He comes forth as King of kings and Lord of lords, and on His head are many crowns.

The scene is in heaven, but news of what is happening is released on earth, with the result that the nations are enraged. They want no king but Caesar. One is tempted to linger long over this passage because the next two chapters are scant indeed of blessing, being occupied with the purposes of the evil one. Two truths are set before us here. The third woe on earth is described, and the thankful worship in heaven is described. The two events stand in stark contrast of each other. Judgment on earth, jubilation in heaven; rage on earth, rejoicing in heaven; cursing on earth, crowning in heaven; woe on earth, worship in heaven. God balances the one against the other with consummate skill.

(a) THE THIRD WOE ON THE EARTH (11:14-15)

It is soon recorded. *The second woe is past; and behold, the third woe cometh quickly. And the seventh angel sounded; and there were great voices in heaven, saying, The kingdoms of this world are become the kingdoms of our Lord, and of his Christ; and he shall reign for ever and ever.* The whole question of sovereignty is now settled. The revisers have changed the wording of this passage slightly so that it reads, "The kingdom [singular] of this world has become the kingdom [singular] of our Lord." That is what the devil has been after for centuries—to unite the world into a single kingdom—but all his attempts fail. He can no more overcome the disruptive, devisive power of sin than he can escape the ultimate judgment of God.

Back in the beginning of human history, when men first began to organize in their rebellion against God, Satan attempted at Babel to build a world society from which God was to be excluded. Men planned a city and a tower— the city was to symbolize their political unity and the tower their religious unity. They had a common tongue as well, which emphasized their cultural unity. God came down and confounded the whole thing. Man, united without God, was the form taken by the first apostasy after the Flood. It will be the form of the final apostasy too.

Note carefully the offer made by Satan when he tempted the Lord in the wilderness. Luke tells us that "the devil, taking him up into an high mountain, shewed unto him all the kingdoms of the world in a moment of time. And the devil said unto him, All this power will I give thee, and the glory of them . . . If thou therefore wilt worship me, all shall be thine" (Luke 4:5-7). He offered the kingdoms, the power, and the glory. The Lord spurned the offer. He had not come for the divided, disunited kingdoms of the earth; He had come for the *kingdom.* And so, the kingdom of this world becomes the kingdom of our Lord. That is the theme of heaven's song. But if it is wonderful news in heaven, it is woeful news on earth, for the transition will take place not by evolution, but by divine intervention in wrath. The kingdom is to be arbitrarily imposed on men by God, and terrible judgments lie between the crowning of the King in heaven and the crowning of that same King on earth. Satan, although he is fighting a losing battle, will not relinquish without a fierce struggle his evil hold upon the planet he has dominated for so long. His rage is all the more intense because, with the Beast riding high, it seems that his ancient goals are about to be realized at last.

(b) THE THANKFUL WORSHIP IN HEAVEN (11:16-19)

The twenty-four elders burst into songs of loudest praise. Their reaction to the announcement is full of interest and practical instruction. The way they respond to divine truth is the way we should respond. Notice, they are *instantaneous in their response to the Word of God.* We read, *And the four and twenty elders, which sat before God on their seats, fell upon their faces and worshipped God.* What they say we are not told. Perhaps the language of Psalm 45 pours from their lips and hearts, 'My heart is inditing a good matter: I speak of the things . . . touching the king . . . Thou art fairer than the children of men . . . Gird thy sword upon thy thigh, O most mighty. And in thy majesty ride prosperously . . . Thy throne O God is for ever and ever: the sceptre of thy kingdom is a right sceptre." They know so well over yonder what it means for Jesus to be absolute Lord that the bare idea that others will come to know it too brings them down off their thrones and down at His feet.

Notice also that they are *intelligent in their recounting of the ways of God.* They acknowledge His titles. They say, *We give thee thanks, O Lord God Almighty, which art, and wast, and art to come; because thou hast taken to thee thy great power, and hast reigned.* We have met these titles before. In fact, the Apocalypse begins with their display. They are titles of singular majesty and power. Satan seeks to imitate these titles, and his wretched little puppet is called "the beast that was, and is not, yet is" (17:8), but it is a poor and shoddy imitation of the titles of dignity and honor our Lord bears in glory.

They acknowledge His triumphs. They say, *Thou hast taken to thee thy great power, and hast reigned. And the nations were angry, and thy wrath is come.* The throne rights of the Lord are not only asserted, they are assured. Within a few more chapters (all of them more or less parenthetical) the wrath of God will be poured out in the emptying of the vials. Nothing will stand before that wrath. The Lord's power is rightly called "great power."

The Lord is coming to receive no mere constitutional monarchy, but absolute, untrammeled, unhindered power. Heaven's ideal form of government for earth is a totalitarian monarchy with complete power vested in the Person of the Lord Jesus. On June 2, 1952, Elizabeth II was crowned Queen of England in Westminster Abbey. The Archbishop of Canterbury presented her to the vast assemblage of people and asked, "Do you take Elizabeth to be your true and lawful liege lord?" From the assembled multitude rolled back a single word, "Aye!" She then took the coronation oath, received a Bible, celebrated Communion, and was seated on the coronation chair. She was anointed, clothed in a cloak of gold, given the orb, the ring, the scepter—the insignia of power—crowned with the glorious crown of St. Edward, and pledged the homage of her people. The guns of London fired a salute, and the new monarch left the abbey in grand and colorful procession for a banquet of state. But from that day to this, Queen Elizabeth II has never made a single decision affecting the government of her kingdom. The Prime Minister of England and the members of the English Parliament do that. All she does is sign their decisions into law. That is a constitutional monarchy—a monarchy in which the king is such only in name and in which all the real power is in the hands of the people. That was the kind of kingdom the devil offered the Lord in the wilderness, and it is the same kind of sovereignty many professing believers offer Him in their lives today. That is not the kind of monarchy God intends Him to have. He is going to be Lord of all. "Thou hast taken to thee thy great power and has reigned."

They acknowledge His timings, especially as those timings concern both the crowning of the redeemed and the crushing of the rebels. They say, *And thy wrath is come, and the time of the dead, that they should be judged, and that thou shouldest give reward unto thy servants the prophets, and to the saints, and them that fear thy name, small and great; and shouldest destroy them which destroy the earth.* The martyrs of God, the messengers of God, the men of God, the multitudes of God all stand before Him for the time has come that they be rewarded for their faithfulness. The elders take note of it and rejoice. And the destroyers of the earth, His earth, are to be themselves destroyed.

Finally, the twenty-four elders are *instrumental in their relation to the will of God*. We read, *And the temple of God was opened in heaven, and there was seen in his temple the ark of his testament: and there were lightnings, and voices, and thunderings, and an earthquake, and a great hail.* Over and over again, things are opened in this book. A door is opened (4:1), the seals are opened (6:1-9), the abyss is opened (9:2), the temple is opened (11:19), the Tabernacle of the testimony (the Holy of Holies) is opened (19:11), and the books are opened (20:12). Here is opened up to human view, the true, eternal temple in the heavens. The opening of the temple displays the Ark that in Old Testament times was always concealed, thus signifying that God is about to act on behalf of beleaguered Israel. In the Old Testament, the Ark was connected with the Tabernacle and Moses, the land and Joshua, the kingdom and David, the Temple and Solomon. It thus stood connected with Israel's law, Israel's land, Israel's Lord, and Israel's light.

The twenty-four elders are closely associated with the worship that takes place in that heavenly temple. Their praise is directly linked to the opening of the heavenly temple and the subsequent rumblings of judgment heard on earth. Their occupation with the Word, the ways, and the will of God is linked with the onward march of the divine purpose. What a lesson for God's people in all ages!

Go back to the early days of the Medo-Persian Empire for an illustration. Daniel was a very old man, probably in his nineties. He had been in Babylon for seventy years and was ceaselessly occupied with the Word, the will, and the ways of God. He was reading the prophet Jeremiah and came to what is now chapters 25 and 29, the great prophecy of the seventy years. He gave himself to prayer, and heaven began to move. Soon the pioneer group of repatriated Israelites was moving westward toward the ancestral land, and the tides of history were turned. There can be little doubt that behind Zerubbabel and his valiant little band was the shadow of an aged man in Babylon, his back bowed in the presence of God, and his finger firmly planted on the promises of God.

"Thy wrath is come!" cry the elders, and their cry is heard. They become instrumental in relation to the will of God. What they did, Daniel did. What Daniel did, we can do. And God's purposes on earth will be advanced.

b. THE PURPOSES OF HELL REVEALED (12:1–13:18)

God's glorious plans have been revealed, and now Satan's schemes are unmasked. We are shown what he has been after since the dawn of time. His plans for this planet include the eradication of all who in any way remind him that God has a purpose on earth, the unification of the world under a single head, and the adoration of the entire human race. The next two chapters of the Apocalypse review much that has been left unsaid in previous descriptions of the trumpet era. They tell us how the Great Tribulation is brought about and how the great tyrant is brought in. Satan's ruling passion is the theme of chapter 12 of Revelation, and Satan's regent prince is the theme of chapter 13.

(1) SATAN'S RULING PASSION (12:1-17)

In a word, Satan's ruling passion is to exterminate the Jews. There are four great things mentioned in this chapter—a great sign, a great red dragon, a great eagle, and a great wrath. We can be assured that the Holy Spirit's use of the word "great" is discriminatory. Chapter 12 has to do with the woman, the war, and the woe.

(a) THE WOMAN (12:1-6)

The Holy Spirit warns us that He is about to describe a great wonder, or sign, from which we gather that what is actually seen is symbolic; it is a sign of something else. Interpretations that take the woman to be the virgin Mary lead us into difficulty. Interpretations that view the woman as the church cannot be correct either, for the church did not bring God's Son into the world. He had come and gone before ever the church was born.

Three things concern us about the woman. There is *the prophetic signifi-cance of the woman*. She represents the nation of Israel, a fact that becomes increasingly clear as the chapter unfolds. John draws our attention to *the glorious dignity that was Israel's*. He says, **And there appeared a great wonder in heaven; a woman clothed with the sun, and the moon under her feet, and upon her head a crown of twelve stars.** This takes us back to the story of Joseph in Genesis 37, the only Scripture that bears any correspon-dence with this sign. Joseph dreamed that the sun, the moon, and the eleven stars made obeisance to him. He understood from this that his parents and his brethren would bow down to him. His dream was a revelation from God that Israel would be preserved through him. This chapter in Revelation gives us a glimpse of the glorious dignity that, in God's thinking, clothes the nation of Israel. The nation has failed repeatedly through the ages, but just the same, Israel belongs to God; its glory is, therefore, the glory of the heavens. For this reason Abraham's seed is likened to the stars (Gen. 15:5). No wonder Satan hates this people. She reminds him of all that once was his and of the heights from which he fell.

John draws our attention also to *the glorious destiny that was Israel's*. He says of the woman that **she being with child cried, travailing in birth, and pained to be delivered.** This takes us back even futher in the book of Genesis to chapter three, to the first great promise and prophecy of Scripture, the promise that the seed of the woman would crush the serpent's head. The promised Seed, of course, was to come through Israel, as later Scriptures make plain. That was the great hope of the nation, the ringing theme of the prophets, the grand climax toward which all else pointed. Every devout Jewish mother hoped that through her would come that Seed. The nation agonized throughout its long history for the coming of the promised Messiah. Israel's grand destiny was to be the nation through which blessing would come to all mankind; through her would come the Seed. "Who are Israelites," cried Paul, "to whom pertaineth the adoption, and the glory, and the covenants, and the giving of the law, and the service of God, and the promises; whose are the fathers, and of whom as concerning the flesh, Christ came, who is over all, God, blessed for ever, Amen" (Rom. 9:4-5).

Then the text speaks of *the prolonged sufferings of the woman*. No nation on earth has suffered so severely and for so long as Israel. We are left with no doubt as to the cause of Israel's sufferings. John says, **And there appeared another wonder in heaven; and behold a great red dragon, having seven heads and ten horns, and seven crowns upon his heads.** The word *dragon* occurs a significant thirteen times in Revelation (eleven times here and once each in chapters 16 and 20). A dragon is a flying serpent, a biblical symbol for Satan (20:2). The heads, horns, and the crowns of the dragon are symbols of earthly power that Satan claims. Satan is the "prince of the power of the air, the spirit that now worketh in the children of disobedience" (Eph. 2:2) and he is also the "prince of this world" (John 12:31). He is pictured here as a great red dragon, an eloquent symbol for cruelty, blood-lust, and power. He is the cause of the woman's sufferings.

We are told that this dread creature with his tail *drew the third part of the stars of heaven, and did cast them to the earth.* This takes us back to the beginning of things, to Satan's initial rebellion in heaven. It would seem that a third part of the angelic host followed him in his great rebellion. Now these hosts are to be marshaled against Israel. They have been active against Israel before, as Daniel tells us, and they will be active again.

It might be appropriate here to consider briefly the course of Israel's sufferings. Both sacred and secular history tell the long tale. The first large-scale attempt to exterminate the Jews was made by Pharaoh. Significantly, the turning point came in Moses' life when he saw, in the desert, that mysterious burning bush, which flamed and blazed away but, for all the crackling of the fire, was not consumed. That bush clearly symbolized Israel, which cannot be consumed despite the ceaseless hatred of her foes, because God is in her midst. Israel cannot be assimilated into the nations, nor can she be exterminated by the nations. She is a burning bush in the wilderness, a gulf stream in the ocean of mankind.

The Jew today is the purest-blooded and proudest-descended people in the world. What he was when Tyre fell or when the Temple went up in smoke, that he is today. His language, his literature, and his customs are much the same. The Jew has been persistently hated and hunted by the Gentiles. Even England, long the refuge of the downtrodden and the outlawed, did not always offer asylum to the Jew. Canute banished them all from England a thousand years ago. Edward I drove every last one of them from England's shores. In France and Germany, they were blamed for the black plague and were terribly treated. The same year that Columbus discovered America, Spain drove all Jews from the kingdom. The Inquisition wreaked its cruelties upon them in the name of Christ.

Says A. W. Kac,

Next to the survival of the Jews, the most baffling historical phenomenon is the hatred which he has repeatedly encountered among the nations of the earth. This hostility to the Jews, which goes under the name of antisemitism, is as old as Jewish existence. It is endemic, i.e., like many contagious diseases it is always with us to some degree. But under certain circumstances it assumes epidemic proportions and characteristics. It is prevalent wherever Jews reside in sufficiently large numbers to make their neighbours aware of their presence. "The growth of antisemitism," Chaim Weizman declares, "is proportionate to the number of Jews per square kilometre. We carry the germs of antisemitism in our knapsack on our backs."[5]

In modern times, anti-Semitism has reached epidemic proportions indeed. In 1882, there were outbreaks of atrocities against the Jews in Russia. In France, in 1894, the Dreyfus Affair was an attempt to make a Jew the scapegoat for national problems and to give the French anti-Semites an opportunity to oust Jews from the higher ranks in the army. In Germany, the rise of Jews to prominent positions in the professions, industry, commerce, science, literature, and the arts gave the lie to German theories of the racial superiority of the German peoples. Ultimately there came Hitler and the death camps. Now the mantle of chief persecutor of the Jews is worn by the Arab states and Russia. But the end is not yet. The worst is yet to come. No wonder the woman is set forth as a figure of suffering Israel.[6]

The next thing to consider is *the promised Seed of the woman*. For in the fullness of time Christ was born of the virgin, a woman of the royal house of David, of the tribe of Judah. In this connection we see that Satan *could not harm Him, for He came.* John says, *And the dragon stood before the woman which was ready to be delivered, for to devour her child as soon as it was born.* Herod was Satan's tool that time. Having ascertained the place from the scribes and the time from the wise men, Herod slew all the babes of Bethlehem under two years of age, but all in vain. Christ came. He escaped the edge of the sword.

Satan could not halt Him either, for He conquered. We read, *And she brought forth a man child, who was to rule all nations with a rod of iron: and her child was caught up unto God, and to his throne.* He was manifest that He might destroy the works of the devil. Demons, disease, death, and disaster all fled before Him. He invaded death at Calvary and tore its bars away. He rose in victory, having spoiled principalities and powers, triumphing over them openly in His cross. And now He is seated at God's right hand in glory. Satan could not halt Him even for a moment.

Satan could not hinder Him, for He controls. John says, *And the woman fled into the wilderness, where she had a place prepared of God, that they should feed her there a thousand two hundred and threescore days.* Satan will certainly try to hinder His plans. The period of 1,260 days mentioned here is the period of the Great Tribulation—three-and-a-half years. During that time, Satan will do his worst, but his plans will be foiled. God has prepared a place already where the fleeing Jews will be safe. Many think that

5. A. W. Kac, *Rebirth of the State of Israel* (Chicago: Moody, 1958), p. 306.
6. See John Phillips, *Exploring the World of the Jew* (Chicago, Moody Press, 1981).

place is the ancient city of Petra. The main gorge by which this rock-hewn city is approached, looks down on a rivulet that threads its way along its entire length. Its rocky steeps are red and brown, purple and yellow. Its valley, with its branching tributaries, is about 4,500 feet long and is flanked on all sides by beetling sandstone cliffs. An invading army would have to creep down that narrow, precipitous canyon, twisting and turning through the mountains, before ever the main citadel itself could be seen. Satan will do his worst, but God will not allow him to succeed. He will not even have the satisfaction of hindering for a moment God's plans, all of which proceed on schedule. Even the exact number of the days involved in the Tribulation has been written in the Word of God for centuries.

(b) THE WAR (12:7-12)

Again the veil is torn aside, and we are given a glimpse of those mysterious principalities and powers that rule in the unseen spirit world. Notice *where the war is fought.* John says, *And there was war in heaven.* That is about the very last place one would expect to find war. War in heaven! No wonder that at the end of the Apocalypse God makes both a new heaven and a new earth, for Satan has defiled both realms. Sin is much older than mankind. It did not originate on earth; it originated in heaven and began, not in a human breast, but in the soul of Lucifer. So this war is fought in heaven.

We observe *why the war is fought.* This is unquestionably one of the most important battles in the entire history of the universe. The records of this war will not be found in secular histories, but they are set forth in a Book more accurate, more enduring than all the history books of earth. Two reasons are given for the fighting of this all-important battle.

It was fought *to cast Satan down from heaven.* The record reads, *Michael and his angels fought against the dragon; and the dragon fought and his angels, and prevailed not; neither was their place found any more in heaven.* It is evident from Daniel 10 that behind the kingdoms of this world is a satanic empire in the spirit world divided into kingdoms synonymous with those on earth. Satanic angels, or "principalities" as they are called, supervise on Satan's behalf the affairs of the nations over which they secretly rule. When God called Abraham out of Ur of the Chaldees, He said to him, "I will make of thee a great nation" (Gen. 12:2). In God's time, this nation emerged as a power to be reckoned with on earth. It was a new and divinely-created nation, and Satan had no angelic prince over it. On the contrary, an angel of God, Michael, "one of the chief princes," was set over Israel in the spirit world. Michael is called "your prince" and "the prince which standeth for thy people" (Dan. 10:13, 21; 12:1). He is also called by Jude "the archangel." Michael defends Israel and God's interests in this nation against the ceaseless attacks of Satan's emissaries.

Revelation 13 describes the casting down of Satan and his hosts from their strongholds in the air. He will no longer be "the prince of the power of the air," but will be confined to earth. This is the second in a series of falls that mark his career. Already he has been cast out of heaven into the air, next he will be cast from the air to the earth, then from the earth into the abyss, and finally from the abyss into the lake of fire.

This war, then, will be fought to cast Satan down from heaven. It is also fought *to cast Satan down to earth.* Two things are worth considering about this. We can note *the efficiency of this operation.* John says, *And the great dragon was cast out, that old serpent, called the Devil, and Satan, which deceiveth the whole world: he was cast out into the earth, and his angels with him.* There can be no mistake, for four of our ancient foe's titles are given. The campaign against Satan does not last long. All his followers are flung with him from the sky in one clean sweep. To borrow a famous statement from Israel's persecuted past, not a hoof will be left behind! Satan may be mighty, but he is not almighty. This event probably takes place in connection with the blowing of the third trumpet (8:10-11).

We can note also *the effect of the operation,* which was twofold. There was a double proclamation, one having to do with heaven and the other having to do with earth. *The great proclamation in heaven* is described first. John says, *And I heard a loud voice saying in heaven, Now is come salvation, and strength, and the kingdom of our God, and the power of his Christ: for the accuser of our brethren is cast down, which accused them before our God day and night. And they overcame him by the blood of the Lamb, and by the word of their testimony; and they loved not their lives unto the death. Therefore rejoice, ye heavens.* The great proclamation in heaven has to do with the Savior, with Satan, and with the saints. The sense of relief and rejoicing that sweeps over heaven is real. For countless ages, Satan has had access to the presence of God. We read of his accusations in connection with Job and in connection with Joshua the high priest. Ever he came with a smirk and a sneer to tell spiteful tales about the faults and failings of the people of God. It is all too evident that Satan, liar that he is, does not need to come into the presence of God to lie about the saints. There is more than enough in our lives to be grist for his mill. He goes into God's presence to tell the truth about us, and heaven has groaned again and again at the long recital of the sins of the saints. Satan has enjoyed himself to the full, relishing the tales he has been able to tell. But over and over again he has been defeated by the high priestly work of our Advocate.

Now, the door is shut! Satan's way into the presence of God is bolted and barred forever. Now, in the presence of God, instead of the vices, are rehearsed the victories of the saints. They tell each other in glory of the *cleansing* of the saints, how they overcame Satan by the blood of the Lamb. They tell of the *confession* of the saints, how they overcame Satan by the word of their testimony. They tell of the *courage* of the saints, how they loved not their lives unto death. Well might this proclamation in heaven end with the joyful summons, "Rejoice therefore ye heavens!"

The great proclamation in heaven is followed by *a grim proclamation on earth.* The voice continues, *Woe to the inhabiters of the earth and of the sea! for the devil is come down unto you, having great wrath because he knoweth that he hath but a short time.* Soon after this woe is pronounced, the woe trumpets begin. Satan is now like a caged lion, enraged beyond words by the limitations now placed upon his freedom. He picks himself up from the dust of the earth, shakes his fist at the sky, and glares around, choking with fury for ways to vent his hatred and his spite upon humankind (see trumpet three). Woe indeed to the inhabiters of the earth and of the sea! Remember, the Lord has planted His feet upon both so that even in this scene to which he is now confined, Satan discovers he is checkmated and mastered by the One he hates most of all.

(c) THE WOE (12:13-17)

For we are not long left in doubt as to the form Satan's rage will take. It is directed against Israel and the saints of God. He cannot touch the manchild, so he attacks the woman who brought Him into the world. How symmetrical is the unfolding of divine truth. The Bible begins with the story of the woman, the serpent, and the Seed; and here it comes full circle and traces that Edenic struggle to its final end.

Three factors come into view in connection with the woe. First, there is *the time factor.* John says, *And when the dragon saw that he was cast unto the earth.* Satan has always detested Israel. Now his animosity and antagonism beggars description. He has been cast down to earth—woe betide God's earthly people. The devil himself will personally supervise the last bloodbath of anti-Semitic persecution.

The second factor is *the tribulation factor,* for the verses that follow tell how Israel will be hated and hidden and hunted and helped during the coming trial. John says, *And when the dragon saw that he was cast unto the earth, he persecuted the woman which brought forth the man child. And to the woman were given two wings of a great eagle, that she might fly into the wilderness, into her place, where she is nourished for a time, and times, and half a time, from the face of the serpent. And the serpent cast out of his mouth water as a flood after the woman, that he might cause her to be carried away of the flood. And the earth helped the woman, and the earth opened her mouth, and swallowed up the flood which the dragon cast out of his mouth.* As Israel in ancient times fled into the wilderness (Ex. 15:5), so in a future day will she flee again. The Lord Jesus spoke of this flight in His Olivet discourse. "Pray," He said, "that your flight be not in the winter, neither on the sabbath day" (Matt. 24:20).

Israel's plight will be desperate, but even so, God will raise up among the Gentiles those who will render help. They will shield and shelter the Jews at great personal risk and will be numbered among the sheep at the judgment of the living nations when the Lord returns (Matt. 25:31-46). But Israel's chief hiding place will be in what is called here "the wilderness." The greatest flight will be from Jerusalem and the land of Israel, the focal point of the Beast's hatred, and God will repeat His former miracles and furnish for His beloved refugees a table in the wilderness.

What a time of terror lies ahead for Israel! The world has seen dress rehearsals for this coming onslaught already—the knock on the door at dead of night; the dreaded secret police; the swift ride through the darkened streets to the sidings where the boxcars wait; the dreadful ordeal of days and nights without food, drink, or sanitation, with men and women and children herded like cattle in the dark, and with little babies flung on top of the struggling heap of humanity like so many sacks of flour; the lonely sidings; the barbed wire, the concentration camps; the callous treatment and cruel tortures; and then the gas ovens and the firing squads. It has been rehearsed already in preparation for the full stage production of terror. No wonder God Himself intervenes to provide a place of hiding for those who exercise saving faith in His Word and flee.

Last of all, our attention is drawn to *the triumph factor.* John says, **And the dragon was wroth with the woman, and went to make war with the remnant of her seed, which keep the commandments of God, and have the testimony of Jesus Christ.** Satan cannot win. Just as the blood of the martyrs has proved to be the seed of the church, so during the Tribulation, persecution will but drive many Jewish people into the arms of the Lord Jesus. Satan, in his rage, displays a notable lack of imagination and originality. He has tried persecution many times before, and it has always failed to deter faith and conversion. That he tries it again is a mute confession of failure, the last resort of a desperate and darkened mind. The godly Jews will not recant. They will only scatter far and wide, bearing as they go the gospel of the kingdom and their triumph will be complete. What can Satan do with the likes of these? Lock them up in prison, and they convert their jailors; torture them, and they become partakers of Christ's sufferings and heirs to a great reward; martyr them, and they go straight to be with Christ; turn them loose, and they evangelize the world!

(2) SATAN'S REGENT PRINCES (13:1-18)

One of the last of Judah's kings was Jehoiakim. The great prophet Jeremiah poured out his sob-choked prophecies in the days of this weak king and his few successors. It was Jehoiakim who took the prophecies of Jeremiah and cut them up with a penknife and cast them into the fire. When Jeremiah came to write up his prophecies, he treated Jehoiakim to a dose of his own medicine, cutting up all matters pertaining to this king, putting a piece here and a piece there. In chapter 13 in the Apocalypse, we note a similar principle. This is the very last of the Gentile kings, crowned by an apostate world as both Lord and Christ. A greater than Jehoiakim is here in his scorn and contempt for the things of God. So God, harking back to Jeremiah's inspired treatment of Jehoiakim, takes the story of this last king of the Gentiles and cuts it up in pieces and strews the wreckage of it here and there throughout the book of Revelation. We have to piece the story together as best we can, picking up a scrap of information, first in one chapter and then in another. Thus chapter 13 really goes back to chapters 8 and 9, and chapters 18 and 19 go back to chapter 13. God drives wedge after wedge into the story of the beast, splitting it up like so much kindling for the fire.

In chapter 12 the record is given of *Satan's ruling passion*—to do as much harm as possible to the people of God before being flung headlong himself into the pit. In chapter 13 the record is given of *Satan's regent prince,* the Beast, the man of sin. Actually there are two beasts in the chapter—there is the false prince and the false prophet.

(a) THE FALSE PRINCE (13:1-10)

The Lord Jesus said, "I am come in my Father's name, and ye receive me not: if another shall come in his own name, him ye will receive" (John 5:43). He was referring to the coming of Satan's messiah. We are now to learn how he comes. Our attention is directed to *the parentage of this false prince.* If ever there was a man on earth whose father was the devil, this is he. We immediately recognize *the family likeness.* John says, *And I stood upon the sand of the sea, and saw a beast rise up out of the sea, having seven heads and ten horns, and upon his horns ten crowns, and upon his heads the name of blasphemy.* Turning back to the previous chapter, we read this description of Satan: "Behold a great red dragon having seven heads and ten horns and seven crowns upon his heads" (12:3). There is no mistaking the family likeness in the number of heads and the number of horns. In chapter 17 where a further description of the Beast is given, we learn that he, too, is scarlet. The word for "crowns" is not the usual word employed in Revelation. It is the word for diadem, only used of the dragon (chap. 12) and of the Beast (chap. 13) and of Christ (19:12). And there, in that last reference, the "many diadems" of

Christ are surely in deliberate contrast with the ten diadems of the Beast and the seven diadems of Satan.

So much, then, for the family likeness. The Lord Jesus could say of Himself, "He that hath seen me hath seen the Father." Here is Satan's imitation of the incarnation. He conjures up a man, a beast, who bears all the characteristics of Satan himself. Whatever Satan is in his person, his nature, and his personality, so is the Beast. He is the visible expression of the invisible devil. He who has seen the Beast has seen the father of lies himself in his outward manifestation. Every line of Satan's character is faithfully reproduced in the character of the Beast. He and his father are one in family likeness.

We recognize, moreover, *the family lineage.* John tells us, *And the beast which I saw was like unto a leopard, and his feet were as the feet of a bear, and his mouth as the mouth of a lion.* This takes us back to Daniel 7:4-6 where the lion, the bear, and the leopard have already been seen in apocalyptic vision. The lion symbolized the empire of Babylon, the bear stood for the Medo-Persian Empire, and the leopard signified Greece. Just as the Roman Empire gathered into itself the Macedonian swiftness of conquest, the Persian tenacity of purpose and the Babylonian appetite for conquest, so will this Beast, the last of a notable line, gather up the characteristics and imperial lust of all three. He is the heir of the ages, the last and worst of all the Caesars, Genghis Khans, Napoleons, Hitlers, and Stalins who have plagued this sin-cursed earth. He is the last Gentile claimant to the throne of the world, heir and successor of Nebuchadnezzar, to whom that throne was given long centuries ago.

He is both *a real person* and a representative person. Think of him first as a real person. His body is like that of a leopard, his feet are like those of a bear, and his mouth is like that of a lion. The body of a leopard is covered with spots. "Can the Ethiopian change his skin, or the leopard his spots?" cried the prophet in describing the ingrained, immutable character of Judah's sins (Jer. 13:23). The Beast has the body of a leopard, full of spots. This is a picturesque way of describing how ferocious, wild, harmful, and immutable is his nature. Now look at the Lord Jesus. He is no leopard; He is the Lamb "without blemish and without spot" (1 Pet. 1:19). Could any contrast be greater or more pronounced? Satan has his spotted leopard; God has His spotless Lamb.

The Beast has feet like those of a bear. A bear has great, ugly claws, and it hugs its prey in a tenacious grip. It rends and tears, and it walks with a swift but ugly shuffle. Now stand with John at Jordan "looking upon Jesus as he walked" (John 1:36). What a contrast between the menacing waddle of the bear and the magnificent walk of Jesus. The Beast leaves a trail of blood behind him; the Lord Jesus walked cleanly through life.

The Beast's mouth is likened to the mouth of a lion, raging and tearing and harmful; and out of his mouth proceed great blasphemies. Now look again at Jesus. "His mouth is most sweet," and His lips are like lilies (Song of Sol. 5:11,16). Men marveled at the gracious words that fell from His lips and said, "Never man spake like this man." Could contrast be greater between the stinking maw of the Beast and the sweet mouth of Jesus?

His lineage is all too apparent—he is a beast. Perhaps it is not for nothing that for the past century, scientific investigation has been largely dedicated to proving that man is a lineal descendant of the beasts. He is not, of course; but Darwin, Huxley, their fellows, and their successors have been at pains to brainwash the human race with this colossal lie. Since men wish to claim kinship with the beasts, then God will justly give them a beast, the incarnation of everything beastly. He will be a real person but will embody the passions, instincts, and appetites of the beasts, along with the intellect of a genius, all touched with more than a dash of the spirit of Satan. So then, looking at the Beast as a real person, he is everything that Christ is not, in his ways, his walk, and his words.

The Beast, however, is not only a real person, he is *a representative person*. Totalitarian states have frequently arisen in which the state and the head of the state have been closely identified. The Beast, as head of state *is* the state. The Beast of Revelation 13 is both an emperor and an empire.

The tide in this direction is now in its flood. It first began to set in, so far as recent times are concerned, when Machiavelli published his book *The Prince*, in 1513. Machiavelli was infatuated with Caesar Borgia, Duke of Valentino, one of the most unscrupulous rulers of all times. Profligate, violent, ferocious, and treacherous, Borgia combined audacity with diplomacy, cruelty with fraud, self-reliance with avoidance of half measures. The only motive he recognized was expediency, and the only method he understood was force. Mussolini acknowledged his debt to *The Prince*. "The State is God," he said, "and Machiavelli is his prophet." Hitler is reported to have kept a copy of *The Prince* at his bedside.

Another philosopher whose writings have played a major part in the development of the modern totalitarian state is Hegel. Nearly every principle guiding Soviet Russia today was first proposed by this German philosopher, especially Russian and communist thought regarding the state. Hegel taught that the state is, in its final expression, the complete embodiment of social and ethical ideals, the nearest approach to divinity. He believed the state to be final and absolute and the highest court of appeal. He taught that all the worth an individual possesses and all his spiritual reality he possesses only through the state. According to him, no moral principles should govern the state in its dealings with other states. Only the strongest and best organized states should survive.

All modern totalitarian governments—fascist Italy, Nazi Germany, communist Russia, and China—have been modeled upon these ideas. In a complete dictatorship, the head of state *is* the state. When people thought of Germany under Hitler, they thought of Hitler. This trend will be consummated in the Beast, who will be a truly representative person. He will not only head the revived Roman Empire, he will be the empire. He will speak for it, act for it, think for it, decide for it.

When God ordained that political ascendency over the nations be taken away from Israel and given to the Gentiles, He said to Nebuchadnezzar, "Thou O King, art a king of kings: for the God of heaven hath given thee a kingdom, power, and strength, and glory. And wheresoever the children of men dwell, the beasts of the field and the fowls of the heaven hath he given into thine hand, and hath made thee ruler over them all. Thou art this head of gold" (Dan. 2:37-38). Nebuchadnezzar, the first Gentile world ruler, possessed only a tithe of his inheritance. A glance at a map will show that the Babylonian was the smallest of all the world empires of Scripture. But, in principle, world dominion was given to him. What Nebuchadnezzar, the first world ruler, did not take, the Beast, the last world ruler, *will* take. Ultimately his authority will be universal. He will take his authority, however, directly from the devil, rather than from God.

We are still considering the parentage of this false prince. We have pondered the family likeness and the family lineage. We must now consider *the family legacy*. It is summed up in a brief sentence. John says, *And the dragon gave him his power, and his seat, and great authority.* He will have the power to do everything, and he will have the authority to do everything. What the Lord Jesus refused to take from the devil (Luke 4:6-7), the Beast will gladly accept. This is exactly what we have in 2 Thessalonians 2:9, where we are told of the man of sin, the son of perdition, that his coming is "after the working of Satan with all power and signs and lying wonders."

The word for "power" is *dunamis,* power to do anything—untrammelled, unhindered power. Before the resurrection of Christ, Satan's power in the world was designated by the use of this word. But after the resurrection, Satan's power was put under restraint. In the present age, *dunamis,* untrammelled, unhindered power, is given to the believer for witness and soul winning (Acts 1:8; Rom. 1:16). Satan no longer has *dunamis,* the kind of power he had in Luke 10:19, where it speaks of "all the power of the enemy." All Satan has during the present age is *exousia,* power subject to another power. He does not have real power, only permission. Thus in Ephesians 2:2, Satan is called "the prince of the power *(exousia)* of the air." In Colossians 1:13 believers are "delivered from the power *(exousia)* of darkness." Paul told Agrippa that his commission was to preach to men and to "open their eyes and to turn them from the power *(exousia)* of Satan unto God."

The Lord Jesus was manifested that He might destroy the works of the devil (1 John 3:8) so, since Pentecost, Satan has been put under restraint. The mighty Spirit of God is holding back Satan, but at the rapture, with the church gone and the Restrainer no longer hindering in the direct way He is today, Satan will receive back his *dunamis.* This unhindered power he will invest in his superman, the Beast.

Our attention is next directed to *the popularity of the false prince.* What a man he will be in the eyes of the world! The world will go delirious with delight at his manifestation. He will be the seeming answer to all its needs. He will be filled with all the fullness of Satan. Handsome, with a charming, rakish, devil-may-care personality, a genius, superbly at home in all the scientific disciplines, brave as a lion, and with an air of mystery about him to tease the imagination or to chill the blood as occasion may serve, a brilliant conversationalist in a score of tongues, a soul-captivating orator, he will be the idol of all mankind.

We are told *the reason for his popularity.* John says, *And I saw one of his heads as it were wounded to death; and his deadly wound was healed.* Looking upon him as a representative man, this is evidently a reference to the revival of the Roman Empire as it will be in its final form. But the Beast is also a real man, so it would seem from this Scripture and from 17:9-11 that the Beast is to be slain and brought back to life again. It does not take much imagination to see what that would do to his impact upon the world and his hold upon the minds of men. More will be said of this when we come to chapter 17.

There is a terrific battle of miracles centering on this entire period of the Apocalypse. The two witnesses perform many miracles, smiting the earth again and again and shutting up heaven itself. Their miracles are their protection, their invincible coat of mail. We are not told so, in so many words, but, since the Beast is their inveterate foe, it may well be that they themselves strike him with that deadly wound from which he dies. But, be that as it may, the death-stroke of the Beast is healed, and the beast returns to life. With this master stroke of miracle, the devil brings the world to the feet of his messiah. From henceforth the Beast is, in reality, the beast from the abyss. It is in this character that he slays the two witnesses. No doubt the fact that he himself is a resurrected man helps take the edge off the impact made upon men by the subsequent resurrection of the two witnesses. It is this miracle of his resurrection that is given as the reason for the popularity of the Beast. No doubt the whole thing will be stage-managed by Satan and the false prophet to make the greatest possible impact upon men. Their propaganda machine will see to it that the miracle is magnified and elaborated to the fullest extent, just as the miracle of the resurrection of the two witnesses will be played down in the same way.

We are then told *the result of his popularity.* John says, **And all the world wondered after the beast. And they worshipped the dragon which gave power unto the beast: and they worshipped the beast, saying, Who is like unto the beast? who is able to make war with him?** Behind all the machinations of Satan in this chapter is his single goal—to get men to worship him. Everything about the Beast makes it easy for men to first adulate him, then adore him, then, through him, worship the devil himself. The Beast will usher in Satan's brief season based on sin and the gratification of every human wish. Great secrets of nature, possibly surpassing any discovered thus far, will be revealed to men, and seducing spirits will inspire the arts, philosophies, and sciences. Men will think that the Beast is the greatest benefactor the world has ever known. A deceptive peace will settle upon the world after the collapse of Russia and the brilliant power play of the Beast. The nations will regard the Beast as invincible, and even those who are jealous of him will not dare to make war with him. They will implement his policies, many of which will appeal to them. As a resurrected man, he will bestride the world like a colossus, the greatest and last of all the Caesars. And men will worship him, and they will worship the dragon who gives him his power.

The world has witnessed several dress rehearsals for this event in recent times. Modern totalitarian regimes exploit the hunger in the human heart for a visible god. Mussolini, Hitler, Stalin were all granted semideification as a result of clever use of pageantry and publicity. It is one of the ironies of history that Communism, which brands religion as "the opiate of the people," has turned Lenin's tomb into a holy of holies for its materialistic faith, and Lenin's body into a sacred relic to be venerated by the devout.

In recent times it was in China that Satan staged one of his greatest preparatory displays. There are some billion people in China, and Mao Tse-tung transformed them into dutiful, obedient puppets. Mao was a living god. His thoughts became the creed of his people. The little red book of his sayings was the bible of a quarter of the earth's inhabitants. Giant posters of Mao were never far from view. Terrifying purges and campaigns of intimidation made sure that the people toed the line. In China, Mao was god.

When we see Hitler's goose-stepping legions parading hour after hour past his reviewing stand, shaking the ground beneath their feet and thundering out their "Heil Hitler!" and when we see long lines of Russians patiently waiting in arctic cold for a brief moment of adoration before the coffin of a mummified corpse, and when we see China's millions dutifully consulting, a dozen times a day, the sayings of a wicked old man, then we can see that the world is putting the stage in order for the coming worship of the Beast.

We have considered the parentage, the power, and the popularity of the Beast. Next we must see what is said about *the purposes of this false prince.* They are four in number. First and foremost he wishes *to defy the God of heaven.* John says, *And there was given unto him a mouth speaking great things and blasphemies; and power was given unto him to continue forty and two months. And he opened his mouth in blasphemy against God, to blaspheme his name, and his tabernacle, and them that dwell in heaven.* Everything in any way related to God is the subject of this man's blasphemous tongue. He cannot lay a finger on God, nor on the heavenly sanctuary, nor on the glorified saints, but he can and does revile them with his tongue. So far as the person of God is concerned, so far as the positon of God is concerned, and so far as the glorified people of God are concerned, the Beast is impotent. He is reduced to name calling! There have been daring blasphemers on earth before, but none like the Beast. He will have a vocabulary for invective and vituperation never equaled on earth. Blasphemies will well up from the dark satanic depths of this man's abysmal soul and will flow like sulfurous lava from his lips. God in heaven has noted well what this Beast will say and do.

His second purpose is to *destroy the saints of God.* John tells us, *And it was given unto him to make war with the saints, and to overcome them.* He cannot harm the glorified saints in heaven, but he can harm the believers on earth, at least those not specially sealed against him. The age-old mystery of the suffering of the saints is again brought into focus. It was given unto him to make war with the saints and to overcome them, just as it was given unto Herod to imprison and behead John the Baptist, just as it was given to Satan to persecute Job, and just as it was given to Pilate to pass sentence of death upon Jesus. It is all a deep mystery now, but it will be an eternal weight of glory for the sufferers when God gives out the martyrs' crowns.

"And it was given unto him to make war with the saints," says John. For a brief period of forty-two months he is permitted to use all his powers against the saints of the Most High. The Great Tribulation is unleashed as the Beast extends himself to the utmost to rid the earth of every last believer in God. To war he goes with his Torquemadas, his Dukes of Alva, his Simon de Montforts. To war he goes with the refurbished equipment of the Inquisition, with the rack, the thumbscrew, the stake, the boiling oil. To war he goes with his firing squads, gas chambers, long-prepared concentration camps, death pits. The experience learned in sixty centuries of torture and terror will be put at his disposal as the annals of hell itself are combed for ideas to expedite the work and make it as fiendish as Satan desires. This is the devil's last fling against the people of God. The great red dragon will drink his fill of blood, and the Beast, summoned from the sea and from the pit, will be unmasked at last for what he is, a monster with a quenchless thirst for blood.

His third purpose is *to dominate the nations of the earth.* John says, *And power was given him over all kindreds, and tongues, and nations.* The old Roman world will be his base, but it will not be big enough for him. He must dominate the globe. North and South, East and West, all peoples must yield obedience to him. It will not last long, it is true; but for a brief season his power and authority will be acknowledged worldwide. Satan will achieve his goal of unifying the nations, dazzling some, browbeating others, cementing the whole rickety structure together with the mortar of the indulgence of every evil passion and with the epoxy of horrible, merciless, unrelenting persecution.

His fourth purpose will be *to delude the masses of mankind.* John writes, *And all that dwell upon the earth shall worship him, whose names are not written in the book of life of the Lamb slain from the foundation of the world. If any man have an ear, let him hear. He that leadeth into captivity shall go into captivity: he that killeth with the sword must be killed with the sword. Here is the patience and the faith of the saints.* There is poetic justice in all this. Those who act as the Beast's agents in executing his will upon the people of God will, in turn, be given over by him to the same fate. God, in His grace, gives prior warning to those who might be tempted to buy an easy immunity by acting as henchmen for the Beast.

The majority will take out the insurance of compliance with the Beast and will worship him. All those without a living faith in God will bow the knee in adoration. This corresponds with 2 Thessalonians 2:4, where we are told concerning the man of sin that he "opposeth and exalteth himself above all that is called God, or that is worshipped; so that he as God sitteth in the temple of God showing himself that he is God." Satan is not against religion. In fact, he is the author and inspirer of all false religion. It is a most useful tool to further his ends, for through religion he can channel worship to himself.

The Beast will be the incarnation of all the world's religious hopes. He will be the Christ of the cults, the reincarnate Buddha of Buddhism, the Madhi of Islam, the seeming messiah of Israel—the kind of messiah the Jews have always wanted. Men will unite in worshiping him. "He that hath an ear to hear, let him hear." For the last time the cry goes forth. Groups of God's people are no longer in focus; it has come down to individuals now. One here, one there will stand out against the rising floodtide of popular enthusiasm and religious fervor for the Beast. Captivity, execution, torture await the faithful; patience and faith will be needed. There will be those who will respond.

(b) THE FALSE PROPHET (13:11-18)

The first part of the chapter deals with the coming of Satan's false prince; the remainder of the chapter has to do with a second mysterious person conjured up by Satan to act as the propaganda chief for the Beast. This person is called the false prophet. The first beast is possibly a Gentile, or at least partly a Gentile, since he comes up from sea. The second beast, the lamblike beast, is probably a Jew. He comes up out of the earth (a Bible symbol for the Hebrew nation and for God's earthly people). The great function of the second beast is to glorify the first beast. Thus Satan, the Beast, and the false prophet form a satanic trinity.

This second beast has *a deceptive appearance*. John says, **And I beheld another beast coming up out of the earth; and he had two horns like a lamb, and he spake as a dragon.** The first beast has ten horns; the second one has two horns. *Territory* is symbolized by the ten horns of the first beast (17:12); *testimony* is symbolized by the two horns of the second beast and, of course, it is false testimony. The second beast looks like a lamb and is thus most deceptive in appearance. Nobody is afraid of a lamb. A lamb is gentle, harmless, innocent, and, in Scripture, ceremonially clean. When the false prophet appears, he will, at first, seem to be all these things. Nobody will be frightened of him, for like a lamb, he will seem to be meek and lowly and will therefore be grossly underrated by mankind. But that is part of Satan's plan.

If the second beast has the horns of a lamb, he speaks like a dragon. The very voice of Satan is heard when he speaks. The idiom of Satan's language is the lie; he is the father of lies (John 8:44). The time has come when men must believe *the* lie, what Paul calls "the strong delusion" (2 Thess. 2:11). Attracted by the dynamic of the Beast and assured by the seeming docility of the false prophet, men will take at its face value the monstrous lie they are now to be told. In the Satanic trinity now formed, the Beast is the anti-God (13:6); the false prophet is the anti-Christ,[7] and Satan is the anti-Spirit, the spirit that now works in the children of disobedience (Eph. 2:2).

The false prophet has *a dynamic appeal*. We are told that **he exerciseth all the power of the first beast before him, and causeth the earth and them which dwell therein to worship the first beast, whose deadly wound was healed.** The two work hand in glove. The false prophet becomes the chief executive officer of the new regime under the Beast. He is the organizer and propagator of a new religion centered in the Beast, and he is the head vicar of the new Caesar cult. The authority of the false prophet is derived from the

7. Some believe him to be *the* Antichrist. Others assign this title to the Beast. Indeed, there is much confusion about the identity of the Antichrist. The term occurs only in 1 John 1:2, 18, 22; 4:3; 2 John 7; and the statements made there are not sufficient for the title to be dogmatically given to either one of the two beasts of Revelation 13. An assortment of disjointed, although biblical, ideas have been gathered around the somewhat nebulous title "the Antichrist." It is best to avoid this controversy and stick to the biblical terms used in the passage, namely the Beast and the false prophet.

Beast. The first beast is the man of sin, the son of perdition in whom Satan invests his power (2 Thess. 2:1-12). The conspiracy is intended to channel worship to Satan through the person of the Beast.

The role of the false prophet will be to make the new religion appealing and palatable to men. No doubt it will combine all the features of the religious systems of men, will appeal to man's total personality, and will take full advantage of his carnal appetite. The dynamic appeal of the false prophet will lie in his skill in combining political expediency with religious passion, self-interest with benevolent philanthropy, lofty sentiment with blatant sophistry, moral platitude with unbridled self-indulgence. His arguments will be subtle, convincing, and appealing. His oratory will be hypnotic, for he will be able to move the masses to tears or whip them into a frenzy. He will control the communication media of the world and will skillfully organize mass publicity to promote his ends. He will be the master of every promotional device and public relations gimmick. He will manage the truth with guile beyond words, bending it, twisting it, and distorting it. Public opinion will be his to command. He will mold world thought and shape human opinion like so much potter's clay. His deadly appeal will lie in the fact that what he says will sound so right, so sensible, so exactly what unregenerate men have always wanted to hear.

The false prophet has *a deadly approach*. He is deadly in the way he *blinds* mankind. Signs from heaven and signs from hell will be tricks in his bag, and men will be so bemused that they will not be able to tell one from the other. John says, *And he doeth great wonders, so that he maketh fire come down from heaven on the earth in the sight of men.* This will be no mere sleight of hand, no sham hocus-pocus of a stage magician. This will be a real miracle, convincing the most skeptical of men—all, in fact, except the saints of God. The memory of the two witnesses will be fresh in the minds of men. They summoned fire from heaven; the false prophet will do the same. The unbelieving Jews demanded of Jesus that He show them a sign from heaven, and He positively refused to perform such a miracle to support His claims. Not so the false prophet! He will delight to set the sky ablaze.

He blinds men with signs from hell also. John says, *And he deceiveth them that dwell on the earth by means of those miracles which he had power to do in the sight of the beast; saying to them that dwell on the earth that they should make an image to the beast, which had the wound by a sword, and did live. And he had power to give life unto the image of the beast, that the image of the beast should both speak, and cause that as many as would not worship the image of the beast should be killed.* The Jerusalem Temple will have been rebuilt by this time. The Beast, having turned against the Jew, will march his troops into the Temple, set up his image in the holy place, and command that it be worshiped. This is the "abomination of desolation" referred to by the Lord Jesus in His great prophetic discourse (Matt. 24:22; Dan. 12:1). This image is referred to seven times in Revelation (13:15; 14:9, 11; 15:2; 16:2; 19:20; 20:4). To worship this image will be the crowning act of blasphemy for mankind. For this sin there will be no forgiveness, either in this life or the next. Yet to refuse to worship will be to incur the wrath of the Beast and to court imminent death. The bringing to life of the image is an unexplained miracle of Satan. Perhaps the devil himself, lurking behind the idol, will lend the wood and stone his own life force. So then, the false prophet, the agent both of the Beast and of Satan, will blind mankind with the strong delusion, making Beast-worship the universal religion of lost mankind.

The false prophet is deadly not only in the way he blinds mankind but also in the way he *binds* men. He does this *cleverly*, and he does it *completely*. John tells us how cleverly he binds them. He says, **And he causeth all, both small and great, rich and poor, free and bond, to receive a mark in their right hand, or in their foreheads.** In the days of the Roman Empire, a citizen had to offer a pinch of incense on a pagan altar as a token of his loyalty to the Caesar cult. That was all—just a pinch of salt. Christians refused to do it and perished by the thousands for their loyalty to Christ. In a coming day, the last of the Caesars will make a like demand. He will require a simple mark, stamped on forehead or hand, as a token of allegiance.

One and all the unregenerate of earth will line up to receive the brand of the Beast in a universal display of solidarity. Some will receive the mark because they are *convinced*. The world, they think, has long needed to unite in a binding federation to end war and waste. These will be convinced that in the Beast can be centered a common government, a common market, and a common faith. Others will receive the mark because they are *careless*. It will make no difference to them one way or the other. They might just as well bow to the Beast as to some other dictator and, as for his mark, well, so what? Others will receive the mark because they are *craven*. Not to receive that brand will be highly dangerous, for it will put a person into a very unpopular and small minority—a minority opposed to a pan-world federation for peace, progress, and prosperity under the highly popular Beast. So then, for one reason or another, men will accept the mark (the word is *charagma*, always connected in the days of imperial Rome with the emperor, and connected too with an official seal). Cleverly, in the name of world unity and under guise of the good of mankind, the false prophet binds mankind.

He binds them *completely* as well. John draws our attention to *the sweeping extent* of the success of his scheme. He says **that no man might buy or sell, save he that had the mark, or the name of the beast, or the number of his name.** There will be a total economic enforcement of the will of the Beast. Every human being will be required to display the passport of the slavebrand, for without that identifying mark no transaction great or small will be made. Whether it be the industrialist trying to close a billion-dollar international deal or the child buying an ice cream cone at the corner store, the rule will be—no seal, no sale! From one end of the earth to the other, not a single wheel of commerce will move without the sign of the seal. Nor will any black market system either dare or desire to defy the will of the Beast. The boycott will be complete.

But if John tells us of the sweeping extent of the success of this scheme, he also tells of *the single exception* to that success. He says, *Here is wisdom. Let him that hath understanding count the number of the beast: for it is the number of a man; and his number is Six hundred three score and six.* There will be an enlightened remnant who will see through the whole sordid scheme, and they will recognize the Beast for who and what he is by the number of his name.

The Greek and Hebrew alphabets have numerical values attached to the letters of their respective alphabets. The Beast's name, when it is known, will yield the number 666. This number, mystic and mysterious as it is, has taxed the ingenuity of commentators from the very beginning. People have seen in it an identification mark for the pope on the one hand and Nero on the other. It has been pointed out that the number 666 is the sum of all the numbers that make up the square of 6. It has been claimed that the symbol of the ancient mysteries was SSS, or 666. Gallons of ink have been spilled in seeking to interpret the meaning of the number "six hundred three score and six."

When the Beast comes, the enlightened will recognize him by the number of his name. Being thus forewarned, they will be forearmed and will be able to make swift and secret arrangements to get away into the wilderness to await the Lord's return from glory.

Part Three (Continued):
Visions of Government (4:1–20:15)

Part Three (Continued):
Visions of Government
(4:1–20:15)

c. THE WORLD RESCUED BY GOD (14:1–20:15)
1. THE FORMAL WARNINGS DESCRIBED *(14:1–15:8)*

The picture that has unfolded thus far in the Apocalypse is that of a world ruined by man. As the seals have been broken and restraint removed, passions in the human heart, long restrained by God, have been allowed to come to full flower and fruit. The harvest has been one of complete chaos on earth. With the blowing of the trumpets, the picture has taken on the even darker hue of a world ruled by Satan. Satanic power has been unleashed, and the evil one's plans for the subjugation of the race have been allowed to mature. The world has united beneath the banner of the Beast. He has been hailed as messiah, and worship has been offered both to him and the dragon. Satan's schemes have been allowed at long last to reach this high tide mark.

With chapter 14 there comes a change and a turning of the tide. The ebb sets in and flows faster and ever faster, as God takes over in direct and determined intervention in the affairs of men. From here on, we have set before us a picture of a world rescued by God. This is a long section of the book and covers a very long period of time. It runs on to the end of chapter 20, and thus covers the final throes of the Great Tribulation, the Battle of Armageddon, the golden millennial age, the final rebellion of Satan, the great white throne judgment, and on to the edge of eternity.

The section is in three parts. First *the formal warnings* are described, as God reveals to men the high cost of Beast worship. Next *the fatal war* is described, as the vials are outpoured and the maddened nations swirl into the maelstrom of Armageddon. Last of all, *the final woes* are described, as Satan is loosed at the end of the Millennium and God finally clears the stage for the judgment of the last day. We are going to consider here the formal warnings that usher in the entire closing movement of those visions of government that occupy such a prominent place in Revelation.

The two chapters now to be explored carry us back up to heaven. In our study of the Apocalypse, God never leaves us to breathe for long the polluted atmosphere of the Beast's earth. He lifts us again and again above its mists and miasmas so that we can breathe deeply the pure air of heaven. That the heavens do rule is one of the dominant themes of the Apocalypse. Time and again this truth is hammered home.

a. THE SPECIAL COMPANY IN HEAVEN (14:1-5)

We have met this company before, only last time they were on earth. This is the illustrious company of the 144,000 who are sealed from twelve of Israel's tribes (Rev. 7). These sealed ones have been preserved unharmed throughout the Great Tribulation, despite the rage of the dragon and the Beast. Unscathed, they have marched right down those dreadful years with horrors abounding on every hand and with every demon from the pit clutching at them in vain. Psalm 91 is their marching song: "He that dwelleth in the secret place of the most High shall abide under the shadow of the Almighty. I will say of the Lord, He is my refuge and my fortress, my God; in him will I trust. Surely he shall deliver thee from the . . . noisome pestilence . . . Thou shalt not be afraid for the terror by night: nor for the arrow that flieth by day. Nor for the pestilence that walketh in darkness; nor for the destruction that wasteth at noonday. A thousand shall fall at thy side, and ten thousand at thy right hand: but it shall not come nigh thee . . . There shall no evil befall thee, neither shall any plague come nigh thy dwelling. For he shall give his angels charge over thee, to keep thee in all thy ways. They shall bear thee up in their arms. . . . Thou shalt tread upon the lion and adder: the young lion and the dragon shalt thou trample under feet."[1]

In chapter 7 this company is seen in anticipation of the Great Tribulation, which then lay ahead. They are seen now in anticipation of the glorious triumph that lies ahead. Four things are told us about them.

(1) THEY ARE AN EXALTED COMPANY (14:1)

This is evident from what John says. *And I looked, and lo, a Lamb stood on the mount Sion, and with him a hundred forty and four thousand, having his Father's name written in their foreheads.* Not one of the number is missing. There were a 144,000 before the Tribulation began; all are safe now in heaven. The heavenly Zion is evidently in view, because the Lord has not yet descended to earth. Also, events in the immediate context seem clearly connected with the activity of heaven. We are not told how or when these Jewish believers were caught up to heaven. But there they are, the

---

1. See John Phillips, *Exploring the Psalms*, vol. 3 (Neptune, N.J.: Loizeaux, 1986).

firstfruits of the Tribulation harvest (14:5), standing now in the very location described by John in chapters 4 and 5; standing before God, before the living creatures, and before the twenty-four elders.

(2) THEY ARE AN EXULTANT COMPANY (14:2-3a)

John tells us what this exalted company is doing in heaven. *And I heard a voice from heaven as the voice of many waters, and as the voice of a great thunder: and I heard the voice of harpers harping with their harps: and they sung as it were a new song before the throne, and before the four beasts, and the elders.* The book of Revelation, so full of sorrow, strife, and tears, is also a book filled with song! Bring the Lamb into the picture, and immediately there is song! The Lord has an amazing ability to make His people happy. One of the wonders of the God of the Bible is that He is a *happy* God! The gods of the pagans are fierce, wicked, and cruel, delighting in the tears and tremblings of men and feasting on human fear. But our God is a happy God. He picks us up from the horrible pit, plants our feet upon the rock, and puts a new song into our mouth. One of the greatest lessons we can learn in life is simply that there can be no real happiness apart from true holiness. God is altogether holy; therefore He is altogether happy. When we are filled with the Spirit, we sing! (Ps. 40:2-3; Eph. 5:18-19). This exalted company of God's people is also an exultant company. They fill the courts of heaven with their song until the very hills thunder back the sound.

(3) THEY ARE AN EXCLUSIVE COMPANY (14:3b)

There are not many like them, even in heaven. John says, *And no man could learn that song but the hundred and forty and four thousand, which were redeemed from the earth.* Their experiences are almost unique. Not many, even of God's choicest saints, have walked through the flood and the flame as God's untouchables. There has been a Meshach, a Shadrach, an Abednego, perhaps, and a Daniel in the lions' den, saints "who through faith subdued kingdoms, wrought righteousness, obtained promises, stopped the mouths of lions, quenched the violence of fire, escaped the edge of the sword, out of weakness were made strong, waxed valiant in fight, turned to flight the armies of the aliens" (Heb. 11:33-34). There have been some, but their ranks are thin. No other age has produced a company like this, a veritable army of militant believers marching unscathed through every form of danger. It has been theirs to defy the dragon, to bait the Beast, and to give the lie to the false prophet. Their calling has been to preach the gospel from the housetops when even to name the name of Christ called for the most dreadful penalties. They have been surrounded, these latter-day Jobs, with impenetrable hedges, able to laugh to scorn all the grand inquisitors of hell. They have walked the streets in broad daylight, careless of the teeth-gnashing rage of their would-be torturers and assassins, true witnesses of Jehovah in the most terrible era of the history of mankind. The devil knows about this coming band of conquerors, and writhes already in an agony of anticipation. By way of revenge he has built a cult already to parody these witnesses. It is a typical attempt of his to pour scorn on everything divine. These saints are not sealed and set apart by God in this present age of grace, but they will appear on earth after the church has gone. They will triumph gloriously while on earth, and then they will celebrate that triumph in a new song before the throne. The words of that song will be theirs alone to sing. No one else will be able to learn its words never having had their unique experience.

(4) THEY ARE AN EXEMPLARY COMPANY (14:4-5)

They are exemplary in five ways. First, they are *exemplary in their conduct*. John says, *These are they which were not defiled with women; for they are virgins.* This may be a figurative reference to their separated, sanctified spirituality, for no doubt these people will be marked by lofty standards of separation from the world and by spiritual sanctity. However, there is more than a figurative reference to spirituality here. These witnesses have separated themselves absolutely, in a practical, purposeful way from the Babylonish, worldly religious system of the Beast. The religion of the Beast, in common with so many pagan religions, will have at its base a vile immorality that will openly pander to every lust of the human heart. With the man of sin enthroned, lust will be applauded. It will be consecrated as an act of worship as it was by the ancient Canaanites and has been in fertility cults ever since. This company sets itself apart from all that.

Second, they are *exemplary in their consecration*. We are told, *These are they which follow the Lamb whithersoever he goeth.* Their reward for such conduct while on earth will be to accompany Him as His constant companions in heaven. Absolute devotion to Christ is the driving force behind their godly lives on earth. Like Caleb, their testimony is that they wholly follow the Lord. They allow no rivals, no refusals, and no restraint to mar their dedication to Him. Does He need someone to stand upon the steps of the Vatican and cry out against the marriage of Christendom to the Beast? There are 144,000 ready to go! Does the Lord need someone to beard the Beast at some high function of state and roundly denounce him, his policy, his statecraft, his religion, his economic boycott, his mark, his ministers, his alliance with Satan? There are 144,000 eager to go! Does the Lamb need evangelists to proclaim to the untold millions the gospel of the coming kingdom of God? to climb the highest Himalayas, to cross the desert sands, to blaze evangelistic trails through steaming jungles, or to mush huskies across wide arctic wastes? There are 144,000 ready to go! And though the Beast's gestapo dog their footsteps and wreak upon their converts his direst vengeance, yet on they go undaunted and undeterred. That was the very spirit of their consecration as they followed the Lamb whithersoever He led them on earth, and their reward is in kind.

They are also *exemplary in their calling.* John says, **These were redeemed from among men, being the firstfruits unto God and to the Lamb.** Israel kept an annual feast of firstfruits. Each year the farmer went into his fields of swiftly ripening grain and cut out one sheaf. This sheaf was then presented to God. It was not the whole harvest, but it represented the whole. It was a token of a work well done. This company make up the firstfruits of those who throughout the Tribulation will make their calling and election sure.

Next, they are *exemplary in their conversation.* How simple is the statement, **And in their mouth was found no guile.** When preaching the gospel, they do not conceal from their hearers that faith in Christ will be followed by swift retribution from the Beast. They tell the truth, the whole truth, and nothing but the truth. "In their mouth was not found the lie" is the way some render it. Others are mouthing the slogans of the Beast, chanting the vile creeds of his new world cult, and hailing him as the revealer of secrets, the savior of mankind, but these victorious believers refuse to pay lip service to him. They refuse to sing the praise of the Beast. In their mouth is not found the lie.

They are, moreover, *exemplary in their character.* John says, **For they are without fault before the throne of God.** They have entered into the truth of Jude 24, "Now unto him that is able to keep you from falling, and to present you *faultless* before the presence of his glory with exceeding joy." They have entered fully into the righteousness of Christ of whom we read that He "offered himself *without spot* [faultless] unto God" (Heb. 9:14). The word implies that they are without blemish, just as the Old Testament sacrifices were without blemish. Animals offered on Jewish altars were scrutinized to make sure that they were perfect. Here, then, is a company of God's people who are saved, sealed, separated, sanctified, and spotless! Yet we, in this age, members of the Body of Christ, are of a higher and holier order than they! What manner of people ought we to be!

b. THE SPECIAL COMMISSION IN HEAVEN (14:6-13)

Three angels now appear, commissioned with messages, announcements, and warnings for earth.

(1) THE PROCLAMATION CONCERNING BELIEF (14:6-7)

This proclamation is God's last call to the Gentiles. It is given during the Great Tribulation, and many are saved by it. The world "gospel" simply means "good news." We use the word today to describe the gospel of the grace of God (Acts 20:24), which is the good news for this age. Any person who tampers with this gospel is accursed (Gal. 1:8). But there are other aspects of the good news, aspects that apply to ages other than ours. There is the gospel of the kingdom, for example, and what is called here "the everlasting gospel." This everlasting gospel is only a very small portion of the gospel that is preached today. Its message is designed for the terrible hour of the Beast's triumph, but it contains the essence of the gospel in any age, namely a living faith in a living God.

The *nature of this gospel* is first described. It is *eternal in its significance,* and it is universal in its scope. John says, **And I saw another angel fly in the midst of heaven, having the everlasting gospel to preach.** It is everlasting because it has to do with eternal verities. The one basic evangel, in whatever form it is cast, is fear God! glorify God! worship God! The special significance of the everlasting gospel lies in the fact that the Beast is saying to men, fear me! glorify me! worship me!

The gospel is not only everlasting in its significance, it is *universal in its scope.* The angel's commission was **to preach unto them that dwell on the earth, and to every nation, and kindred, and tongue, and people.** Angels do not preach the gospel of the grace of God, but they do preach the gospel of the government of God. These shining ones have watched with greatest interest throughout the long years of the Christian era as redeemed ones have told forth the story of God's grace. They have looked on in amazement at Christians wasting priceless opportunities for telling others the good news, hiding their light under a bushel, investing in the tinsel trappings of earth, time, talent, and money that might have been invested in preaching the gospel to every creature under heaven. But now an angel is given a chance to tell out a fragment of the good news. And he *flies!* What a rebuke to our tardy, dawdling way of doing the King's business!

The *news of this gospel* is next described. It *involves conviction,* conversion, and consecration. The angel is heard "saying with a loud voice, Fear God!" The fear of God is the beginning of wisdom. At this point in the world's history, there will be so much fear on earth that all values will be distorted and all perspectives destroyed. The gospel puts the priorities straight—fear God! It is the word of conviction, smiting the conscience and bringing the terror of the Lord to an awakened soul.

The gospel *involves conversion.* The angel says, **Fear God, and give glory to him; for the hour of his judgment is come.** It is not merely the day of judgment now, but the hour of judgment. The unregenerate man always denies God glory, the saved man always gives God glory and thus comes into harmony with God's great goal both in creation and in redemption—to bring glory to Himself. In his unregenerate days, C. S. Lewis had trouble with the insistent demand by religious people that we "praise God." His ingrained dislike for the kind of person who demands continual assurance of his own virtue, intelligence, or delightfulness did nothing to minimize this. He found the psalms particularly troublesome, with their frequent exhortations to praise the Lord. After his conversion, however, he came to see how mistaken he was in his attitude. When we say we admire a picture, for example, we mean that admiration is the correct, adequate, and appropriate response to it, and the person who fails to admire a great work of art shows his own deficiencies. As C. S. Lewis came to see, the appropriate thing for a believer to do is to praise God. Giving glory to God is the evidence of his own conversion, proof that he has entered into a new world, one to which he had been deaf and blind before.[2]

The gospel *involves consecration.* The angel cried, **Worship him that made heaven, and earth, and the sea, and the fountains of waters.** Worship is the highest, holiest, and happiest function of a rational, complete human being. it is the overflow of a heart filled with wonder, love, and praise for God. Intelligent worship is pouring out one's being as a drink offering to God, the laying of one's life upon the altar, the giving back to God of the life we owe. This then is the first proclamation. It concerns belief.

(2) THE PROCLAMATION CONCERNING BABYLON (14:8)

If the first proclamation was good news, the second was great news. John says, **And there followed another angel, saying, Babylon is fallen, is fallen, that great city, because she made all nations drink of the wine of the wrath of her fornication.** This is the first mention of Babylon in the Apocalypse, but it is by no means the last. It gathers up into itself, in one brief preliminary statement, all that is later unfolded in chapters 17 and 18. This proclamation anticipates the complete collapse of the political, economic, and religious system of the Beast. This note is sounded here in view of the warning that follows, for those alive on the earth at this time will have a dire choice before them. That choice is the subject of the third proclamation. This second proclamation puts things into perspective for them and thus helps them decide. The trimph of Babylon will be brief.

(3) THE PROCLAMATION CONCERNING THE BEAST (14:9-12)

The issues are now made clear, the alternatives unmistakable. "Worship me," cries the Beast, "or be doomed!" "Worship me," cries the Lamb, "or be damned!" The proclamation is in two parts. First is described *the doom of those who deify the beast.* This doom is twofold. Those who take this step can expect *undiluted torment* from an angry God. John says, **And the third angel followed them, saying with a loud voice, If any man worship the beast**

---

2. C. S. Lewis, *Reflections on the Psalms* (New York: Harcourt Brace, 1958), pp. 90-98.

and his image, and receive his mark in his forehead, or in his hand, The same shall drink of the wine of the wrath of God, which is poured out without mixture into the cup of his indignation; and he shall be torment-ed with fire and brimstone in the presence of the holy angels, and in the presence of the Lamb. The message is urgent; it is proclaimed by an angel, and it is heralded in a loud voice. It is short, it is blunt, it is plain, and it is one of the most unique proclamations in Scripture, for it depicts the horrors of hell with a fullness of detail rare indeed in the Bible. There will be no hope for those who worship the Beast, bow before his image, or receive his mark. They can expect nothing but the wrath of God poured out upon them in undiluted strength.

Those who worship the Beast, moreover, can expect *undying torment* from an angry God. John says, *And the smoke of their torment ascendeth up for ever and ever: and they have no rest day nor night, who worship the beast and his image, and whosoever receiveth the mark of his name.* Their torment begins on earth. They find it impossible to rest, for their days become one long horror of anguish, and their nights become black nightmares of torment. And, after that—eternity, an awful eternity of woe.

In happy contrast with the doom of those who deify the Beast is *the destiny of those who defy the beast.* Two things are said of these as well. They will be *resisted.* John says, *Here is the patience of the saints: here are they that keep the commandments of God, and the faith of Jesus. And I heard a voice from heaven saying unto me, Write, Blessed are the dead which die in the Lord from henceforth: Yea, saith the Spirit, that they may rest from their labours; and their works do follow them.* Except for the 144,000, those who defy the Beast can anticipate death in a thousand fiendish ways, but it is death instantly transformed by God into blessing! "I'll make you suffer!" screams the Beast. "You'll make us saints!" reply the overcomers. "I'll persecute you to the grave," roars the Beast, "You'll promote us to glory!" reply the overcomers. "I'll blast you!" snarls the Beast. "You'll bless us!" reply the overcomers. The Beast's rage against these noble martyrs will all be in vain. He will utterly fail at last.

They will be *rewarded. Yea, saith the Spirit, that they may rest from their labours; and their works do follow them.* Their troubles will be over. They will enter into reward on the shining banks of the crystal sea.

c. THE SPECIAL COMMAND IN HEAVEN (14:14-20)

In the Old Testament, harvest and vintage preceded the Feast of Taberna-cles, that great annual feast of jubilation and joy. It is the same here. The golden age is soon to come, the long-awaited millennial reign of Christ; but first the ripened harvest must be reaped, and the reddened vintage must be trod. Both are scenes of judgment.

(1) THE GOLDEN HARVEST (14:14-16)

The Lord's great parable of the wheat and the tares casts light upon this harvest. Satan sows his tares among the wheat, and both wheat and tares grow together toward the harvest. In the early stages, Satan's weeds are so much like the wheat that the difference is hard to detect. But no longer! The black, ugly darnel stands now in stark contrast with the golden grain of the wheat. The good seed and the bad are exposed by their fruits, and the time has come to separate the one from the other forever. The tares are to be bundled for the fire, and the wheat is to be gathered into the barn of the millennial earth.

Mention is made of *the reaper of the harvest.* John says, *And I looked, and behold a white cloud, and upon the cloud one sat like unto the Son of man, having on his head a golden crown, and in his hand a sharp sickle.* This is none other than the Lord Himself. He was the Sower in Matthew 13, now He is the Reaper. Incidentally, this is the last time we read of Him as the Son of man. The first time is in Matthew 8:20 where we read, "The foxes have holes, the birds of the air have nests; but the Son of man hath not where to lay his head." That reference had to do with His first advent; this one refers to His second advent. Then His poverty was in view, now it is His power. The title first occurs in Psalm 8, a messianic psalm, and it relates to His dominion over the earth. The title occurs eighty-four times in the New Testament, eighty of them in the gospels and Acts.

Next we are told of *the ripeness of the harvest.* John says, *And another angel came out of the temple, crying with a loud voice to him that sat on the cloud, Thrust in thy sickle, and reap: for the time is come for thee to reap; for the harvest of the earth is ripe.* The darnel was not merely a weed, it was a dangerous weed capable of hindering the growth of the wheat and was poisonous if eaten. It symbolizes those described by the Lord Jesus as "sons of the evil one." These wicked people are related spiritually to the devil as intimately as the sons of the kingdom are related to God. In His parable, the Lord explained that the harvest will take place at the end of the age and will be in two stages. First the weeds will be gathered into bundles, and then later they will be flung into the flames. The great separation of the wheat from the tares is now to take place.

Next is described *the rapidity of the harvest.* A few swift strokes of the sickle, and it is all over. *And he that sat on the cloud thrust in his sickle on the earth; and the earth was reaped.* For two thousand years the saints have watched satanic cults spring up and flourish. After the rapture of the church no doubt they will prosper even more, cultivated with a lavish hand by Satan and his demon hosts. The believers during these days of consummation will find themselves beset on every hand with weird and wicked cults as false prophets abound, deceiving many. The Lord, however, makes no mistakes

when harvest times comes and swiftly separates the false from the true. The
burning comes later. "His angels," the Lord Jesus said, "shall cast them into a
furnace of fire: there shall be wailing and gnashing of teeth" (Matt. 13:41-42).

(2) THE GORY VINTAGE (14:17-20)

The harvest has to do with Christendom—or what is left of it, for the
sphere of the harvest is religious. The vintage has to do with the world, and
mention of it makes it clear that the time of God's vengeance has come. The
harvest depicts the final separation of the false from the true; the vintage
describes the final subjugation of the foes of the truth. The vintage pictures
the Lord stepping down into the arena of Armageddon to trample down the
Beast and all those gathered to his standards in this final conflict of the age.

The judgment symbolized here is *timely.* John says, *And another angel
came out of the temple which is in heaven, he also having a sharp sickle.
And another angel came out from the altar, which had power over fire;
and cried with a loud voice to him that had the sharp sickle, saying,
Thrust in thy sharp sickle, and gather the clusters of the vine of the earth;
for her grapes are fully ripe. And the angel thrust in his sickle into the
earth, and gathered the vine of the earth, and cast it into the great
winepress of the wrath of God.* Isaiah foresaw this and wrote, "Who is this
that cometh from . . . Bozrah? . . . Wherefore art thou red in thine apparel, and
thy garments like him that treadeth the winefat? I have trodden the winepress
alone; and of the people there was none with me: for I will tread them in mine
anger, and trample them in my fury; and their blood shall be sprinkled upon my
garments, and I will stain all my raiment" (Isa. 63:1-3). Joel saw it also and
said, "Come, get you down; for the press is full, the fats overflow; for their
wickedness is great. Multitudes, multitudes in the valley of decision: for the
day of the LORD is near in the valley of decision" (Joel 3:13-14). The grapes are
ripe at last. The time has come.

The judgment symbolized here is also *terrible.* The description is graphic
indeed. *And the winepress was trodden without the city, and blood came
out of the winepress, even unto the horse bridles, by the space of a
thousand and six hundred furlongs.* What an appalling scene! From Dan to
Beersheba was sixteen hundred furlongs, that is, about two hundred miles.
Flowing from Armageddon, a deep crimson tide of human blood is seen.
Outside the city where He was crucified, down there in the valley of Jehosha-
phat, the valley of judgment, the Lord will complete the trampling down of His
foes. What is signified is a vast destruction of human life, a slaughter beyond
anything the world has known, a slaughter that begins at Armageddon and
that continues on to the end of the judgment of the living nations spoken of in
Matthew 25:31-46.

d. THE SPECIAL COMMEMORATION IN HEAVEN (15:1-8)

The chronological movement of the Apocalypse is soon to be carried forward another giant step in the outpouring of the vials of wrath. But before describing that dreadful happening, John must give us one more glimpse of heaven.

(1) THE PERIOD OF WAITING (15:1-4)

God is in no hurry to proceed; He never is. Things ever proceed according to His timetable, not man's. With calm, majestic poise He invites us to *look at the scene*. We read, *And I saw another sign in heaven, great and marvellous, seven angels having the seven last plagues; for in them is filled up the wrath of God. And I saw as it were a sea of glass mingled with fire: and them that had gotten the victory over the beast, and over his image, and over his mark, and over the number of his name, stand on the sea of glass, having the harps of God.* There it shimmers, in the light that streams out from the throne of God with currents of fire glowing in its crystal depths, the sea of glass! There they stand, a glorious throng, those who have triumphed over the Beast and all that for which he stands! Now comes a sight indeed! In slow, solemn parade, stately as the stars, appear seven messengers of God, the angels with the last seven plagues. We are invited to look at the scene.

We are invited to *listen to the song*. And what a song it is! *And they sing the song of Moses the servant of God, and the song of the Lamb, saying, Great and marvellous are thy works, Lord God Almighty; just and true are thy ways, thou King of saints. Who shall not fear thee, O Lord, and glorify thy name? for thou only art holy: for all nations shall come and worship before thee; for thy judgments are manifest.* It is a twofold song, the song of Moses and the song of the Lamb. The song of Moses was sung at the Red Sea, the song of the Lamb is sung at the crystal sea; the song of Moses was a song of triumph over Egypt, the song of the Lamb is a song of triumph over Babylon; the song of Moses told how God brought His people out, the song of the Lamb tells how God brings His people in; the song of Moses was the first song in Scripture, the song of the Lamb is the last. The song of Moses commemorated the execution of the foe, the expectation of the saints, and the exaltation of the Lord; the song of the Lamb deals with the same three themes. The song of Moses was sung by a redeemed people; the song of the Lamb is sung by a raptured people.

The song is in two parts. The first part tells *what the ransomed will sing.* They will sing, "How great Thou art!" They say, *Great and marvellous are thy works, Lord God Almighty.* They will sing, "How good Thou art!" They say, *Just and true are thy ways, thou King of saints.* They will sing, "How glorious Thou art!" They say, *Who shall not fear thee, O Lord, and glorify thy name?*

The second part of the song tells us *why the remnant will sing.* They sing because of the majestic virtue of God. They say, *Thou only art holy.* They sing because of the magnificent victory of God. They say, *For all nations shall come and worship before thee.* They sing because of the manifest vengeance of God. They say, *For thy judgments are made manifest.*

That is the song! We are given just the barest outline of it. Each line could be expanded into a whole book. It commemorates in heaven the triumph soon to be enacted on earth, a triumph as complete and guaranteed as heaven itself.

(2) THE PLACE OF WORSHIP (15:5-8)

We are now to be taken into the Holy of Holies in the heavens and given a description of divine splendor such as is rarely surpassed even in this closing book of the Bible. Even God's wrath ministers to His glory.

Three things are associated with the Holy of Holies, the central place of worship in the universe. A description is given of *the messengers of wrath.* John says, *And after that I looked, and, behold, the temple of the tabernacle of the testimony in heaven was opened: And the seven angels came out of the temple, having the seven plagues, clothed in pure and white linen, and having their breasts girded with golden girdles.* They emerge from the inner sanctuary of the Temple. They do not act with impatience or in a spirit of independence, but in strict accord with the will of God. They come out from His presence to face a world that has reached the climax of its wickedness, a wickedness made all the worse by sordid contrast with the heavenly Temple's holiest shrine. They are characterized by *divine righteousness,* for they are arrayed in pure linen. What they are about to do is terrible, but it is absolutely right. No stain nor spot of sin is mingled with their acts. They are characterized by *divine restraints,* for they are girted across the breast with golden girdles. No hot passion of their own is mingled with their acts. They are calm and dispassionate in what they do. The surgeon who plunges his knife into quivering flesh does so without passion; false pity does not hold him back from what he knows must be done. Surgery at times is needful, urgent, and in the end, healing, even though the process may seem drastic, painful, and unkind.

A description is given of *the mediators of wrath.* John says *And one of the four beasts give unto the seven angels seven golden vials full of the wrath of God, who liveth for ever and ever.* The mediators are the four living creatures, one of whom acts here for them all. These living creatures are possibly the cherubim, ever associated in Scripture with God's creatorial and redemptive rights over the earth. Their faces are those of the lion, the calf, a man, and a flying eagle. Since the whole creation groans and travails, it is fitting that these representative beings mediate the short, sharp pains that result in the final removal of the curse. We are not told which of the cherubim handed the ominous bowls to the angels of doom, but perhaps it was the one with the human face, since man has been the chief cause of the curse and since creation's redemption is intertwined with his (Rom. 8:19-21).

Finally, a description is given of *the manifestation of wrath*. John says, *And the temple was filled with smoke from the glory of God, and from his power; and no man was able to enter into the temple, till the seven plagues of the seven angels were fulfilled.* The awesome Shekinah fire resided within the Holy of Holies in Israel's Temple. Once a year, a priest was permitted to enter there carrying a bowl of blood in his hand. Since Calvary, the way into the holiest in heaven has been opened to all, because the blood of Christ has blazed a highway to the heart of God. But now, for a brief spell, that royal road is barred. God's wrath, once poured out upon His Son on man's behalf, is to be outpoured again. The world that crucified the Lamb and that now has crowned its rebellions with the worship of the Beast, is to be judged to the full. So bright glory burns within the Temple, filling it with smoke and standing guard at the door. The way into the holiest is barred again for a while.

2. THE FATAL WAR DESCRIBED *(16:1–19:21)*

For chapter after chapter now in the Apocalypse it has been like a torrid summer's day. There has been a stillness in the atmosphere—the quiet, ominous calm before the storm. Against the splendor of the sky, the thunder clouds have marshaled into place. Occasional distant rumblings have been heard—nothing much, but enough to intimate the dimensions of the coming storm. The warning angel has flashed across the sky, sounding the alarm against succumbing to the Beast. The fall of Babylon has been announced. But for the most part, things have been muted and low. And yet the tension has been there, steadily mounting, and the heat has become oppressive. The chapters have been pregnant with doom. And now the time has come for the storm to break in all its pent-up fury and to crash from verse to verse of this chapter in a stupendous roar. Mercifully, the storm will be short, and best of all it will leave the skies sunny and clear for a thousand years.

a. THE TERRIBLE BOWLS SPILLED (16:1-21)

A world ruined by man and a world ruled by Satan has been described. Now the time has come for the world to be rescued by God. Down into the arena of human affairs He comes, shortening the days and making a swift, sudden end of the Beast and his hideous strength. The vials, shallow bowls used in the temple worship, are filled now with wrath and are swiftly outpoured.

(1) THE JUDGMENT COMMANDED (16:1)

John says, *And I heard a great voice out of the temple saying to the seven angels, Go your ways, and pour out the vials of the wrath of God upon the earth.* Much that follows is reminiscent of the plagues called down by Moses on the land of Egypt—boils, water turned to blood, darkness, frogs, thunder, and hail. For this reason, much that follows, more so than in the other judgments, is probably literal. The judgment angels, standing in solemn line with the bowls in their hands, are now issued the word of command, and like a lightning flash, forth they go on their errands of doom.

(2) THE JUDGMENT COMMENCED (16:2-9)

The exodus of these avenging angels is no wild stampede. It is an orderly procession, as each angel in turn peels off from the descending formation to pour out his bowl.

(a) THE UNEXPECTED CANCER OF THE SEAL (16:2)

What happens first is most fitting. John says, *And the first went, and poured out his vial upon the earth; and there fell a noisome and grievous sore upon the men which had the mark of the beast, and upon them which worshipped his image.* Men had been well warned what would happen if they accepted the slavebrand of the Beast, that ceaseless torment would be theirs, and that they would not be able to rest day or night. Who can rest when tormented by a great, festering, painful sore? There, on the right hand, a horrible, putrifying, incurable cancer! There on the face, a loathesome, ugly, disfiguring, and agonizing blotch! Men become horrible to look upon, and their pains never end.

(b) THE UNEXPLAINED CONTAMINATION OF THE SEA (16:3)

The environment suffers next. John says: *And the second angel poured out his vial upon the sea; and it became as the blood of a dead man: and every living soul died in the sea.* In Moses' day, it was the Nile that was turned to blood; now it is the sea itself. What a sight! The heaving billows become one vast stench of crimson putrefaction, rolling in from the deep toward the coastlines of the world, heaving themselves upon the reefs and rocks, breaking with a vile stench upon the shores. The retreating waves of blood litter the sand with the rotting carcasses of its dead. The globe is girdled by death.

From time to time, off the coast of California and elsewhere, a phenomenon known as "the red tide" occurs. These red tides kill millions of fish and poison those who eat contaminated shellfish. In 1949, one of these red tides hit the coast of Florida. First the water turned yellow, but by midsummer it was thick and viscous with countless billions of dinoflagellates, tiny one-celled organisms. Sixty-mile windrows of stinking fish fouled the beaches. Much marine life was wiped out, even bait used by fishermen died upon the hooks. Eventually the red tide subsided, only to appear again the following year. Eating fish contaminated by the tide produced severe symptoms caused by a potent nerve poison, a few grams of which, distributed aright, could easily kill everyone in the world. An unchecked population explosion of toxic dinoflagellates would kill all the fish in the sea. The phenomenon is well known, but scientists do not know what causes the proliferation of these creatures or what normally limits it. One theory is that it is caused when cobalt in an area reaches a certain density. Using the sea as a dumping place for nuclear and other waste may one day raise the level of cobalt to the point that it triggers a dinoflagellate plague. That may not fully explain what will happen when the second vial is outpoured, but it certainly illustrates it. The disaster described is quite credible.

(c) The Unexaggerated Corruption of the Streams (16:4-7)

The description of this next judgment is somewhat longer. Our attention is drawn to *the reality of this judgment*. John says, *And the third angel poured out his vial upon the rivers and fountains of waters; and they became blood*. An ecological disaster in the sea is bad enough, but what will it be like when rivers and lakes, fountains and streams are likewise corrupted? When all sources of fresh water turn to blood, as they did in Egypt in the days of Moses, men's horror and despair will know no bounds. The Lord's first miracle was to turn water into wine; now He turns water into blood.

We observe next *the righteousness of this judgment*. This is clearly stated. *And I heard the angel of the waters say, Thou art righteous, O Lord, which art, and wast, and shalt be, because thou hast judged thus. For they have shed the blood of saints and prophets, and thou hast given them blood to drink; for they are worthy*. This statement shows that angels have authority over what men call "the forces of nature." Earlier in the Apocalypse we read of angels standing at the four corners of the earth holding the winds (7:1). The angel, whose sphere it is to guard the water supplies of earth, instantly recognizes the poetic justice of God in turning the rivers and fountains into blood. The Beast and his followers have shed the blood of the martyrs in rivers, and now they are given blood to drink. God pays down their wages with a firm and a righteous hand and with a just but terrible coin.

Our attention is then drawn to *the response to this judgment*. John says, *And I heard another* [angel] *out of the altar say, Even so, Lord God Almighty, true and righteous are thy judgments*. Some versions render this: "And I heard the altar say." The altar speaks! The altar referred to is the brazen altar, the altar of consuming judgment, the fires of which were to burn with ceaseless flame. Beneath that altar have been sheltered the souls of those who were slain for their faith. The altar itself is now given tongue and voice to shout its loud "Amen" to the judgment of God. The Bible begins with a martyrdom and with the blood of murdered Abel crying out for vengeance. Now the altar itself cries out with a glad and thankful endorsement of the true and righteous judgment of God.

(d) THE UNEXAMPLED CATASTROPHE OF THE SUN (16:8-9)

The statement of what happens next is remarkably brief when compared with the dimensions of what happens. *And the fourth angel poured out his vial upon the sun; and power was given unto him to scorch men with fire. And men were scorched with great heat, and blasphemed the name of God, which hath power over these plagues: and they repented not to give him glory.* The false prophet had confirmed the Beast in his position of power by calling down fire from heaven (13:13). Now God pays back that lying miracle. This is one of those "signs in the sun" of which the Lord Himself spoke (Luke 21:25). When God's Son died upon the cross of Calvary, He put out the sun. Now it will be quickened to renewed and terrible life.

The sun, in its normal state, pours out a continuous stream of high-energy particles that race toward the earth at a peak speed of 3 million miles an hour. The earth is surrounded by a field of radiation, the magnetosphere, which protects it from full exposure to this deadly assault. The solar radiation that penetrates the magnetosphere is trapped in turn by the Van Allen belts. Should anything happen to the magnetosphere, the earth would be bombarded by these highly dangerous particles. Some scientists believe that, from time to time, the earth's magnetic field reverses itself. The changeover is thought to take place about every five thousand years, at the midpoint of which the magnetosphere is reduced to a mere five percent of its normal strength. During such a change, the cosmic rays, normally trapped by the magnetosphere, bombard the earth in full force, producing death or drastic mutation to all life forms. Such a change has not taken place during man's tenure of the earth, but there are signs that it could be happening again. Since the year 1670, the earth's magnetic field is thought to have been reduced by fully 15 percent and, at the present rate of decrease, will have almost completely disappeared by the year 3990. One geologist predicts that man will go the way of the dinosaurs.

That is one possibility, but the Lord certainly does not have to wait another two millennia to subject the earth to cosmic radiation. The sun itself is subject to violent weather patterns. From time to time, tongues of flame leap out from the seething surface of the sun, erupting hot solar plasma as far as a million miles from the sun, and projecting X-rays, radio waves, light waves, electronic clouds, and destructive high-energy protons toward the earth. When the earth is in a direct line with those eruptions, magnetic storms occur on earth that disrupt communication systems and play havoc with sophisticated modern equipment. These giant flares, which follow three well-known cycles (one of eleven-year intervals, one of eighty-year intervals, and one of four hundred-year intervals), cause the phenomena in the sun known as sun spots. One such flare occurred at 2:37 P.M. on November 12, 1960. The resulting cloud of solar hydrogen gas measured 10 million miles across, trailed halfway back to the sun, 93 million miles away, and bombarded the earth at a speed of 4,000 miles a second. It set off violent week-long disturbances on and around the earth and precipitated an electrical and magnetic storm of enormous proportions. Compass needles wavered eratically, communications were blacked out, and the northern lights flared majestically. Yet that was a mere ripple in the steady flow of energy from the sun. The disaster on earth caused by the fourth vial might easily result from some such explosion in the sun.

Or perhaps the sun will die a premature death. The sun, known to astronomers as a "second generation star" is built up of cosmic dust and gas. It has been radiating for only a comparatively short time, astronomically speaking, and its hydrogen content has been only moderately depleted. But the sun will not continue to radiate at its present rate. The hydrogen and helium in the sun do not mix thoroughly. The helium is concentrated in the sun's central core, while the atomic fusion reaction takes place at the surface of this core. As the sun continues to radiate, the helium core will become more massive, and there will be a corresponding increase in the temperature at the sun's center. In time, helium fusion will begin, resulting in a gradual expansion of the sun until it becomes a red giant. When that happens, the heat on earth will become unbearable, the oceans will boil away, and life will be scorched from the planet.

It may or may not happen like that, but happen it will. Men will be scorched by great heat and will blaspheme God, hating Him and blaming Him for what is happening. For all their warm embrace of God-denying and God-defying creeds, for all their ready worship of the Beast and the hearty endorsement of the lie, men will still know that there is a God and will tacitly acknowledge, by their very blasphemies, that He alone has power to cause the disasters now overtaking the earth.

So, thus, the judgment is commenced. God begins the rescue of a world held in a thralldom by Satan and his beasts. With the remaining vials, the judgment of God will come home in giant strides to the heartland of the rebellion, as the Beast, his domain, and his capital city are attacked and overthrown. The end will come with breathtaking speed.

(3) THE JUDGMENT COMPLETED (16:10-21)

God's rescue of the world proceeds in three stages.

(a) THE DOMAINS OF THE BEAST ARE RAVISHED (16:10-11)

John says, *And the fifth angel poured out his vial upon the seat of the beast; and his kingdom was full of darkness; and they gnawed their tongues for pain, and blasphemed the God of heaven because of their pains and their sores, and repented not of their deeds.* So far the Beast has been immune, but now his throne is shaken, and, like Pharaoh of old, he is powerless to defend himself. Darkness sweeps in as Joel long ago foretold: "The day of the LORD cometh . . . A day of darkness and of gloominess, a day of clouds and of thick darkness" (Joel 2:1-2). In His Olivet discourse, the Lord warned that the sun would be darkened and the moon would withhold her light. Since men have chosen the powers of darkness as their spiritual guides and have scorned the Light of the world, God gives them what they want—darkness, thick darkness, a darkness like that of Egypt, which could be felt. It is a foretaste of that "blackness of darkness for ever" (Jude 13) that will be the eternal lot of these evil ones.

Men will writhe in that horrible darkness, gnawing their tongues for the pains of the terrible sores that have erupted upon their bodies, caused perhaps by the radiation from outer space. The crescendo of hurt brings a crescendo of hate, and in a thousand tongues and dialects, men lift up their voices to heaven in one long shrieking blasphemy and curse. The Beast, the wonderful Beast they have exalted and extolled, will be powerless to help, for now his throne is under attack from on high, and he knows it full well. He is not long in reacting, however.

(b) THE DIRECTIVES FOR THE BATTLE ARE RELEASED (16:12-16)

The time has come for the fighting of that final war of the age, the name of which has become a byword among men since John first wrote it down—Armageddon! The Holy Land has been chosen by God as the stage upon which two crucial events take place, one on a mountain and one on a plain. Mount Calvary and the Plain of Megiddo are the two altars of sacrifice that dominate the history of the world. On Mount Calvary, grace redeemed the world by the sacrifice of God's Son; on the plains of Megiddo vengeance offers up the armies of the world in a sacrifice of doom. Both are blood baths; both are the descent of wrath upon sin; both are brought about by God's bitterest foes who work out, despite themselves, God's perfect and sovereign will. Across both can be written the words of Peter, "The Gentiles, and the peoples of Israel, were gathered together, for to do whatsoever thy hand and thy counsel determined before to be done" (Acts 4:27-28). From each proceeds a supper, one a feast of remembrance for the people of God, and the other a feast of retribution for the carrion. At Calvary there rang up to the gates of heaven a victorious cry, "It is finished!" And at Armageddon there rings down to earth an answering cry from the temple gates in glory, "It is done!"

We are told three things about the armies that now begin their fateful march toward Megiddo. We are told *where those armies are delayed.* John says. *And the sixth angel poured out his vial upon the great river Euphrates; and the water thereof was dried up, that the way of the kings of the east might be prepared.* Babylon and all it stands for is about to be overthrown. History repeats itself in a way, for ancient Babylon was overthrown when the armies of Cyrus the Persian diverted the waters of the Euphrates to expedite their march into the city. But here is a suggestion of delay. Before the armies of the East can converge on the capital of the Beast, a hindrance must be removed. That hindrance is described as "the great river Euphrates." The drying up of the Euphrates could be literal, for the river is indeed a great river. It is eighteen hundred miles long and in places it is thirty-six hundred feet wide and thirty feet deep. In ancient times it was a formidable barrier to an invading force from the east, and for centuries it has been the dividing line between East and West. A literal interpretation of the text is likely enough, but that does not seem to exhaust the meaning of the text. A mere river, no matter now deep or wide or long, is not much of a barrier to a well-equipped, determined, and well-led modern army.

The Euphrates has been mentioned before in connection with the trumpets. At that time it was associated with Russia's stranglehold on the Middle East. At that time the fall of Russia enabled the Beast to seize control of the world, and made it possible for him to command even the obedience of China and the Eastern powers. But the time has now come for those tremendous hordes of the East to assert themselves, to mobilize, and to hurl themselves westward. So far they have been held back by an impassible barrier, but that barrier, "the Euphrates," is now removed. For a hundred years it was the British Empire that sat astride the Euphrates and that held down the East. In recent times, Russia has dominated this key area. Later on, it will be held by the revived Roman Empire commanded by the Beast. But his kingdom is now in turmoil, and his power in the East has dried up, making it possible for China, India, Japan, and other Eastern powers to unite. The nightmare that has haunted world leaders for generations becomes a reality. The industrial might of Japan is wedded to the manpower and nuclear knowhow of China and to all the manpower of the East. The way of the kings of the East is prepared, and at long last the awakened millions of Asia see their way clear to avenge themselves on the hated powers of the West.

We are told *why these armies are deluded.* Two reasons are given for this delusion. They are deluded, first of all, by reason of *the permissive will of God.* John says, *And I saw three unclean spirits like frogs come out of the mouth of the dragon, and out of the mouth of the beast, and out of the mouth of the false prophet. For they are the spirits of devils, working miracles, which go forth unto the kings of the earth and of the whole world, to gather them to the battle of that great day of God Almighty.* This is the final delusion of mankind before the millennial reign of Christ. Frogs and toads are cold-blooded amphibians, denizens of two worlds. Many of them have poison in their skin, and many of them can change color at will. They have the ability to leap remarkable distances. The demons that are now spewed out by the satanic trinity are like frogs—swift-paced, cold-blooded fiends; creatures of two worlds, full of venom and poison for mankind. Forth they go, working miracles, deluding men, inciting to war, dangling dreams of dazzling victory first before this king, then before that one, sowing seeds of hate, inflaming passions, stirring up the world, summoning together the countless armies of the world—East against West, West against East, all against God. Perhaps the nations of the East think they can wrest world empire from the Beast; perhaps the Beast thinks the time is ripe for a final showdown with the potentially dangerous hordes of the East, or perhaps he thinks that, if need be, he can rechannel the martial ardor of the Eastern powers into some kind of a confrontation with heaven, which now is drawing too near for anyone's comfort. In any case, the nations are deluded by the permissive will of God and converge on Armageddon for a battle that must be decisive for the future of mankind.

The nations are deluded, moreover, by *the purposeful will of God.* It is not merely that He permits this convergence of nations; He plans it. God has goals and purposes far beyond the dreams of men. He has a people on earth, and for them this war has a purpose too. To them He says, *Behold, I come as a thief. Blessed is he that watcheth, and keepeth his garments, lest he walk naked, and they see his shame.* His coming as a thief suggests surprise. The suffering saints on earth are now told that the Lord's coming is no longer imminent, but immediate. They are to be ready, walking circumspectly, avoiding contamination from the world around. The pressures upon them will be unbearable. Perhaps the Beast will offer them some kind of amnesty if they will join in his confrontation with his foes. All around them, there is a new pulse of excitement as the nations rush to mobilize. The siren call to arms, the temptation to become involved in politics, the possibility of being swayed by the deceptive propaganda of the pit is a dire peril to their souls. They must stand aloof. This last great war is, for them, the last test of their loyalty to a greater throne than Caesar's.

Still concentrating on the mobilization of the world's armies, John tells us *where these armies are deployed.* He says, *And he gathered them together into a place called in the Hebrew tongue Armageddon.* They are drawn there for various reasons—to stamp out by united action the last living Jew on earth and the last known believer in God, to settle their own bitter animosities, to decide once for all who will control the world, and to fight against God and thus meet their doom.

(c) THE DESTRUCTION OF BABYLON IS REALIZED (16:17-21)

The hour of "that great city," Babylon, the Beast's new capital, has come. John tells us of *the voice that precedes the destruction of Babylon.* He says, *And the seventh angel poured out his vial into the air; and there came a great voice out of the temple of heaven, from the throne, saying, It is done.* The temple is seen at the close of each of the three series of judgments. It will be seen no more in the Apocalypse after this, because in the new heaven there will be no temple. Ezekiel's millennial temple is not a subject of mention in Revelation, for the closing book of the Bible looks upon that golden age from heaven's perspective, not earth's. *It is done!* cries the voice, and one can almost hear the great sigh of relief that must surely go up from every lover of God in the universe.

John then tells of *the violence that precipitates the judgment of Babylon.* There is a thunderstorm, an earthquake, and a hailstorm. Mention is made first of the thunderstorm. John says, *And there were voices, and thunders and lightnings.* Similar phenomena accompanied the breaking of the seventh seal (8:5) and the blowing of the seventh trumpet (11:19), as though dumb nature found for herself a voice with which to tell deluded men that the heavens do rule. The earth is now besieged by an unprecedented thunderstorm. Blinding flashes of lightning burn and blaze across the sky, deafening peals of thunder crash and roll like some celestial cannonade, thunderballs of fire skip and roll around the earth, terrible voices rumble through the skies. How men must tremble!

These portents, which herald the approaching demise of the last Roman Caesar, remind us of the portents that Shakespeare says surrounded the assassination of the first one. Shakespeare has Casca, one of the conspirators, say to Cicero:

> Are you not moved, when all the way of earth
> Shakes like a thing infirm? O Cicero,
> I have seen tempests, when the scolding winds
> Have rived the knotty oaks, and I have seen
> The ambitious oceans swell and rage and foam,
> To be exalted with threatening clouds:
> But never till to-night, never till now,
> Did I go through a tempest dropping fire.
> Either there is civil strife in heaven,
> Or else the world, too saucy with the gods,
> Incenses them to send destruction.
>
> (*Julius Caesar* 1.3.3-13)

The time has come for the second death to swallow up the last Caesar of Rome. Fierce, fiery warrior-clouds in ranks and squadrons marshal in the darkening sky. The blazing of heaven's dread artillery deadens every sound on earth. The fiery darts of the living God flame across the sky, striking earthward in sheets and forks of lurid flame.

John tells them of the earthquake that God uses to bring down the city of Babylon in crashing ruins. As to the *severity* of his earthquake, we are told that *there was a great earthquake, such as was not since men were upon the earth, so mighty an earthquake, and so great.* As to the *significance* of it, we are told that *the great city was divided into three parts, and the cities of the nations fell: and great Babylon came in remembrance before God, to give unto her the cup of the wine of the fierceness of his wrath.* As to the *scope* of this earthquake, we are told *every island fled away, and the mountains were not found.*

The next two chapters of the Apocalypse will give a detailed description of Babylon and of all that is centered there. Expositors have ranged far and wide in their efforts to interpret the significance of Babylon in the Apocalypse. Some have thought it to be Rome; some have seen it as a symbol for Jerusalem; some conceive a rebuilt, literal Babylon; some have gone so far as to see it as a symbolic reference to the United States of America.

There are good reasons for believing that ancient Babylon will be rebuilt as the final capital city of the Beast's empire. It will have a special strategic significance once he has overpowered the East. Many Old Testament prophecies focus on Babylon, some of them have been fulfilled, others still slumber, awaiting the dawn of a coming day. Whole series of statements (e.g., Isa. 13-14) await fulfillment. The destruction of ancient Babylon, foretold by Isaiah, had only a partial fulfillment. The complete fulfillment of many of Isaiah's statements about Babylon await the coming "day of the Lord," when there will be mighty disturbances in the sun, the moon, and the stars (Isa. 13:6, 9-10, 13). Babylon was never destroyed by Cyrus; it lingered on as an important city of the world. It was not until 293 B.C., when Seleucus built Seleucia as his capital, that Babylon began its long and slow decline. It has never been violently overthrown in a way that satisfies Old Testament predictions. That violent overthrow is still future (as we learn from Revelation 18), a point that argues strongly for the rebuilding of the city in a coming day.

Napoleon, the master strategist, recognized the importance of the site of Babylon. He is reported to have surveyed the Euphrates valley with a view to rebuilding Babylon, and presumably his campaigns in Egypt and Palestine had this ultimate goal in mind, for in his view, whoever held Babylon held the key to India and the world. Britain's commanding world position as a major power soon waned when she lost her grip on this important area, and Russia's star has ascended in step with her penetration of the Euphrates valley. Russian engineers have built a giant dam on the Euphrates.

The magnificent Babylon of a coming day will never grow old, for soon after being built it will be thrown violently down in an earthquake that has no equal in the entire history of the human race. Many other cities of the world will be shaken to pieces in this coming disaster. No doubt, when it comes, this earthquake will follow zones of fracturing and rifting well mapped by geologists into a worldwide rift system. The entire western coast of America, from Alaska to the southern tip of Argentina, is embraced in these fault lines, and so is all the eastern coast of Asia from Siberia to New Zealand. The faultline takes in all of southern Europe and the entire coastline of the Mediterranean, and it follows on eastward in a broadening band all across central Asia. No doubt the whole of this potentially hazardous area will burst wide open when this final earthquake comes.

Finally, John tells us about the hail storm. He says, *And there fell upon men a great hail out of heaven, every stone about the weight of a talent: and men blasphemed God because of the plague of the hail; for the plague thereof was exceeding great.* The earth will be bombarded by hailstones weighing a talent apiece! A talent was the highest weight in the Hebrew metric scale, and it represented the full weight an able man could carry. Imagine the destruction caused by hailstones weighing a hundred pounds, each hurtling down from the sky in solid missiles of ice! Picture the menace of these screaming projectiles as they shatter into millions of ricocheting fragments and coat the earth with a solid blanket of ice! And for the third time we are told that men, demented by their torments, will blaspheme God.

b. THE TWO BABYLONS SPOILED (17:1–19:6)

She was old, incredibly old, so old that Horace Holly refused to believe what she said about her age. She was beautiful too, beyond words to describe. For that reason she went veiled, lest her beauty drive men mad. She was wise and clever and had a fund of knowledge and experience gleaned over a score of centuries. She was ambitious. Her soaring plans to conquer the world left Holly and Leo Vincey aghast. Rider Haggard tells us all this as he spins the web of one of his most famous works of fiction, *She.* She was called Ayesha and had vast powers at her command as well, secrets she had wrung from nature in long and lonely vigils over the years. She was fascinating, with her varying moods, spellbinding charm, imperious will, daring courage, and vacillating hopes and fears. She was evil. She was a woman old and beautiful, wise and ambitious, fascinating and evil. At the end of volume one of the story, Rider Haggard tells of a climax, sudden, startling, and unexpected. Ayesha, the glorious, takes Leo Vincey to bathe in the mysterious fires from whence had come her beauty and her length of days. To demonstrate the virtue of the flames, Ayesha stepped into them first, but something went horribly wrong. The process was reversed, and instead of emerging glorified anew, she suddenly turned visibly old.

"Her face was growing old before my eyes," says Holly. "Her glorious eyes grew dim. She put her hand to her head and touched her hair—and oh, horror of horrors, it all fell out upon the floor. She was shrivelling up; smaller and smaller she grew; her skin changed color and in place of its lustre it turned dirty brown and yellow, like withered parchment. Her hand became a claw, like that of a badly preserved mummy. Smaller she grew and smaller yet, till she was no larger than a monkey. Now her skin was puckered into a million wrinkles, and on that shapeless face was the stamp of unutterable age. She who but minutes before had gazed upon us the loveliest, noblest, most splendid woman the world has ever seen lay before us, no larger than a monkey, and hideous—ah, too hideous for words!"

The whole tale is only fiction, but there is another woman. This woman too is old, so old that man cannot count her years. She was born before the founding of Rome, before the days of David, before the calling of Abraham from Ur of the Chaldees. She is beautiful too, if worldly splendor is beautiful. She is wise, well versed in the ways of mankind. She is ambitious, for from the very beginning she has wanted to rule the earth, and to a great extent has succeeded, for her fingers are in every political pie. This woman, too, is fascinating and attracts all manner of men to herself. She has a thousand wiles for bringing her lovers to her feet. And she is evil, although her wickedness is, for the most part, well masked and veneered. Beneath her smiles, her heart is as black as pitch. Her hands drip red with blood, and her history is the annals of hell. This woman's name is written in bold, black letters in the chapter before us. She is *MYSTERY, BABYLON THE GREAT, THE MOTHER OF HARLOTS AND ABOMINATIONS OF THE EARTH.* In this section of the Apocalypse, all this woman's disguises are stripped away. Her beauty drops off like a mask, and she stands exposed for what she is, a repulsive, ugly old woman, grown ancient in sin.

(1) THE GREAT BABYLONISH SYSTEM (17:1-18)

The next two chapters of Revelation deal with the whole question of Babylon. In this chapter we have *the Babylonish system* to consider, in the next one, *the Babylonish city.* Thus there are two Babylons, and the one grows out of the other. The Beast controls the first and creates the second.

The Babylonish system is both religious and political. The religious system paves the way for the political system. In the beginning, the religious system supports the political system, but in the end the political system supplants the religious one. The religious system is symbolized in Revelation

17 as the Babylonian mother; the political system is symbolized as the Babylonian monster.

(a) THE BABYLONISH MOTHER

THE FIRST DEVELOPMENT OF THE SYSTEM (17:1-6)

Five things are stated about this woman and the religious system she represents. First, mention is made of *her universal power* (17:1-2).

John says, *And there came one of the seven angels which had the seven vials, and talked with me, saying unto me, Come hither; I will shew unto thee the judgment of the great whore that sitteth upon many waters: With whom the kings of the earth have committed fornication, and the inhabitants of the earth have been made drunk with the wine of her fornication.* The scene is dramatic indeed! The angels with their terrible bowls have just wreaked unimaginable havoc on the earth. The din and noise of it all are still ringing in John's ears, and the dust and debris of a devastated world still fill the air. Then one of the angels, swinging an empty bowl strolls over to where John stands aghast and begins to chat with him as though the whole thing were an interval in a football game. He explains the whys and the wherefores of all that has happened, laying bare the power structure of the Beast's empire. The whole thing began with religion.

The scarlet woman has one master craving—power! To get that power, she has abandoned every principle. She will do anything for power. Do the kings of the earth have power? She will court them, cajole them, or command them; she will give them anything they want so long as they give her power in exchange. Do the masses of the earth have power? She will intoxicate them with her filthy brews and filch that power from them while they are drunk. She must have universal power. For that she has lived and outlasted every system and every nation on earth, including Israel. The name of the woman is printed out in bold capitals. Her name is BABYLON. Her home is in the city of the seven hills (vv. 9, 18), and she is identified prophetically with Rome. She is an apostate religious system linked with Rome. But in actual fact she is far older than Rome, having a history already hoary at the time of Constantine, who wedded Christianity to the ancient mysteries of Babylon. In her final form she gathers up into her embrace all the false religious systems of earth. From Babylon they first began their migration across the globe; to Babylon they will return.

The church first acquired its taste for temporal power in the days of Constantine the Great. On the eve of a crucial battle that was to make him master of the world, Constantine saw in a vision a fiery cross bearing the words *in hoc signo vinces* ("in this sign conquer"). He took the cross as his symbol, won the battle, and imposed Christianity as state religion on the empire of the world. It was one of the most fateful single acts ever performed by a human being. Since then, a segment of the church, especially the Roman church, has hungered for secular power. An addiction was formed that calls for massive infusions of the imperial drug.[3]

Administratively, today the Roman system is organized like a super state. At the head of the hierarchy is the pope; beneath him are the cardinals, who form a kind of papal senate. Next comes the curia with its departments, tribunals, offices, and commissions. Then follows the papal diplomatic corps, made up of nuncios, internuncios, and apostolic delegates. Still further down the structure of power is the ordinary government and the extraordinary government. Then come the clergy—the priests, monks, and nuns. Last of all are the rank and file, the laity.

For centuries the Roman system has exerted temporal power. At times she has ruled the nations wtih an iron hand; sometimes she has guided affairs with a velvet glove. Sometimes her power has waxed until a dozen nations would put their armies in the field at her slightest nod. Sometimes her power has waned beneath the hammer blows of Renaissance, Reformation, or revival. But ever Rome has sought after power. Lecky, the historian, has aptly summed her up. "In the minority, a lamb," he said; "in equality, a fox; in power, a tiger." Today Rome is playing a waiting game, for the time is not yet come when the chapter before us is to be fulfilled. Today she is in an ecumenical mood, wooing the apostate, liberal Protestant church and making overtures to the great, separated religious Orthodox church of the East. For as mystery Babylon emerges in her final form, she will embrace all of Christendom and all other religious systems of the world as well. She is gathering new sources of wealth and power in the U.S., making new alliances, absorbing the shock of change, and biding her time. In a coming day, she will resume her autocratic mantle of power, and the rulers of the earth will again become ensnared in her wiles. A marriage of convenience will be arranged. The church and state will wed, each thinking to use the other as a fresh source of power. And in the beginning the religious system will win. John is shown how.

We next see *her unique position* (17:3). John sees her astride a scarlet colored beast. He says, ***So he carried me away in the spirit into the***

---

3. There is a difference between devout Roman Catholics, some of whom are genuine believers in the Lord Jesus Christ and are trusting Him alone for salvation and are displaying a real love for the Word of God, and the Romish *system*, which is clearly included in the system identified with the city of Rome in this passage of Scripture.

It should be noted that Protestantism, too, bears many of the marks of Babylonianism—lust for power, wealth, the persecution of dissenters and so on. The Romish system is described in this commentary because it most graphically illustrates the text centering on the city of seven hills (Rome). Rome was the mother of the Protestant churches, and they will eventually return to their mother, once the rapture has come and all genuine believers are removed. The move toward greater ecumenicism indicates that trend.

The Organization of the Roman Catholic Church

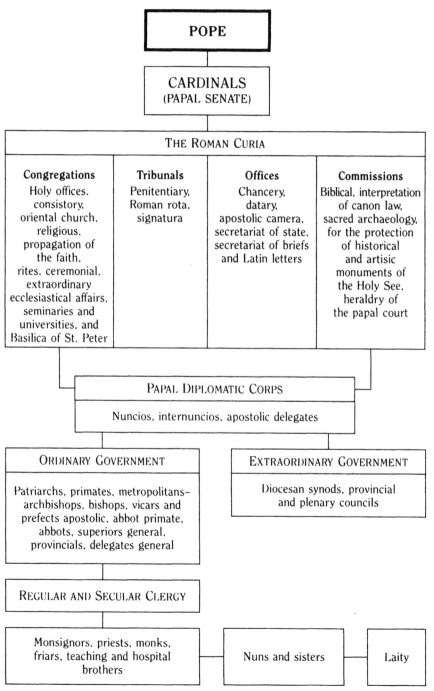

POPE

CARDINALS
(PAPAL SENATE)

THE ROMAN CURIA

Congregations	Tribunals	Offices	Commissions
Holy offices, consistory, oriental church, religious, propagation of the faith, rites, ceremonial, extraordinary ecclesiastical affairs, seminaries and universities, and Basilica of St. Peter	Penitentiary, Roman rota, signatura	Chancery, datary, apostolic camera, secretariat of state, secretariat of briefs and Latin letters	Biblical, interpretation of canon law, sacred archaeology, for the protection of historical and artisic monuments of the Holy See, heraldry of the papal court

PAPAL DIPLOMATIC CORPS

Nuncios, internuncios, apostolic delegates

ORDINARY GOVERNMENT

Patriarchs, primates, metropolitans–archbishops, bishops, vicars and prefects apostolic, abbot primate, abbots, superiors general, provincials, delegates general

EXTRAORDINARY GOVERNMENT

Diocesan synods, provincial and plenary councils

REGULAR AND SECULAR CLERGY

Monsignors, priests, monks, friars, teaching and hospital brothers

Nuns and sisters

Laity

wilderness: and I saw a woman sit upon a scarlet coloured beast, full of names of blasphemy, having seven heads and ten horns. The scarlet beast represents the final stage of a Gentile world empire headed up by an individual, the Beast, who embodies all its characteristics, ambitions, and powers. This empire is administered by ten subordinate kings. It is a blasphemous empire, thoroughly antichrist in character and opposed to everything holy and true. It is scarlet in color, for it is sinful and blood-thirsty beyond anything known on earth before. The scarlet woman sits upon this bestial empire like a queen enthroned, although it is a matter of conjecture as to whether that means she has subdued the empire or whether the empire supports her. In any case, hers is a precarious perch, though she does not seem to realize that.

For a brief space, the apostate religious system seems to achieve its heart's desire. The woman sits astride the Beast with everything seemingly under control. Yet Rome has been torn more than once by the tiger. In France, for example, she still bears the scars left upon her by the French Revolution. Napoleon, archetype of the coming world dictator, thrown up by the red tide of revolution, humbled the papacy in the dust. He summoned Pius VII to Paris in 1804 to preside over his coronation. Then at the last moment, without a word to anyone, he changed the ritual. Waiting until the pope lifted up the crown, he rudely pushed the pope aside, seized the crown in both hands, and placed it on his own head. That was but a mild rebuff to what the woman is to experience before long.

The next reference is to *her unlimited prosperity* (17:4a). John says, **And the woman was arrayed in purple and scarlet colour, and decked with gold and precious stones and pearls, having a golden cup in her hand.** It is Rome's wealth that dazzles the kings of the earth and makes them dance to her tune. At one time the total wealth of the Roman system in the United States alone was estimated to be about 34.2 billion dollars—only slightly less than the worth of the American Telephone and Telegraph Company before it was broken up by law into separate companies. Most of that wealth is in real estate. In a tax dispute between the Vatican and the Italian state, it was revealed that the church's portfolio of securities alone was worth 5.6 billion dollars. The total wealth of the church worldwide is estimated to be in the region of 70 billion dollars. The Vatican is an international financial power. It has extensive holdings in hotels, transportation companies, and industry. The Vatican's liquid assets are deposited mostly in American banks and are protected by a small army of financially expert Jesuit priests.[4]

Other churches are wealthy, but Rome exceeds them all. Rich and poor

4. This information was culled from various sources, including the *Chicago Sun-Times*, 23 May 1965; James Gollin, *Worldly Goods* (New York: Random, 1971); and *Time* (8 Nov. 1971).

alike are made to contribute to her bulging coffers. Many of the worst scandals in her history have been connected with her lust for this world's goods. It was the sale of indulgences, for example, which gave impetus to the Reformation.

In recent years fresh scandals have erupted. They have been widely reported by the media and some of them have been the subject of some very sensational books.[5]

One scandal involved the biggest bank fraud in modern Italian history climaxing in the failure of Italy's eleventh largest bank, Milan's Banco Ambriosiano, as the result of an audit that found that as much as $1.2 to $1.4 billion missing. Involved were shadowy figures from the underworld, a powerful Masonic lodge, mysterious deaths, dubious Vatican investments, and schemes to print large amounts of fraudulent securities. Involved, too, was the Instituto per le Opere di Reliogione (I.O.R.), better known simply as the Vatican Bank, and Archbishop Marcinkus, the bank president and often termed "God's banker" by the media.

The story makes sorry reading. Most would be able to empathize with Italian Treasury Minister Beniamino Andreatta who has long urged the Vatican to conduct its financial affairs in public. "As a Catholic," he declared, "I am against this strange, secret, uncontrolled, scandal-filled administration." Andreatta explained further that he thought the Vatican ought not to be in the banking business at all.

John refers next to *her unholy passions* (17:4*b*-5). He says, *Having a golden cup in her hand full of abominations and filthiness of her fornication: And upon her forehead was a name written, MYSTERY, BABYLON THE GREAT, THE MOTHER OF HARLOTS AND ABOMINATIONS OF THE EARTH.* The word *abomination* in Scripture is a common appellation for idols. Idolatrous worship is never far removed from all kinds of immorality.

The name "MYSTERY, BABYLON" reveals that the idolatrous system, now associated with the city of the seven hills, is very ancient indeed. It has been traced back to Nimrod and the building of the tower of Babel. Nimrod is described in Scripture as a mighty hunter. He was the world's first empire builder and the founder of great and lasting cities. He taught men to throw off their fears of God. Upon his death he was deified and worshiped under various names. At first that worship was secret, and only selected ones were initiated into its mysteries. The religious systems of Egypt, Greece, and Phoenicia all stemmed from Babylon as did all the false religious systems of antiquity. The

---

5. Those wishing to study this subject further could consult *In God's Name—An Investigation into the Murder of Pope John Paul I* by David A. Yallop, and *Rich Church, Poor Church,* by Malachi Martin. Malachi Martin is a Jesuit priest. He estimates Rome's wealth at over $300 billion and draws attention to gold deposits that exceed those of many industrial nations and to real estate holdings larger than the total area of many countries.

chief priest of the old Babylonian religion was known as the pontifex maximus. All knowledge and learning was concentrated into the hands of the priestly hierarchy. The Babylonians taught that Nimrod had reappeared as a posthumous son, supernaturally born by his widow. The worship of Nimrod very quickly became the worship of the mother and the child, the mother being known as the Queen of Heaven. Traces of this system of religion are discernable in all parts of the globe even to this day.[6]

When Babylon was captured by the Medes and Persians, the headquarters of the Babylonian religion was moved to Pergamos. Attalus III bequeathed Pergamos to Rome when he died in the year 133 B.C., and the Babylonian mysteries eventually found their way to Rome. When Julius Caesar became head of state, he was elected pontifex maximus as well, and the title was held by the Roman emperors down to Gratian. When Constantine became a professing Christian, the ancient Babylonian mysteries were simply transferred bodily into the church. Pagan temples became Christian churches, pagan gods became Christian saints, pagan festivals became Christian feasts, pagan customs became the customs of the church. The virgin Mary became the queen of heaven. Little by little, all the trappings of paganism became an established part of the religion of Christendom. Such Babylonian articles of religion as the worship of the mother and child, the dogma of purgatory, the use of holy water, bells, and candles, absolution by a priest, the celibacy of the priesthood, and the dedication of virgins all became articles of Roman faith. In A.D. 378, Damascus, then bishop of Rome, was appointed pontifex maximus and became at once head of the professing church and legal successor to the sovereign pontiffs of Babylon.

Mystery Babylon! The system has survived the centuries, and it lives on in many a pagan religion in the world today and reigns supreme in Rome. Rome is certainly not the *mother* of harlots and abominations, for that title belongs to ancient Babylon—but she certainly is included. The intoxicating wine of idolatry with all its accompanying vileness was already bottled and labeled three thousand years before Rome was dreamed of; but Rome is a major purveyor of this merchandise. The whole worldwide system of idolatry, possibly coached and led by Rome, will unite at last under the Beast. Idolatry will be the cornerstone of his world religion; once the Beast rids himself of the Roman system, it will all be headed up in himself and his image. Twice in Revelation 17, the woman is identified with Rome. The fact that she sheds the blood of the martyrs of Jesus aids in her prophetic identification, for certainly ancient Babylon did not shed the blood of *Christian* martyrs. In the last days Rome, as a religious system, is clearly linked with Babylon, and Babylon with Rome.

6. Those wishing to study this further can read *The Two Babylons*, by Alexander Hislop (Neptune, N.J., Loizeaux Bros., 1948).

The woman is described as being morally filthy. When Father Chiniquy, a most successful Roman Catholic priest, was a young vicar, he was greatly troubled by the evils of the church and took his doubts and disillusionments to his superior. His superior admitted that once his friend Bishop Plessis had been plagued by similar misgivings. He told Chiniquy how the bishop had revealed his uneasy feelings to him. He had opened before his bishop the pages of the history of the church, written by Cardinals Baronius and Fewry, pointing out to him the names of more than fifty popes who had evidently been atheists and infidels. He read aloud the lives of Borgia, Alexander VI, and a dozen others who deserved to be publicly hanged for the crimes of adultery, murder, and debauchery of every kind, which they had committed in Rome, Avignon, Naples, and elsewhere. He read to his bishop the record of the public and undeniable crimes of several of the Alexanders, the Johns, the Piuses, and the Leos, supposed successors of the apostles, who had sunk deep into the abyss of every kind of iniquity. For five hours the reading had gone on as Chiniquy's superior had read to his bishop the sad catalog of crime, and the crisis had passed. Now the priest, grown old and gray in the service of Rome, was confronted by Chiniquy, his own young vicar, troubled with similar doubts.[7]

Turning to the young priest, he said,

When Satan tries to shake your faith by the scandals you see, remember that Stephen, after having fought with his adversary, the Pope Constantine II., put out his eyes and condemned him to die. Remember that other Pope, who through revenge against his predecessor, had him exhumed, brought his dead body before judges, then charged him with the most horrible crimes which he proved by the testimony of scores of eyewitnesses, got him (the dead Pope) to be condemned to be beheaded and dragged through the muddy streets of Rome, and thrown into the river Tiber. . . . Remember that more than twelve Popes have been raised to that high and holy dignity by the rich and influential prostitutes of Rome, with whom they were publicly living in the most scandalous way. Remember that young bastard, John XI., the son of Pope Sergius, who was consecrated Pope when only twelve years old, by the influence of his prostitute mother, Marosia, who was so horribly profligate that he was deposed by the people and the clergy of Rome.

Then concluded the aged priest to the young Chiniquy,

If our holy Church has been able to pass through such storms without perishing, is it not a living proof that Christ is her pilot, that she is imperishable and infallible because St. Peter is her foundation?[8]

---

7. Charles Chiniquy, *Fifty Years in the Church of Rome* (New York: Agora, 1885), pp. 107-12. A more recent book is *The Decline and Fall of the Roman Church*, by Malachi Martin (New York: Bantam, 1983).
8. Ibid., 112.

Chiniquy remained unimpressed by this summary of vileness.

When the priest was exhibiting to me the horrible unmentionable crimes of so many of our popes, to calm my fears and strengthen my shaken faith, a mysterious voice was repeating to the ears of my soul the dear Saviour's words: "A good tree cannot bring forth evil fruit . . . by their fruits ye shall know them.[9]

Finally, John relates *her untold persecutions* (17:6). He says, *And I saw the woman drunken with the blood of the saints, and with the blood of the martyrs of Jesus: and when I saw her, I wondered with great admiration [wonder]*. John was astonished beyond measure at what he saw. That pagan Rome should hate and persecute the people of God was no cause for wonder, but that this woman, this apostate church of the end times, should be drunken with their blood, was astonishment indeed. The atrocities wreaked upon God's people by Rome fill whole books of church history. In the Middle Ages she ravaged like a tiger. Torquemada, for example, the first Inquisitor General, was appointed to his office in 1483. He celebrated his promotion to the so-called holy office by burning alive some two thousand prisoners of the Inquisition. Sovereigns, princes, royal ladies, learned men, magistrates, prelates, ministers of state, all were suspect. Torquemada burned at the stake upward of ten thousand people. During the regimes of his three immediate successors, another eight thousand were similarly destroyed. Some two hundred thousand people suffered lesser punishments in the torture chambers of the Inquisition.

Nor has Rome finished her brutal work. At the present, she treads softly, but when again she sits supreme, her old bloodlust will come upon her once more. John sees her as she is at the end of her days, sodden, drunken with the blood of the saints of God.

This, then, is the Babylonian mother, and this is the beginning of the system. It begins with religion. It begins with a total apostasy of Christendom in alliance with powers older far than the church and playing for high stakes with the kings of the Western world.

(b) THE BABYLONISH MONSTER
THE FINAL DEVELOPMENT OF THE SYSTEM (17:7-18)

There is no mistaking the identity of the Beast now described. It is the same beast that was introduced in chapter 13. The method whereby the Beast came to power is now described. John says, *And the angel said unto me, Wherefore didst thou marvel? I will tell thee the mystery of the woman, and of the beast that carrieth her, which hath the seven heads and ten horns.* The subject of the beast is developed in two stages. Mention is made of its advent, and then of its advancement.

9. Ibid.

First we see *the advent of the beast* (17:7-11). The only thing said about this Beast in Revelation 13 is that John saw it standing on the sand of the seashore. Now we are told how that Beast left the coastline of the Mediterranean to make its way to the heights of world dominion.

The first matter of interest is *whence the beast comes.* John is told, **The beast that thou sawest was, and is not; and shall ascend out of the bottomless pit, and go into perdition.** The emphasis in chapter 17 is not so much on the beast as an empire but on the Beast, the emperor. It is his personal history that is chronicled. It is no doubt true that the Roman Empire will be revived, but the language here goes far beyond that. An empire cannot emerge out of the abyss and later be consigned into perdition. Such language describes an individual's history, not that of a nation. Behind the whole story, as depicted here, there is a revived empire; but the verses primarily have to do with the Beast himself, the head of the bestial empire.

The empire is already envisioned as being hand in glove with the woman when the history of the Beast himself is described. He comes up out of the abyss, for the narrative concentrates on that part of his history, which is plainly supernatural. It begins with a satanic miracle of the highest order, for the Beast is to be a resurrected man. The language used even at this stage to describe the Beast is reminiscent of that used of the Lord Jesus (1:17-18). We are told here, of the Beast, that "he was and is not; and shall ascend out of the bottomless pit." Satan will duplicate , as far as possible, the miracle of Christ's resurrection. The sensation caused by that miracle can well be imagined. We can readily picture what would happen, for example, if, on some great occasion of state when the television cameras of the world were focused on the Kremlin, the body of Lenin were suddenly to arise! The man's authority on earth would be absolute! Something similar to that is going to happen on earth someday.

At first, the Beast will be a normal human being. He will be a world figure in his own right by virtue of his personality, genius, and political skill. He is to be killed, and then before the eyes of the world, he will come back to life. His authority will be absolute on earth after that, at least for a while. So we are told whence this beast comes. He comes out of the abyss. He is Satan's man, and his second coming will take the world by storm.

John next tells us *why the beast comes.* He comes for a specific reason forordained long ago by God. He comes to deceive the Christ-rejecting masses of mankind. John says, **And they that dwell on the earth shall wonder, whose names were not written in the book of life from the foundation of the world, when they behold the beast that was, and is not, and yet is.** Centuries ago the prophet Isaiah gave form to the principle behind this. He wrote, "Yea, they have chosen their own ways, and their soul delighteth in their abominations, I also will choose their delusions" (Isa. 66:3-4). Writing of the Beast, the man of sin, Paul stated the same truth. He tells us that his coming will be "with all deceivableness of unrighteousness in them that perish; because they received not the love of the truth, that they might be saved. And for this cause God shall send them strong delusion . . . That they all might be damned who believed not the truth, but had pleasure in unrighteousness" (2 Thess. 2:10-12).

It is inevitable. When a person turns his back upon the truth, he automatically embraces a lie. The principle holds good whether the truth involved is a mathematical truth, a biological truth, a medical truth, or a spiritual truth. In a coming day, those who fill up the measure of unbelief by rejecting the truth will be given the lie to embrace. In his superhuman appearing the Beast, emerging triumphant from the abyss, still bearing in his body the marks of his deadly wound, will fire the imaginations of men and lead them captive at his will. Men will gaze after him in awe and wonder with their mouths agape. Their names are not written in the book of life, and they are ready for the lie of lies.

It is vitally important that we pay careful heed to what we believe. Many people collect the articles of their faith on the same principle that they collect their articles of furniture. They are concerned that their beliefs be comfortable, convenient, and conformed to their taste. The devil has a large stock of error from which to furnish such empty souls.

The next thing we are told is *where the beast comes*. We are now told exactly where the beast concentrates his power at first. It is at Rome. John says, *And here is the mind which hath wisdom. The seven heads are seven mountains, on which the woman sitteth.* This pinpoints the seat of imperial power. Rome is the city of seven hills and has been known as such from the earliest times. Rome, as a center of political power, is not of much importance today, but it will be. The headquarters of the United States of Europe, federated under the Beast, will be there, at least until the Beast builds his new city of Babylon.

There are indications in the world already of what is to come. One of the most important treaties of modern times was signed in 1957 by a half-dozen European countries. It is known as the Treaty of Rome and brought the Common Market into being. The history of the Common Market, or the European Economic Community (E.E.C.) has been stormy. Here are the highlights:

1. March 25, 1957. The Treaty of Rome brought France, Belgium, West Germany, Luxembourg, Italy, and the Netherlands into economic union.

2. January 6-7, 1958. Nine commissioners, designated to serve as the main administrative body of the E.E.C., were sworn into office in Brussels.

Their number was later enlarged. The commissioners have their headquarters in Brussels, and they employ more than 12,000 people.

3. July 30, 1962. A common agricultural policy was adopted for E.E.C. members.

4. January 29, 1963. President Charles de Gaulle of France vented his personal spite against Great Britain by vetoing Britain's application for membership in the E.E.C. He charged that Britain was not a European nation and that its membership would weaken the E.E.C.

5. July 1, 1968. The members of the E.E.C. abolished customs duties between themselves and agreed on applying a common customs tariff to non-member nations.

6. July 18, 1968. All restrictions on movement of workers between E.E.C. countries were abolished, and the universal rights for workers within the E.E.C. were established.

7. January 1, 1973. Great Britain, Denmark, and Ireland became members of the E.E.C., bringing the total number to nine.

8. June 7-10, 1979. The E.E.C. countries voted, for the first time, by direct election, to seat a European Parliament. Sixty percent of an electorate of 180 million people participated. The results were as follows:

France (35.1 million voters)	81 seats
Great Britain (41.0 million voters)	81 seats
West Germany (42 million voters)	81 seats
Italy (41.6 million voters)	81 seats
The Netherlands (9.7 million voters)	25 seats
Belgium (6.6 million voters)	24 seats
Denmark (3.5 million voters)	16 seats
Ireland (2.1 million voters)	15 seats
Luxembourg (.2 million voters)	6 seats
	410 seats

The ideology of the members of the parliament were as follows:

Socialists	109 seats
Christian democrats	107 seats
Liberals and democrats	40 seats
European progressive democrats	22 seats
European conservatives	63 seats
Communists and allies	46 seats
Unattached	23 seats
	410 seats

9. October 10, 1979. The last of several treaties was signed forming alliances with most former colonies of E.E.C. members, providing for a system of nonreimbursable aid and preferred trade status.

10. January 1, 1981. Greece became a member, raising total E.E.C. membership to ten countries. (This raised fanciful speculation among some would-be prophets that the 10-nation confederacy, spoken of in Daniel's prophecies and in the Apocalypse, had arrived.)

11. April 1985. The ten foreign ministers of the E.E.C. voted to accept Spain and Portugal as full members, bringing the number of member nations to twelve, effective January 1, 1986. (Thereby spoiling the theories of the would-be prophets. Lesson: Beware of pinning current events too closely to prophecy. It is not until after the rapture of the church that end time events will finally be enacted.)

At the present time the E.E.C. is a customs union that enables free movement of goods, labor, and capital in Europe. It has a common commercial policy for trade with countries outside the community. It also has a common agricultural policy and is developing shared policies in industry, energy, transport, fisheries, social and regional policy, aid, environment, education, scientific research, and company law.

In 1979 the leaders of the E.E.C. formally inaugurated the European Monetary System, designed to link together the currencies of Common Market members as a bulwark against sharp fluctuations in the U.S. dollar and the Japanese yen. Members of the E.M.S. are to pool twenty percent of their foreign reserves to create a fund that may eventually give rise to a joint currency. The fund is denominated not in marks, francs, or dollars but in the new European Currency Units (ecus). Britain, Italy, and Ireland have held out from the E.M.S. for the time being, afraid that the price of belonging might be too high.

The E.E.C. has its own democratic institutions:

1. *The European Commission,* which is responsible for administering the E.E.C. Its members are appointed by unanimous agreement between the governments of the member nations. Each member holds a portfolio of responsibilities and acts in the interest of the E.E.C. independently of the governments that proposed them.

2. *The Council of Ministers* of member nations, which decides what major commission proposals should be adopted. Ministers attending meetings vary according to the subject under discussion. European heads of government meet regularly three times a year in summit meetings.

3. *The European Parliament,* consisting of directly elected representa-

tives who are consulted by the commission and the council on all major decisions. They have the power to veto the community budget and to dismiss the commission.

4. *The Court of Justice* interprets the treaties. It is the supreme court for European community law, and its judges can make rulings on states, institutions, and individuals.

5. *The Economic and Social Committee.* Those belonging to this committee of at least 150 members represent interest groups who advise the institutions.

6. *A Court of Auditors.* This group keeps a check on the spending of the E.E.C.

7. *The European Investment Bank* promotes energy investments and regional development in poorer areas of Europe and in the Third World countries linked to the community.

The E.E.C. is the world's largest trading unit. It accounts for nearly 25 percent of world trade. It is also a force in international politics. Some 114 countries have diplomatic missions accredited to the Community. Over 60 African, Carribbean, and Pacific (ACP) nations, former European colonies, have special trade aid relationships with the E.E.C.

The E.E.C. and the United States are economically independent. Visible trade between them, however, totals more than $100 billion a year, and investment across the Atlantic by European and U.S. firms is worth over $130 billion. High-level consultations between the E.E.C. and the U.S. Administration are held on a regular basis.

The E.E.C. has come a long way, but it has its own problems. Some of them are serious. One of the great hindrances to European federation was France's Charles de Gaulle. He blocked the institutional development of the Treaty of Rome, paralyzing development and stunting the E.E.C.'s political growth.

Paul-Henri Spaak, once Belgium's far-sighted Prime Minister, declared that if Stalin had not existed, the Common Market would not have existed. "The problem," he said, "was that Stalin died too soon."

General de Gaulle's cynicism and jealousy reportedly led him to say once: "Europe when it was just nations that hated one another had more reality than the Europe of today... good luck to this federation without a federator... no doubt about it, we're watching the end of Europe."

De Gaulle was wrong. Bible prophecy makes it clear that the future, for a brief while at least, belongs to a wholly reunited Europe, a revived Roman Empire indeed, to be headed by the last of the Caesars, a man the Apocalypse calls the Beast. When he comes on stage the E.E.C. will no longer be a "federation without a federator." He will take charge of things with a vengeance and, in short order, will make Europe not only strong, but the dominant world power on earth.

It is far too soon to be able to discern specifically the fulfillment of prophecy in what is happening in Europe. But the present stirrings are of great interest and foreshadow what is to come. The final union will not take place without rumblings, discontent, and conflict, for it will take the coming of the Beast to mastermind the final union. But the trend is discernible at least. The new United States of Europe, when it is finally forged, will need a capital city. What more logical city than Rome, already the seat of the scarlet woman, who, doubtless, will have a meddlesome finger in the pie? Once Rome ruled Europe, and traces of her empire still remain in most of the countries that once owned her sway. One day Rome will rule Europe again, and not because of some harebrained scheme of a latter-day Mussolini, for Italy has neither the manpower, the resources, nor the force of character to impose itself on Europe as its lord. Rome will become Europe's capital by the popular vote of the member nations in the union, no doubt helped toward their choice by the wire-pulling of Vatican agents. The Beast, when he first comes to power, will be content with the choice, and Rome will suddenly become a city of greater importance in world affairs than Washington, London, Peking, or Moscow.[10]

Finally, we are told *when the beast comes.* John says, *And there are seven kings: five are fallen, and one is, and the other is not yet come; and when he cometh, he must continue a short space. And the beast that was, and is not, even he is the eighth, and is of the seven, and goeth into perdition.* There have been numerous interpretations of this verse. Some have thought that the seven kings represent seven great Gentile empires spanning the Bible from beginning to end. Five of those empires, supposedly, had come and gone by John's day, and the sixth was in power. The empires envisioned are those of Egypt, Assyria, Babylon, Persia, Greece, and Rome. The seventh empire, still future in John's day, would be that of the Beast, the revived Roman Empire, which ultimately would rule the whole earth.

Some have thought that the seven kings represent seven forms of the government of Rome. Five of those had come and gone, and in John's day, the sixth was in power. These five forms of government are said to be the government of Rome by kings, consuls, dictators, decemvirs, military tribunes, and emperors. The seventh form of government, still future, would be that of a great confederacy headed by the Beast.

---

10. Three cities are key in the Beast's career: Rome is his political capital, Jerusalem is his religious capital, Babylon is his financial capital.

These views are interesting, but they do not seem to do full justice to the passage. The seven kings referred to here surely are seven individuals. One of them, the last, is brought up out of the abyss and is eventually cast into the lake of fire (17:8, 11; 19:20; 20:10). This last fate he shares with the false prophet, who is certainly an individual. The kings, then, are actual kings. This view being adopted leads to a most interesting conclusion. Of the kings referred to, five had come and gone at the time John wrote the Apocalypse. We are not told who they are, and we have no means of finding out who they were. We are not told whether they were Roman rulers or rulers from various Gentile empires that preceded that of Rome. One of the succession of kings was alive and ruling when John wrote this chapter and presumably was the emperor Domitian, a cruel, lustful, and blasphemous man who delighted to be addressed, as Seutonius tells us, as "our Lord God." One king was yet future in John's day, and upon his ascension to power, he would "continue a short space." We do not know who this king is or whether he has yet lived on earth. Some have speculated that this seventh Roman ruler is Mussolini, but that is simply conjecture and is probably unfounded.

We are now told when the Beast will appear. He appears at the very end of the sequence. We are told that "the beast . . . he is the eighth and is one of the seven." In other words, one of the seven rulers is to reappear as the eighth ruler. Probably the seventh ruler is the Beast in his human form, the form he assumes when he first appears as the beast out of the sea (13:1); and the eighth ruler is the Beast in his superhuman form, the form he assumes when he reappears, after his assassination, as the Beast out of the abyss. He comes out of the abyss and goes into perdition, a fact that helps us identify him with the man of sin, the son of perdition of 2 Thessalonians 2.

There are several signs of our times that indicate Satan is preparing the stage for the unveiling of his man. A book that has caused a mild sensation in modern times is Ruth Montgomery's book *A Gift of Prophecy*,[11] written about Jeane Dixon, a popular modern soothsayer. The book illustrates Jeane Dixon's apparent ability to foretell future events with some degree of accuracy. The author, a newspaper reporter, confesses that she was skeptical to begin with but that she became increasingly impressed as she investigated the phenomenon. The book itself tells of numerous events of national significance foretold by Jeane Dixon and closes with a vision she had, which, apocalyptically, is of very great interest.

The vision came to her shortly before sunrise on February 5, 1962, a date to which some importance apparently is attached. In her vision the seer saw an exceedingly bright sun, out of which stepped one of the pharaohs and Queen

11. Ruth Montgomery, *A Gift of Prophecy* (New York: Morrow, 1965).

Nefertiti, who was carrying a baby in her arms. The two royal Egyptians, parents of the infant, were magnificently robed, but the babe was clothed in rags. Jeane Dixon felt herself captivated by the child's eyes, which were full of wisdom and knowledge. From the infant emerged rays of light, bright as the sun, and these rays blotted out the pharaoh. The prophetess watched for a while the fate of the child's mother and then, turning back to the infant, discovered it had grown to manhood and that above him had formed a small cross, which began to expand until it covered the earth. People of every race and religion gave worship to the man, and all were as one.

Jeane Dixon's interpretation of her vision follows the clues found in the vision itself. On February 5, 1962, she believes, a peasant child was born in the Middle East who is a direct descendant of Nefertiti and Akhenaton. She saw in this child a coming savior of the world. It is her conviction that the world will begin to feel the impact of this person in the early 1980s, that he will reshape the world without war or suffering, and that by the end of the century all people will understand the meaning of her vision. At that time they will follow this new leader, who will unite mankind in an all-embracing, revitalized, and ecumenical Christianity. One remarkable statement made on the last page of this book is that the prophetess believes that Rome will eventually become the foremost center of culture, learning, and religion.

This vision is of great interest and is not without some significance, but it certainly does not stand the test of biblical revelation and therefore must be rejected as false (Isa. 8:20). Some of the features of the vision are worth noting. It pinpoints the Middle East and particularly Egypt as a crucial area to watch. It foretells the coming of a world leader, already born and growing up somewhere in obscurity, who will unite mankind. This leader is of humble parentage, yet he has the most illustrious of royal ancestries and is semi-divine. (The ancient pharaohs were supposed to be incarnations of Ra, the sun). This is apparently a parallel of sorts to the incarnation of the Lord Jesus. The vision foresees a world united by a dazzling leader and, without war, united into a vaguely Christian form of ecumenical religion. The vision is false for a number of biblical reasons. The Bible does not envision a world peacefully united around New Testament precepts until the return of the Lord Jesus; and He is not to be reborn, nor is He of Egyptian stock, however royal. Perhaps the vision is an attempt to capitalize on the prophecy "out of Egypt have I called my son" (Hos. 11:1), a Scripture already fulfilled by Christ at His birth (Matt. 2:15). From the standpoint of biblical revelation, if this vision has any real significance at all, it must be in connection with the coming of either the Beast or the false prophet. The most significant thing about the vision is the fact that it was given wide publicity. Not only did Jeane Dixon capture the imagination of millions, but this vision of hers, which she describes as the most significant and soul stirring of her life, was given wide coverage by being included in a condensation of Ruth Montgomery's book in the pages of *Reader's Digest*.[12]

So much, then, for the advent of the Beast. Already the minds of men are being prepared for the coming of Satan's messiah. The remainder of the chapter chronicles the impact which the Beast will make, especially after his miraculous resurrection, upon the leadership of the world.

Now we are shown *the advancement of the beast* (17:12-18). The kings of the earth cannot resist him and unanimously give their power to him, acclaiming him as their lord. But if they are united in their liking for the Beast, they are equally united in their loathing for the woman. First, John tells us that the kings of the earth *hail the Babylonian monster.* They are to be united in *acknowledging his lordship.* John says, **And the ten horns which thou sawest are ten kings, which have received no kingdom as yet; but receive power as kings one hour with the beast. These have one mind, and shall give their power and strength unto the beast.** The nations of Europe will be united at last in a ten kingdom federation under the Beast. We are not told how Europe, and possibly all of the Western world, will fall into this ten nation pattern, but we do know that when the time comes, all petty differences will be submerged in an enthusiastic and wholehearted endorsement of the Beast as supreme head of the federation. The ten nations will be quite sure that they are acting sovereignly and that the federation is the crowning achievement of their own diplomacy. But the whole thing is really brought about by the will of the God they ignore. The federation lasts only so long as God permits the Beast to last. The federation rises with him and falls with him. At this stage of world history, the Western world has only one mind: to yield to the Beast and to acknowledge his lordship. He will be the inspiring genius behind the federation, its driving force, and its unifying center. And the leaders of the nations will know it and, for their own self-interest, will hasten to be part of it.

They will be united, moreover, in *acknowledging his leadership.* The Beast has only one real passion, and that is to defy the Lamb. John says, **These shall make war with the Lamb, and the Lamb shall overcome them: for he is Lord of lords, and King of kings: and they that are with him are called, and chosen, and faithful.** The kings of the earth follow the Beast in his insane hatred of the Son of God. The Beast has one infatuation and that is to strike at the Lamb. In that he is similar to King Saul, whose hatred of David grew and grew until it dominated everything he did. His life at last became nothing but an unrelenting and ruthless crusade to persecute David and anyone who took David's side. To that end he harnessed all the resources and manpower of his kingdom. It will be the same with the Beast in

12. Ruth Montgomery, "Crystal Ball," *Reader's Digest* 87 (July 1965): 235-42.

his hatred for the Lamb, even though the final outcome is not for a moment in question. The Beast struts across the stage of human history as a great king, but against him comes the Lamb, the King of kings and Lord of lords. The deluded leaders of the nations, who accept the leadership of the Beast and endorse his hatred of God, will discover too late that they have made a fatal choice.

Next, John tells us that the kings of the earth *hate the Babylonian mother.* They hate her for three very good reasons. They hate her for *practical* reasons. John says, *And he saith unto me, The waters which thou sawest, where the whore sitteth, are peoples, and multitudes, and nations, and tongues. And the ten horns which thou sawest upon the beast, these shall hate the whore, and shall make her desolate and naked, and shall eat her flesh, and burn her with fire.* The kings of the earth hate the woman because she represents a threat to their own power. She wields an authority that they feel rightly belongs to them. It was one thing for them to court the whore and to use the Babylonian religious system to expedite the unification of the empire. To tolerate her and her political meddling once the end has been achieved is another matter. The religious system soon becomes an unwanted encumbrance, and the Beast himself has other ideas about the kind of religion suitable for mankind. As Brutus said of Caesar:

> That lowliness is young ambition's ladder,
> Whereto the climber-upward turns his face;
> But when he once attains the utmost round,
> He then unto the ladder turns his back,
> Looks in the clouds, scorning the base degrees
> By which he did ascend. So Caesar may.
> *(Julius Caesar* 2.1.22-27)

The kings of the earth in a coming day, following the lead of the greatest Caesar of them all, will climb thus to the pinnacle of worldly ambition. Papal Rome might be a useful ladder for their climb, but it will be a positive encumbrance once the goal is reached. The kings have no plans for ever climbing down again. If they come down, it will be by a violent overthrow, not by a humble descent and not at Rome's expense.

So they hate the religious system for very practical reasons. She exerts enormous influence, and the Holy Spirit piles up the words to emphasize the extent of her influence. He speaks of peoples and multitudes and nations and tongues. The woman sits enthroned in a greatness all her own, resplendent with the wealth she has taken from the nations over centuries of time. It makes good political sense for the kings of the earth to clip her wings, pluck her, and roast her in the flames. They do so in five stages.

First, the whore is *detested* by the kings. We read *these shall hate the whore*. The honeymoon between the scarlet woman and the kings of the earth does not last very long, for as in any marriage of convenience, the antagonisms soon surface. Next, she is *despoiled* by the kings. The kings *make her desolate*. They rob her of her wealth, those vast holdings in real estate, those immense liquid assets, those thriving businesses of hers. Just as Henry VIII plundered the Church of Rome in England, so these kings will enrich themselves at Rome's expense. Next, she is *disgraced* by the kings. They *make her . . . naked* and expose all her moral vileness to public view. One can well imagine the sensational trials which will take place in country after country as all the secret scandals are exposed. Then, she is *devoured* by the kings. They *eat her flesh*. They glut themselves upon her, tearing out her vitals. The Romish system ceases to exist as such, and the kings of the earth feed their own imperial hungers upon all that made her what she was. Finally, she is *destroyed* by the kings. They *burn her with fire*. When they have finished with her, there is nothing left at all. Thus, for very practical purposes, they make an end of the religious system centered at Rome—an utter end!

They hate her not only for practical reasons but for *providential* reasons. John says, *For God hath put in their hearts to fulfil his will, and to agree, and give their kingdom unto the beast, until the words of God shall be fulfilled.* Nothing could be further from the minds of these kings than to be fulfilling the divine will, but God makes even the wrath of man to praise Him! For centuries this evil system has flourished, developed, expanded, and prospered. Now, by a sovereign act of God, it is all over. The most insolent, daring, blasphemous, and powerful coalition of nations ever brought together by godless, wicked men is shown here to be a mere tool in the hands of God to wreak His vengeance upon that which has provoked His wrath for centuries.

Finally, the nations hate the woman for *political* reasons. John says, *And the woman which thou sawest is that great city, which reigneth over the kings of the earth.* They hate her because of her claimed right to rule the nations. For centuries not a nation in Europe stirred without a nod from the Vatican. In recent years, Rome's political power has been curbed, and she has had to trim her sails to suit an adverse wind. But she has not relinquished her claims, and although she has muted them for now, she has not abandoned them.

The papacy's pretensions to temporal power grew gradually with the passing of time. They received great impetus in the days of Charlemagne and the founding of what was called "the holy Roman Empire." Her claims were given forceful expression by Pope Gregory VII in the eleventh century. He said:

> It is laid down that the Roman Pontiff is universal bishop, that his name is the only one of its kind in the world. To him alone it belongs to depose or reconcile bishops. . . . He alone may use the ensigns of empire; all princes are bound to kiss his feet;

he has the right to depose emperors, and to absolve subjects from their allegiance. He holds in his hands the supreme mediation in questions of war and peace, and he alone may adjudge contested successions to kingdoms—all kingdoms are held as fiefs under Peter. . . . The Roman church has never erred. . . . The pope is above all judgment.[13]

Thus *the great city* still *reigneth over the kings of the earth.*

In a coming day, the inveterate habit of opportunist intrigue so characteristic of the woman will lead her into an alliance with the last of the Caesars. She will think she can control him, only to find too late that he has used her for his own imperialist ends. The Apocalypse records her last meddling in the political affairs of men. So much, then, for the Babylonian system. The next chapters of the Apocalypse tell of the Babylonian city, its power, its prosperity, and its fall.

(2) THE GREAT BABYLONISH CITY (18:1–19:6)

At the zenith of his pride and power, Nebuchadnezzar the Great looked out over the magnificent city of Babylon with its massive walls, its hanging garden, its broad boulevards, its beauty and its strength, and he cried, "Is not this great Babylon which I have built?" In a coming day, the last of the Gentile world rulers will boast over a rebuilt Babylon. The fact that many Bible prophecies concerning Babylon have not yet been fulfilled and others have been only partly fulfilled make it imperative that Babylon should rise again from the dust in order to meet its final doom. It was foretold of Babylon, for example, that it would be a place of "perpetual desolations" (Isa. 13:9, 12); that no man would dwell there anymore (Jer. 50:1-4, 40-46); that the Arabian would be afraid to pitch his tent there; that it would be the abode of dragons; that it would be "empty and without inhabitants"; and that its destruction would be violent (Isa. 13:9, 12, 20; 25:12; 50:1-4, 40-46; 51:3-43). None of these things have had an adequate fulfillment. Babylon has never been violently overthrown; its slow decline lingered over many centuries, even into the Christian era.

Babylon, founded under Nimrod, became the first center ruled by violence. She was once the world's capital. It is again to become the central city of the world. False religion was first organized at Babylon, and the city will again become the home of idolatry, occultism, demonism, and false religion. The right of world dominion, when taken away from Israel by divine decree, was given to Nebuchadnezzar, a Babylonian king. When the right of world dominion is taken away from the Gentiles, it will be from a king whose seat of government again is Babylon. In modern times, the city and its site has become

---

13. Andrew Miller. *Short Paper on Church History* (Fincastle, Va.: Scripture Truth, n.d.), p. 355.

increasingly important. Napoleon planned to rebuild the city; the Kaiser schemed to build a railway to the area; Russia has plans for the locale; and Toynbee has predicted it will become the world's natural population center.

We are not told what the relationship will be between Babylon and Rome. The great Babylonian system is centered at Rome at first, but when the scarlet woman is crushed by the kings of the earth, it will no doubt be deemed expedient to find a better capital. What better site than ancient Babylon on the banks of that important river that dominates both East and West? Newly built Babylon will become the major religious, economic, and political center of the world.

The Apocalypse is silent as to how and when this great Babylonian city is built. It is concerned only with its fall. *After these things I saw another angel come down from heaven, having great power; and the earth was lightened with his glory*, says John. The advent of this mighty being divides between the two chapters, one dealing with the Babylonian system and the other with the city. The overthrow of the Babylonian system was revealed to John by one of the angels that poured out the vials. The overthrow of the city was the work of another angel, one of exceptional power and glory, as though the destruction of the city were an event even more momentous than the overthrow of the system. There are many differences between chapters 17 and 18, not least of which is that in the former chapter the kings of the earth rejoice over the destruction of the symbolic Babylon, whereas they mourn the destruction of the literal Babylon. The language of chapter 17 is almost entirely symbolic, whereas the language of chapter 18 is almost entirely literal.

(a) THE REASONS FOR THE FALL OF BABYLON (18:1-8)

John is given three reasons this great thriving city is destroyed. The Lord credits this latter-day Babylon with the same guilt as Jerusalem of old. With solemn words, He pronounced judgment on the city that would crucify Him: "that the blood of all the prophets, which was shed from the foundation of the world, may be required of this generation" (Luke 11:50). He gathered up the roll of the martyrs and hung the whole list around the neck of guilty Jerusalem. Now He does the same for the city of the Beast.

Babylon is to be overthrown *because of the magnitude of her sins*. The city is wholly given over to demonism and depravity. In fact, it is to be *the home of demons*. John says, *And he cried mightily with a strong voice, saying, Babylon the great is fallen, is fallen, and is become the habitation of devils, and the hold of every foul spirit, and a cage of every unclean and hateful bird*. Demon worship will have its home there again, as it did in ages past. In Daniel's day, Babylon was the home of magicians, soothsayers, and astrologers who were official counselors of the king. All of today's reviving cults of satanism, spiritism, occultism, witchcraft, and astrology will gravitate toward Babylon. Modern science having proved itself such a poor practitioner for the diseases of the soul, the peoples of the earth are turning more and more to the occult world with both curiosity and credulity. Babylon will be the natural home of every such cult, and long after its fall it will be haunted by the evil spirits soon to be congregated there in great numbers.

Babylon is also to be *the headquarters of depravity.* John says, *For all nations have drunk of the wine of the wrath of her fornication, and the kings of the earth have committed fornication with her, and the merchants of the earth are waxed rich through the abundance of her delicacies.* She will be toasted around the globe as the enlightened, liberated city, hidebound by none of the foolish fads of prudish religious quacks. Her constitution will give free rein to all forms of immorality.

The rulers of the earth will be captivated by the prospect of getting rich through her trade. Possibly the Beast will introduce some novel and ingenious economic system, as revolutionary and as morally seductive as the introduction of joint-stock companies were to the Victorian world. Historians tell us what happened in England, for example, once men discovered the possibilities of getting rich in this remarkable new way. The joint-stock companies conferred on Victorian businessmen the new economic boon of limited liability. Fictitious bodies, enjoying the legal rights of individuals, could incur unlimited financial obligations without their shareholders becoming fully responsible for them. A man could grow rich in security and innocence from business practices that would have outraged his conscience as a private, individual businessman. The Companies Act of 1862 completed the divorce between the Christian conscience and the economic facts of life. Henceforth, an astute man, by abiding by rules that had nothing to do with morality, could grow immensely rich by shifting his most elementary obligations to his fellows. He could not only grow rich by such means, he could become exceedingly powerful. Perhaps the Beast will introduce economic concepts as revolutionary and as far-reaching as that and center their control and operation at Babylon. In any case, Babylon will be sought out by the rulers and the rich of this world.

It may be, too, that the crime syndicate, already enormously wealthy and powerful, feudal, ruthless, and omnipresent, will move its headquarters to Babylon. There can be little doubt that the syndicate, controlling the vice traffic of the world and insinuating itself into all kinds of legitimate businesses, will ultimately look to the Beast as its head. It may be that the Beast will use the syndicate to enforce his economic policies on the rest of mankind. In any case Babylon, wealthy beyond words, will attract the world's commerce to itself, and by pandering to the dictates of the offices of economic opportunity centered there, the kings of the earth will "commit fornication" with her.

Babylon is to be overthrown also *because of the measure of her sins.* John elaborates along three lines. *The enticement of her sins is declared.* John says. *And I heard another voice from heaven, saying, Come out of her, my people, that ye be not partakers of her sins, and that ye receive not of her plagues.* The few believers still left on earth are warned to have nothing to do with the city. Babylon's trade and traffic is accursed by God, and God's people must resist all the enticements offered them to enter her Vanity Fair. A special voice from heaven warns them away.

The enormity of her sin is described. John hears the angel explain, *For her sins have reached unto heaven, and God hath remembered her iniquities.* Thus it was in the world of Noah's day, with the cities of Sodom and Gomorrah, and with Nineveh. There comes a time when the sins of a nation or a city reach to heaven and cry aloud for God to act. The sword of vengeance slumbers long, and heaven seems silent and indifferent to earth's corruptions, calumnies, and crimes. God Himself seems deaf and blind, but then suddenly He acts, and the tale is told.

The end of her sins is decreed. The angel cries, *Reward her even as she hath rewarded you, and double unto her double according to her works: in the cup which she hath filled fill to her double.* In ancient times an earlier Babylon trampled down Jerusalem. The psalmist gave voice, in fierce imprecation, to the heart cry of Israel for God to act in justice. He cried, "O daughter of Babylon, who art to be destroyed; happy shall he be, that rewardeth thee as thou hast served us. Happy shall he be, that taketh and dasheth thy little ones against the stones" (Ps. 137:8-9). The Babylonians visited upon Jerusalem all the horrors of war, its insensate cruelties, its violent lusts, its horrible excesses. "Lord, pay her back in kind," implored the Jews. Jewish law demanded an eye for an eye and a tooth for a tooth, and it was a just and righteous law. The Jews, picking up the broken, lifeless forms of their little babes, held the shattered shapes toward heaven and cried, "A life for a life, O God of our fathers, a life for a life." But now, with this new Babylon—heir of the sins of Nimrod's Babylon and Nebuchadnezzar's Babylon, it is not justice that is decreed, but vengeance. Not just an eye for an eye, but double—three times in one short verse it is written—for all the infamies practiced on others: double!

Babylon is to be overthrown *because of the madness of her sins.* In a word, her crowning sins are pride and presumption. *How much she hath glorified herself, and lived deliciously, so much torment and sorrow give her: for she saith in her heart, I sit a queen, and am no widow, and shall see no sorrow. Therefore shall her plagues come in one day, death, and mourning, and famine; and she shall be utterly burned with fire: for strong is the Lord God who judgeth her.* Babylon will enjoy the good life. But even the opulent standard of living that is ours and which is the envy of the world will be surpassed a thousand times by that of Babylon. Babylon will be the Laodicea of the cities of the world, "rich and increased in goods" and feeling her need of nothing. It will be the rich fool of the nations saying, "I have much goods laid up for many years, I will eat, drink, and be merry." With a crown upon her head and a consort at her side, and with swelling confidence in her heart, this queen of cities will mock at the thought of judgment or, more likely, will not even entertain the thought.

But then it comes, in a single day, the vengeance of God dammed back through millennia of time. The plagues come howling through her streets, sweeping her markets with death, leaving an anguished cry of mourning wailing in their wake. As Jonah, striding through Nineveh with a message of unmitigated doom, brought that city to its knees, so these swift-paced heralds of God, these dire plagues, will bring Babylon to the dust in ruin beyond repair.

(b) THE REACTIONS TO THE FALL OF BABYLON (18:9-20)

There are two basic reactions to the fall of Babylon, and they are opposite the one from the other. There are those who are grieved by it, and there are those who are gladdened by it.

Those who are grieved by the fall of Babylon (18:9-19) are those who have profited from the city's influence, trade, and power, from its wickedness and from its wealth. Three groups are easily recognizable in the text by the repetition of the words "Alas, alas!" The first group said to lament are *the monarchs*. John says, *And the kings of the earth, who have committed fornication and lived deliciously with her, shall bewail her, and lament for her, when they shall see the smoke of her burning, standing afar off for the fear of her torment, saying, Alas, alas, that great city Babylon, that mighty city! for in one hour is thy judgment come.* The kings are probably those allied with the Beast, who helped sponsor the founding and building of the city and whose influence and power was in no small measure centered in the city. They stand afar off, watching the holocaust, afraid to come near, wringing their hands over their losses, and recognizing, godless and blasphemous as they are, that Babylon's fall is a visitation of judgment. The kings are dependent on Babylon for their power, yet with all their armies and all their resources of science and technology, they are impotent to lift a finger to save their city.

The next group said to lament are *the merchants*. John tells us, *And the merchants of the earth shall weep and mourn over her; for no man buyeth their merchandise any more: The merchandise of gold, and silver, and precious stones, and of pearls, and fine linen, and purple, and silk, and scarlet, and all thyine wood, and all manner vessels of ivory, and all manner vessels of most precious wood, and of brass, and iron, and marble, and cinnamon, and odours, and ointments, and frankincense, and wine, and oil, and fine flour, and wheat, and beasts, and sheep, and horses, and chariots, and slaves, and souls of men. And the fruits that thy soul lusteth after are departed from thee, and all things which were dainty and goodly are departed from thee, and thou shalt find them no more at all. The merchants of these things, which were made rich by her, shall stand afar off for the fear of her torment, weeping and wailing, and saying, Alas, alas, that great city, that was clothed in fine linen, and purple, and scarlet, and decked with gold, and precious stones, and pearls! For in one hour so great riches is come to nought.* What a catalog of opulence! What a vivid picture of a great, commercial city, trafficking in every luxury the heart could desire. This is the world's great Vanity Fair. It offers articles of adornment and display, beautiful things to grace the mansions of the world's millionaires. It deals in exotic spices and perfumes, in delicacies for the table, in provisions for banquets, in slaves, and in the souls of men.

And Babylon imported all these things. They flowed into her new and magnificent harbor from the seaports of the world. The business magnates of the earth harnessed their industries, their export trade, their entire commercial enterprise, for Babylon; and the wealth of the world passed through her clearinghouse. Babylon's demand for this world's goods was insatiable; ever it clamored for more and more! But now nothing is left of the city. Her giant warehouses have gone up in smoke; the fabulous markets and shopping centers are reduced to smouldering rubble; her multimillionaires are dead. In one hour, so great riches are brought to nothing, and the merchants, standing out of reach of Babylon, choking the arterial highways that lead into the city, watch with horror as their investments, their inventories, and their fortunes go up in smoke.

The last group said to lament are *the mariners.* John says, *And every shipmaster, and all the company in ships, and sailors, and as many as trade by sea, stood afar off, and cried when they saw the smoke of her burning, saying, What city is like unto this great city! And they cast dust on their heads, and cried, weeping and wailing, saying, Alas, alas, that great city, wherein were made rich all that had ships in the sea by reason of her costliness! for in one hour is she made desolate.* All the great seaports of the world—New York, London, Hong Kong, Tokyo—are to be outstripped by Babylon. "What city is like unto this city?" cried the mariners. The sea lanes of the world, which previously converged on these other giant seaports, in Babylon's day converge on her. But now Babylon is gone, and the world's trade is in ruins. The ships entering the Persian Gulf stand hastily back out to sea. Giant convoys of ships, displaying the flags of a hundred nations, ride at anchor far from the writhing center of the fiery maelstrom of doom. Telescopes are fixed to every eye as the astonished and frightened seamen watch in impotent horror the last agony of Babylon. Ruined shipowners wonder what can be salvaged from the glut of vessels that will choke the harbors of the world now that Babylon, at whose beck and call so many merchant fleets were launched, is gone forevermore.

The great dirge ascends to heaven, alas, alas! And in contrast, the Holy Spirit directs our attention to the hallelujah chorus that opens chapter 19. We are prepared for that by the command to rejoice which intervenes.

Now come *those who are gladdened by the fall of Babylon* (18:20). The angel says, *Rejoice over her thou heaven, and ye holy apostles and prophets; for God hath avenged you on her.* Some versions read, "Rejoice over her thou heaven and ye saints, and ye apostles, and ye prophets." Thus, three classes were grieved by the fall of Babylon, and three classes are gladdened by that fall. Those who rejoice are in heaven. It is a matter of great interest to observe that heaven is still interested in earth! Jeremiah, Ezekiel, Isaiah, Daniel, and all the other prophets have waited long for the fulfillment of their words. Now they can rejoice for their prophecies are carried out to the full.

From one end of heaven to the other the tidings are borne, Babylon is fallen! The flags are run up and adorn the turrets and towers along the walls of jasper. The echoes of the everlasting hills awake and sound back the news. Babylon is fallen!

(C) THE RESULTS OF THE FALL OF BABYLON (18:21–19:6)

The results are far reaching, both in heaven and on earth. On earth the damage is described, and in heaven the delight is described.

There is *holocaust on earth* (18:21-24). With the appearing of this angel, the dramatic act itself is described, and the actual fall of Babylon is brought sharply into focus. So far in the chapter it has been heralded, lamented, and hailed. Now it is actually described. We are told of *the violence of Babylon's fall.* John says, *And a mighty angel took up a stone like a great millstone, and cast it into the sea, saying, Thus with violence shall that great city Babylon be thrown down, and shall be found no more at all.* The hurling into the sea of a great millstone vividly symbolizes the violence of Babylon's overthrow. It is easy to picture the scene—the violent upheaval of the water as the mighty weight makes impact and sinks beneath the surface, the outrushing circles of disturbance, the closing in of the sea, and the eternal disappearance of the stone. Suddenness, violence, and completeness are all portrayed. One moment, prosperous Babylon stands a queen of cities in communication with the rest of the world and is sought out by all nations. The next moment she is gone, forever gone! Mark well the words "no more at all," and note how often the words "no more, no more" are sounded in the dirge that follows.

We are next told of *the vastness of Babylon's fall.* John writes, *And the voice of harpers, and musicians, and of pipers, and trumpeters, shall be heard no more at all in thee; and no craftsman, of whatsoever craft he be, shall be found any more in thee; and the sound of a millstone shall be heard no more at all in thee; and the light of a candle shall shine no more at all in thee; and the voice of the bridegroom and of the bride shall be heard no more at all in thee.* The doom will be complete. The curtain rings down forever on this city of sin. The language used is similar to that of a legal document, as though God were covering the pronouncement from every possible angle to leave no loophole. Babylon will never rise again.

We are then told of *the validity of Babylon's fall.* The reason for the fall is stated again. *For thy merchants were the great men of the earth; for by thy sorceries were all nations deceived. And in her was found the blood of prophets, and of saints, and of all that were slain upon the earth.* The pride, the presumption, the perversity of Babylon makes her the final depository of the sins of the world. She was deliberately built to organize, control, and extend the Beast's policies of godlessness, iniquity, oppression, and persecution. Her fall is just.

There are *hallelujahs in heaven* (19:1-6). The hallelujah chorus is sung in heaven! Four times the two words are lifted high: "Hallelujah! Amen!" Those two words seem to be the same in all the languages of men. They are praise words of heavenly hosts, loaned to men to help them voice their worship of the Lord. They are part of a universal tongue.

Two men once met aboard an ocean liner; the one was white, the other black. They had never met before; both were Christians; both felt out of place among the frivolous and pleasure-seeking crowds on deck. Each carried a Bible in his hand. They met, shook hands, and tried to exchange a few words of Christian greeting. But the barrier of language stood between. Then one of them had an idea. "Hallelujah!" he said, to which the other replied, "Amen!" They had found a common tongue of praise.

The news of Babylon's fall prompts praise in heaven. They sing Hallelujah for *the salvation of God.* John says, *And after these things I heard a great voice of much people in heaven, saying, Alleluia; Salvation, and glory, and honour, and power, unto the Lord our God.* Although it occurs twenty-four times in the Old Testament, this is the first time the word *hallelujah* occurs in the New Testament. It simply means "praise the Lord!" The saints in heaven praise God for His salvation, His splendor, and His strength. They give thanks that His salvation has now been vindicated in power. The overthrow of Babylon marks the end of those organized evils that have plagued the earth for so long. Evil things are so entrenched in society already that no amount of legislation can root them out; the rot has gone too deep. The shout of praise in heaven for the salvation of God is given by "much people." The disciples once asked the Lord if there would be few who would be saved. Here is the answer: much people!

They sing hallelujah for *the severity of God.* They sing, *For true and righteous are his judgments: for he hath judged the great whore, which did corrupt the earth with her fornication, and hath avenged the blood of his servants at her hand. And again they said, Alleluia. And her smoke rose up for ever and ever.* God, in love and patience, has stayed His hand so long that it seems at times He does not care at all for the wrongs being done on earth. The ages roll on, and wickedness ripens, flourishes, and bears fruit and multiplies. But in the end, God always acts. His severity, when at last it is unleashed, proceeds along the lines of truth and righteousness and falls with wrath and indignation upon all that is false and wrong. In heaven they are particularly delighted at the judgment of the whore, the Babylonian system, for without the system there would have been no city. The city was but the final materialization of the system—its physical, material, tangible expression. But now the severity of God has erased both city and system from the earth, and heaven is glad.

They sing hallelujah, for *the sovereignty of God.* John says, *And the four and twenty elders and the four beasts fell down and worshipped God that sat on the throne, saying Amen; Alleluia.* This is the last time the elders and the living creatures are mentioned in the Apocalypse. They appear first when the throne, symbolic of the sovereignty of God, is introduced; and they appear now, at the very end of things, to say a hearty "Amen" to God's judgments and a warm "Hallelujah" because of the glorious triumph of His throne. We leave them prostrate before God in worship, the attitude in which they are always found when God's sovereignty is asserted. From their standpoint in glory, the sovereignty of God, no less than the salvation of God, is seen to be something eminently worthy of praise.

They sing hallelujah for *the supremacy of God.* John says, *And a voice came out of the throne, saying, Praise our God, all ye his servants, and ye that fear him, both small and great. And I heard as it were the voice of a great multitude, and as the voice of many waters, and as the voice of mighty thunderings, saying, Alleluia: for the Lord God omnipotent reigneth.* Could anything be more majestic than that? God is supreme, He is the Lord God omnipotent. Every being in the universe, inspired by a love of God, from the humblest saint to the mightiest of the cherubim, joins in the swelling chorus. It reverberates and rolls, echoes and swells, resounds and grows until it is a mighty waterfall of sound, a thunderous roar—*Hallelujah!* Creatures great and small need authority. Now supreme Authority has spoken, and all whose longing to be properly ruled has been satisfied in God cry out in ecstasy—hallelujah! And with that note rolling like shock waves across the heavenly hills, the Spirit of God turns abruptly, almost in the middle of a sentence, to another theme. Enough of the harlot! Behold now the bride!

Two great events are now to be described, one in heaven and one on earth. One is a wedding; the other is a war. The church and the world both come to the consummation of their ways. Joy, long delayed, is the happy portion of the one; judgment, delayed even longer, is the portion of the other. The Lord Jesus fills both scenes.

c. THE TRUE BRIDE SEEN (19:7-10)

Considerable controversy has raged over the identity of the bride. Some claim the bride is Israel, others that she is the church. It is true that in the Old Testament Israel was said to be the wife of Jehovah; but it was Hosea's great lament that she was divorced for her profligacies and repeated infidelities. Though in a coming day the divorced wife will be forgiven, cleansed, and restored, that hardly satisfies the scene now described. What we have here is the bringing together at last of Christ and His church. Paul declares that his ministry was to espouse believers to Christ so that, as the church, they might be presented to Him as a chaste virgin (2 Cor. 11:2). All believers from Pentecost to the rapture are seen collectively and symbolically as the bride of Christ.

(1) THE BRIDE DESCRIBED (19:7-8)

Two things are recorded about the bride. We are told that *she is ready.* John says, *Let us be glad and rejoice, and give honour to him: for the marriage of the Lamb is come, and his wife hath made herself ready.* The church is the dearest object in all the universe to the Lord of glory, for she is His bride. It is a recurring theme in the Pauline epistles. At the moment of conversion we are espoused to the Lord Jesus and receive the "engagement ring," the earnest, of the Holy Spirit. But the wedding has been postponed these many centuries. The glorious bridegroom is in heaven preparing a place for us, and we have His promise that He is coming again. At the beginning of the Apocalypse, the rapture to glory took place. Now the time of the wedding has come.

The bride is ready! In one sense the bride has always been ready. The moment a person accepts Christ as Savior he is ready. Paul says, "Giving thanks unto the Father, which hath made us meet to be partakers of the inheritance of the saints in light" (Col. 1:12). On the other hand, our lives on earth have to be reviewed at the judgment seat of Christ. That judgment is not particularly described in the Apocalypse, but the light of that throne has now done its work, and the church can be presented to Christ "not having spot, or wrinkle, or any such thing" (Eph. 5:27).

We are next told that *she is robed.* John says, *And to her was granted*

*that she should be arrayed in fine linen, clean and white: for the fine
linen is the righteousness of saints.* The apparel of the bride is in contrast
with the gaudy garments, the flaunted finery, and flashy jewelry of the scarlet
woman. All the woman had was this world's paltry treasure; the bride has her
righteous acts.

During his earthly pilgrimage, the believer prepares himself for this day.
The garments that beautify the bride are said to be given her because any good
work, any righteous deed, any praiseworthy act we do is the work of the Holy
Spirit in us. "Work out your own salvation," says Paul; then he adds at once,
"It is God which worketh in you both to will and to do of his good pleasure"
(Phil. 2:12-13). The righteous acts of the true church, performed while on
earth and from which the world benefits more than it knows, become the fine
linen, clean and white, in which the bride is arrayed to go forth to meet her
Groom.

(2) THE BANQUET DESCRIBED (19:9-10)

Here again, two things are detailed. We are told of *the blessing of the
saints.* John says, *And he saith unto me, Write, Blessed are they which are
called unto the marriage supper of the Lamb. And he saith unto me,
These are the true sayings of God.* There's not a word about what is on the
table! With Jesus there, the bounty of the banquet is scarcely worth a thought.
Attention is drawn to the blessedness of being one of the King's invited guests.
The church is the bride; the redeemed of other ages are the wedding guests,
friends of the Bridegroom. In they come, rank after endless rank—the patriarchs, the prophets, the princes, the priests, the seers, the scribes, the sages,
and the saints—all those whose names are written down in glory. They greet
the Groom and the bride; they take their places at the table; they are full of joy;
they are blessed of God. The Lord's first miracle was at a wedding when, earth's
resources having failed, He transformed water into wine. Now it is His wedding
feast, and He drinks the new wine of the kingdom as He promised long ago; lo,
He has kept the best wine until last!

We are told of *the blunder of the seer.* It was usually Peter who said the
wrong thing, but this time it was John, and he made a terrible mistake. His was
a serious breach of etiquette, and he tells us all, keeping nothing back. John
was carried away by the wonder of the revelations being made to him by the
angel, and he says, *I fell at his feet to worship him. And he said unto me,
See thou do it not: I am thy fellow servant, and of thy brethren that have
the testimony of Jesus: worship God: for the testimony of Jesus is the
spirit of prophecy.* John's great blunder was to attempt to worship an angel—
a blunder that has been often repeated in the history of the professing church.
The angel described himself as "thy fellow servant." The word he used is the
common Greek word for slave. Those glorious beings who surround the

throne, who hang upon the words of Jesus, and who rush to do His bidding; who, at His command, delight to become ministering spirits of the humblest child of God, count it their greatest delight, their highest dignity to be His slaves.

The testimony of Jesus is the spirit of prophecy, said the angel to John. It is exceptional and startling that this angel should speak of the Lord of glory as *Jesus.* It would be impertinent were there not a reason for it. It is common in our day to hear people address Him in this way in prayer. Such a form of address is not common to the Scriptures outside of the gospels, and rarely, if ever, did anyone speak to Him in this way. He said, "Ye call me Master and Lord: and ye say well; for so I am" (John 13:13). He is called Jesus frequently in the gospels, for His humanity is often in view. The use of the word *Jesus* by the angel, then, is significant. The Son of God in His *humanity* is the spirit, the sum, and the substance of prophecy. It all points to Him. As Son of man He came to earth, conquered death, and ascended into heaven. At God's right hand, though Son of God, He is yet a glorified man. He retains humanity with His deity. It is "at the name of Jesus" that every knee will bow to confess Him Lord (Phil. 2:10, see 9-11).

The time has now come for God to settle accounts with the godless crowd that is running the earth. What is now described has been anticipated again and again in the Apocalypse, and now the story must be told of God's reckoning with the Beast, the false prophet, the dragon, and all their adherents.

d. THE TRAGIC BATTLE STILLED (19:11-21)

Just as the wedding is described in two movements, so is the war. This is Armageddon, the last war before the Millennium begins. All its details are not given, although some description of it has already been given in connection with the vials. Once the Lord appears on the scene, it is soon over.

(1) THE LORD'S COMING DESCRIBED (19:11-16)

This is not His coming in the air to receive His church (1 Thess. 4:13-18), for that coming took place at the beginning of the book. This is His coming to the earth *with* His church to deal with His foes by force of arms and to impose upon mankind an era of peace. We should note what we are told about *His nature.* John says, *And I saw heaven opened, and behold a white horse; and he that sat on him was called Faithful and True, and in righteousness he doth judge and make war.* This is the great unveiling! The Lord Jesus is coming to earth again; not with all His glory veiled as when He came the first time, but in pomp and power, in martial splendor, with all His banners of war unfurled.

He is faithful and true. We have become familiar enough with the propaganda techniques of the great aggressors, with the way they attempt to subvert their foes by distorting, dramatizing, and dissembling the truth. At last there comes a King who is faithful and true, for that is His very nature. It is impossible for Him to be anything else. No attempts are made by Him to persuade the world that He is King. Now it is evident to all.

Moreover, in righteousness He judges and makes war. Every nation that takes up arms against its neighbors seizes on some pretext to convince its people and the world that it has a righteous cause. Hitler claimed that his aggressions were just and a righteous redress of the grievances of Versailles. The Western world claimed that its cause was just, for they were fighting one of the most frightful dictatorships the world had ever known. And so it goes. But now here is One who truly claims that in righteousness He judges and makes war.

The Lord is a man of war! It is an amazing title for the Son of God. Says Alexander Whyte, commenting on Bunyan's *Holy War,*

> Holy Scripture is full of wars and rumours of wars: the wars of the Lord; the wars of Joshua and the Judges; the wars of David, with his and many other magnificent battle-songs; till the best known name of the God of Israel in the Old Testament is the Lord of Hosts; and then in the New Testament we have Jesus Christ described as the Captain of our salvation. . . . And then the whole Bible is crowned with a book all sounding with battle-cries, . . . till it ends with that city of peace where they hang the trumpet in the hall and study war no more.[14]

The Lord is a man of war! In righteousness He judges and makes war. The judging has been going on throughout the breaking of the seals, the blowing of the trumpets, and the pouring out of the bowls. Now He makes war. He, who for long centuries has endured patiently the scoffings, the insults, the bad manners of men; who for ages has contemplated Calvary and all that it displayed of human hatred and contempt; and who, through the millennia has made peace through the blood of that cross, now makes war over that blood. For human sin has reached highwater mark and must be put down by force of arms. But there will not be much fighting when the battle is joined; it will all be over in a flash.

We should note, also, what we are told about *His name.* At the beginning of this long section dealing with God's government, we were given a glimpse of a throne in heaven and, connected with that throne, a mystery, a majesty, and a ministry. Now, at the end of this section the same three thoughts are in focus again. His is *the name of mystery.* John says, *His eyes were as a flame of fire, and on his head were many crowns; and he had a name written, that no man knew, but he himself.* The Lord is crowned with many diadems; all possible prerogatives are His. His name is shrouded in mystery. His human

14. Alexander Whyte, *Bunyan Characters* (London: Oliphant, Anderson & Ferrier, 1895), 3:2.

name of Jesus has been used as a curse word by godless men. They have scorned the name by which has been revealed to men the gracious heart of God. Now He bears the name of mystery, and they cannot know Him even if they would. There were always mysteries connected with God's Son, even when He was here as the revealer of God. "What manner of man is this?" cried His most intimate friends. How much more awesome must be the terrible mysteries that surround Him when He reappears with a name that none can know!

His is *the name of ministry.* John says, *And he was clothed with a vesture dipped in blood: and his name is called The Word of God. And the armies which were in heaven followed him upon white horses, clothed in fine linen, white and clean. And out of his mouth goeth a sharp sword, that with it he could smite the nations; and he shall rule them with a rod of iron: and he treadeth the winepress of the fierceness and wrath of Almighty God.* He now has a ministry far different from that which was His when He came as the Word made flesh, full of grace and truth. His ministry now is one of battle and blood. He is heaven's minister, but heaven's minister for war; and His name is called the Word of God. The sword issuing from His mouth is God's Word. In Genesis 1 He only had to speak, and flaming suns sprang into being, and life in myriad forms arose vibrant from the dust. This last battle will be won by a word! He will speak, that's all, and His foes will be smitten where they stand.

His garment is dyed red with blood, and the armies of heaven follow Him, their robes unsplashed by the conflict. "Behold," cried Enoch in the far-off dawn of time, "Behold, the Lord cometh with ten thousands of his saints, to execute judgment" (Jude 14-15). The armies of heaven, on milk-white steeds, follow in his train. These armies are real enough. Elijah caught a glimpse of such armies once. What a sight it will be for wicked men, marshaled by the million in acrimonious discord at Armageddon, yet determined, too, to unite against a common foe! What a sight it will be for them, swayed again by the gifted oratory of the Beast, the false prophet, the dragon, and the frogs, into believing that they can settle accounts with heaven once and for all! What a sight it will be for them to look up, as the skies rend asunder with a roar, and see that Holy One ride forth, followed by rank after endless rank of the redeemed and by heaven's angelic powers! Where now are the Beast's boasted powers?

His is *the name of majesty.* John says, *And he hath on his vesture and on his thigh a name written, KING OF KINGS, AND LORD OF LORDS.* Pilate's contemptuous title: "This is Jesus of Nazareth, the King of the Jews," came close to the mark, but this new title has a wider reach than that. He is not merely the King of the Jews; He is King of the world. The "times of the Gentiles" come to a screeching halt with His appearing. The thigh, on which this title is emblazoned, symbolizes power. Jacob wrestled with the angel until his thigh was out of joint and his power of resistance was broken. The Messiah's sword is seen upon His thigh (Ps. 45:3). The thigh is associated with His power, the vesture with His position. Joseph's brothers took his vesture, his coat of many colors that proclaimed his position as head of the family, dipped it in blood and flung it at their father's feet. The Lord is now arrayed in a vesture dipped in blood indeed, the blood of all His foes, and embroidered thereon is the title by which He will be known on earth for a thousand years.

(2) THE LORD'S CONQUEST DESCRIBED (19:17-21)

In a few graphic sentences we are shown Satan's rickety empire collapsing like a house of cards when the Lord appears. We see that Satan's forces are to be *doomed at Armageddon.* John says, *And I saw an angel standing in the sun; and he cried with a loud voice, saying to all the fowls that fly in the midst of heaven, Come and gather yourselves together unto the supper of the great God; that ye may eat the flesh of kings, and the flesh of captains, and the flesh of mighty men, and the flesh of horses, and of them that sit on them, and the flesh of all men, both free and bond, both small and great.* As the armies, assembled at the cockpit of the earth, stare in amazement at the appearing of the King of glory, their gaze is momentarily directed to the sun. There, standing in its glare, is an angel; at his summons, enormous flocks of birds appear, circling and wheeling around the armies of earth, croaking to one another in anticipation of the coming feast, dipping low over the horrified troops, and climbing again to the skies. The battle has not yet been fought, but the omens are dreadful. With each passing moment, the sky grows darker with these birds of prey. There cannot be a vulture, an eagle, a raven left on earth that has not obeyed the summons and come to the supper of God. Satan's armies are doomed; the fierce fowls know it and have come to bury the dead in the name of the living God.

We are next told how Satan's forces are to be *drawn to Armageddon.* John says, *And I saw the beast, and the kings of the earth, and their armies gathered together to make war against him that sat on the horse and against his army.* Thus, tersely, is the mobilization of the world described. Whatever may have been their original motives in converging on Armageddon, all animosities are forgotten, and the men are united by the challenge from on high.

In recent times, science fiction writers have made much of imagined plots against our planet. They have told of invasions from Venus and Mars and from the deep recesses of space. They have depicted a terrified world suddenly united in a common cause in the face of a threat from the far reaches of the sky. That is what happens here, but it is no fantasy of fiction; this is the real thing. The planet is invaded at last from outer space, not by horrible insectlike monsters, but by the Lord Himself and His glorious hosts. The devil knows his hour has come, but careless of human life, he fights to the bitter end. What the Beast will say to his armies, his allies, and his antagonists can well be imagined:

"Gentlemen, we are at war and have been at war one with another. The time has come for us to unite in a common cause. The things that unite us now are far more important than the things that divide us. It is no longer a question of which of us will rule the world; it is a question of common survival. The time has come for us to take final counsel together against the Lord and against His anointed. He has put Himself in our power. He has dared to appear on earth. The last time He came, we crucified Him; this time we shall cast His bands asunder and cast away His cords from us forever. We have tried uniting for peace; it has not proved a durable bond. Now let us unite for war. Let us deal with this invasion of our planet once and for all. Let us deal with this invasion of white-robed psalm singers. Let us show them how men, freed of all religious opiates, can fight. Let us hurl our defiance in their teeth. Time and again I have given you proofs of my mighty and supernatural powers. That dread lord of darkness whom we serve has defied these heavenly hosts for countless ages and is more than a match for them all. Come, let us rid the world and its atmosphere forever of these unwanted chanters of hymns."

The nations unite, as Psalm 2 foretells. Yet, as the great conference of kings disbands and the heralds proclaim the new resolutions, peal after peal of mocking laughter sound down from the sky for "He that sitteth in the heavens shall laugh; the Lord shall have them in derison" (Ps. 2:4).

It is the same old story. The nations in their folly were united against Christ at His first advent. The early church proclaimed it so: "Lord, thou art God, which hast made heaven, and earth, and the sea, and all that in them is: Who by the mouth of thy servant David hast said, Why did the heathen rage, and the people imagine vain things? The kings of the earth stood up, and the rulers were gathered together against the Lord, and against his Christ. For of a truth against thy holy child Jesus, whom thou hast anointed, both Herod, and Pontius Pilate, with the Gentiles, and the people of Israel, were gathered together. For to do whatsoever thy hand and thy counsel determined before to be done. And now, Lord, behold their threatenings" (Acts 4:24-29). The nations united against Christ at His first coming and will do so again. They did their worst when they crucified Him but only succeeded in accomplishing God's will. They will do the same when they unite against the Lord to oppose His return. The nations will imagine that they are working out their own schemes and plans as they march toward Esdraelon, but they are simply marching in step with God's will. They are drawn to Armageddon.

Finally, we are told how Satan's forces are to be *destroyed at Armageddon*. We read, *And the beast was taken, and with him the false prophet that wrought miracles before him, with which he deceived them that had received the mark of the beast, and them that worshipped his image. These both were cast alive into a lake of fire burning with brimstone. And the remnant were slain with the sword of him that sat upon the horse, which sword proceeded out of his mouth: and all the fowls were filled with their flesh.* With what panoply and pomp the armies march across the plains of Galilee, file through the passes and deploy on the fertile fields of Megiddo! What masses of military equipment are stockpiled in the hills! What fleets ride at anchor in the Red Sea, the Persian Gulf, and along the shorelines of the eastern Mediterranean! What stirring strains of martial music are heard. The ground shakes to the beat of marching feet; the skies darken with aircraft drawn from the ends of the earth. Amazing new weapons, given to men by the Beast, are brought into place. Miracles are wrought by the false prophet to encourage the troops. The final commands are given.

Then suddenly it will all be over. In fact, there will be no war at all, in the sense that we think of war. There will be just a word spoken from Him who sits astride the great white horse. Once He spoke a word to a fig tree, and it withered away. Once He spoke a word to howling winds and heaving waves, and the storm clouds vanished and the waves fell still. Once He spoke to a legion of demons bursting at the seams of a poor man's soul, and instantly they fled. Now He speaks a word, and the war is over. The blasphemous, loud-mouthed Beast is stricken where he stands. The false prophet, the miracle-working windbag from the pit is punctured and still. The pair of them are bundled up and hurled headlong into the everlasting flames. Another word, and the panic-stricken armies reel and stagger and fall down dead. Field marshals and generals, admirals and air commanders, soldiers and sailors, rank and file, one and all—they fall. And the vultures descend and cover the scene.

Thus ends the Battle of Armageddon! For a thousand years there will be peace on earth after that. Men will beat their swords into plowshares and their spears into pruning hooks, their tanks into tractors and their missiles into silos for grain. The ages will roll by, and the words for war in human speech will become archaic fragments of a language dead to mankind.

One can picture a schoolboy reading an ancient book sometime during the second half of the Millennium. "Say, Dad," he says, "what is an intercontinental ballistic missile?" To which the father replies, "Go and ask your mother!" The mother, being questioned, answers, "Some kind of cabbage, I expect. Go and ask your dad." What a day that will be!

3. THE FINAL WOES DESCRIBED *(20:1-15)*
a. THE GREAT WORLD THREAT AT THE END OF THE MILLENNIUM (20:1-10)

The golden age has come. The armies of the nations have been disbanded, and the great military academies have fallen into ruin and decay. The machinery of war has all been smelted down and converted to the implements of peace. Jerusalem has become the world's capital. The throne of David is there, and the twelve apostles are there judging the twelve tribes of Israel, for Israel rules the world. The millennial Temple has been built to crown Moriah's brow, and the nations of the earth come there to worship the living God. Prosperity is evident from pole to pole and from the new river, which now graces Jerusalem, to the ends of the earth. Poverty is unknown. Every man has all that heart can desire. There are no prisons, no hospitals, no mental institutions, no barracks, no saloons, no houses of ill repute, no gambling dens, no homes for the aged and infirm. Such things belong to a past and lesser age. The bloom of youth is on everyone's cheek, for a man is a stripling at a hundred years of age. Cemeteries are crumbling relics of the past, and tears are rare. The wolf and the lamb, the calf and the lion, the cow and the bear, the child and the scorpion, all are at peace. Jesus has come, and the Millennium is here. The golden age, so frequently heralded by the prophets of Israel's past, has dawned at last, and the earth is filled with the knowledge of God. Jesus is Lord, and He rules the nations with a rod of iron. His reign is righteous, and the nations obey. The principles of the Sermon on the Mount are the laws of the kingdom, and men obey them because infractions are not allowed. Sin is visited with swift and certain judgment. The era lasts for a thousand years.

Many of the details are missing from the Apocalypse because they have been told again and again in the Old Testament, and the Apocalypse has other and greater themes to discuss. But if the details are missing, the duration is not. It is mentioned five times in a half dozen verses. Moreover, John will come back to the Millennium before he is through, but will discuss it in the light of eternity. In the meantime, he hurries on to its end.

The two beasts were cast alive into the lake of fire before the golden age began, but not so the devil. He was chained in the abyss, for God is not yet through with him. He has one more evil mission to fulfill.

(1) THE MILLENNIAL POSTPONEMENT OF THE LAST REBELLION (20:1-6)

There is a good reason for the postponement of this last rebellion. God intends to give mankind a thousand years of peace, prosperity, and perfect rule. The Millennium is the last and, in some ways, the greatest of the dispensations. We are told of *the period when Satan* is bound. John says, *And I saw an angel come down from heaven, having the key of the bottomless pit and a great chain in his hand. And he laid hold on the dragon, that old serpent, which is the Devil, and Satan, and bound him a thousand years.* Observe the repetition in the narrative of the phrase "and I saw." Its use begins in chapter 19 and continues on to the eternal state. It denotes a clearly chronological sequence of events and helps establish the fact that the Millennium will be an actual historical period taking its place in a tightly-forged chain of happenings.

The last time the key to the abyss was mentioned, Satan had it and was permitted to open that dread prison and release swarms of foul fiends upon the earth. Now an angel of God has that key. Armed with authority and power from on high, the angel seizes the old dragon, flings a mighty chain around him, and hurls him into the abyss, locking him up for a thousand years. No railing accusations are brought against this ancient foe of God, indeed four of his titles are given—the dragon, that old serpent, the devil, and Satan—which spell out his history since his fall. He is the cruel and cunning one, the accuser, and the adversary.

The devil is chained for the duration of the Millennium. Generation after generation is born, and the earth flourishes as it did in Eden before the serpent seduced mankind. For a thousand years the old deceiver and murderer is chained, and for a thousand years there is heaven on earth. A thousand years—that's the period of it! There can be no mistake, for God writes it down again and again; it is a whole millennium of time.

We are next told *the place where Satan is bound.* John says that the angel *cast him into the bottomless pit, and shut him up, and set a seal upon him.* There is a poetic justice in God's dealings with Satan. Centuries ago, the evil one saw to it that the mortal remains of God's beloved Son were shut up in a tomb and sealed. Throughout the Tribulation era, Satan has opened the abyss to plague mankind, once with horrible demons and once with the recalled soul of the Beast. Now he himself is consigned to that dark hole and sealed in by an act of God, and there he rages in the most secure prison cell in the universe. It is the condemned cell, and he knows it. He has his thoughts to keep him company, and terrible thoughts they are—thoughts of the day of his creation when he sprang mature, magnificent, and mighty from the hand of God; thoughts of the wide world that once he ruled as the anointed cherub; thoughts of the ways in which once he led the worship of the angel hosts; thoughts of God's throne and his attempts to seize it for himself; thoughts of his fall, of his entrance into Eden, of his short-lived triumph over the first human pair; thoughts of the sentence passed upon him and of his futile efforts to prevent the coming of the promised Seed; thoughts of Calvary and of his utter defeat; thoughts of the fleeting moments when he brought the world to the foot of the Beast and had seemingly triumphed at last; thoughts of the lake of fire just ahead. He is given a thousand years in confinement to think.

We are then told *the purpose for which Satan is bound.* It is *that he should deceive the nations no more, till the thousand years should be fulfilled: and after that he must be loosed a little season.* The nations blunder along in darkness and despair, throughout the long ages of time, ever learning but never able to come to a knowledge of the truth. Responsibility for that is laid at Satan's door, but now for a thousand years they will be free of his baneful influence and lies. In the verses that follow, three reasons are given for the incarceration of the devil. Paul promised the Roman Christians, "The God of peace shall bruise Satan under your feet shortly" (Rom. 16:20). This is what is described next.

We observe *the coronation of the saints of God.* John says, *And I saw thrones, and they (that) sat upon them, and judgment was given unto them.* Those on the thrones are not angels, "for unto the angels hath he not put in subjection the world to come" (Heb. 2:5). The church is in view here, and the saints of other ages. When the Lord returns, He is going to depose two different types of ruling classes. He is to "punish the host of the high ones that are on high, and the kings of the earth upon the earth" (Isa. 24:21). The "high ones that are on high" are Satan's angelic princes on their thrones (Col. 1:16; Eph. 6:13). These thrones in the heavenlies will be occupied throughout the Millennium by the triumphant believers from the church age. Paul says, "Do ye not know that the saints shall judge the world . . . Know ye not that we shall judge angels" (1 Cor. 6:2-3). Along with the "high ones" will be deposed "the kings of the earth," the Gentile ruling powers. Their seats of authority will be taken over by redeemed Israel (Isa. 60:12) under the tutelage of the twelve apostles (Matt. 19:28).

The second group to be crowned are those martyred prior to the Great Tribulation. John speaks of *the souls of them that were beheaded for the witness of Jesus, and for the word of God.* These souls are seen under the altar at the time of the breaking of the fifth seal—the firstfruits of those martyred by the Beast. The third class to be crowned are the Tribulation saints themselves. John mentions a great company: *which had not worshipped the beast, neither his image, neither had received his mark upon their foreheads, or in their hands.* These too are crowned. John says *they lived and reigned with Christ a thousand years. But the rest of the dead lived not again until the thousand years were finished. This is the first resurrection.*

We are told of *the character of the saints of God.* John heard the proclamation, *Blessed and holy is he that hath part in the first resurrection.* Their state is described as happy, and their standing is said to be holy. Happiness and holiness always go hand in hand. There is so little genuine happiness among men today because there is so little holiness.

We are told of *the confidence of the saints of God.* John says that *on such the second death hath no power, but they shall be priests of God and of Christ, and shall reign with him a thousand years.* The first resurrection occurs in stages but is not regarded as being complete until the last group of martyrs is raised. Now they are seen as reigning in power, never to die again, forever beyond the reach of the second death. They are kings and priests, exalted with Christ and entrusted with ministries of great dignity and responsibility. While Satan rages in bonds in the dark reaches of the abyss, these are enthroned in light.

(2) THE MALIGNANT PROPAGATOR OF THE LAST REBELLION (20:7-9a)

The long, blissful ages of the Millennium roll by, but as in every dispensation, a test must be given to bring to light the secrets of men's hearts. We are told of Satan's dramatic appearance on earth. John says, *And when the thousand years are expired, Satan shall be loosed out of his prison.* Imagine the fury of the evil one in his cramped cell. Picture a mighty jungle lion caged in solitary confinement, when suddenly the door of the cage is thrown open. With a mighty bound, the beast leaps forth, shaking his mighty mane and roaring until the mountains shake. With furious lashings of his tail, he glares around looking for something or someone on which to vent his rage. Thus Satan bursts forth from the pit. He has lost none of his cunning with the passing of the years. He knows exactly what to do; for a thousand years he has plotted his revenge. Men are still men, and sin is still sin, and well he knows how to bring the two together. He will have one final fling; he will strike out at both God and man; he will make a mockery out of this Millennium and show it up as just another pious fraud. He is back, and sin once more can blaze up in human hearts. The kindling is there, stacked and dry, and he has the fire.

We are told of *Satan's dynamic appeal to mankind.* John says, *And shall go out to deceive the nations which are in the four quarters of the earth, Gog and Magog, to gather them together to battle: the number of whom is as the sand of the sea.* Men have not known the arts of war for a thousand years; but now the master craftsman is back, and it will not take them long to learn.

Throughout the Millennium, righteousness has reigned. The golden age began with a population on earth of soundly saved people, filled with the Spirit, living according to the precepts of the Sermon on the Mount. But, as the ages come and go, countless children are born, disease will be banished, and death will be exceedingly rare. Children born during this age will be born with sinful natures, needing to be saved, just as today. Children of believing parents today sometimes become gospel-hardened; so, during the Millennium many will become glory-hardened. They will submit to Christ's rule and to the stern laws of the kingdom because to rebel will mean instant punishment. During the Millennium, many will render only feigned obedience. Psalm 18:44 says, "As soon as they shall hear of me, they shall obey me [yield feigned obedience unto me]." Psalm 66:3 says, "Say unto God, How terrible art thou in thy works! through the greatness of thy power shall thine enemies submit [yield feigned obedience] unto me." Thus, many will abide by the laws of the kingdom only because they have to. Sin will reign in secret in their hearts, and they will long for the time when the strict rules will be relaxed. The devil will find fertile soil in their souls.

Throughout the Millennium the nations will come up to Jerusalem to worship. There they will have before their eyes a vivid reminder of what happens to rebels. The tour of the glorious city complete, they will be taken out to survey a dreadful scene, all the more terrible because death will be so rare. On one side of the city yawns a fearful gulf. Visitors looking down will see the remains of men who have transgressed the commandments of the King. Their bodies will be seen in that horrible place where the worm never dies and where the fire burns on unquenched. The visitors will be reminded of another place, more dreadful still, where the Beast and the false prophet scream out their torments in quenchless flames.

Still, many will pay no heed to these warnings. Retreating to the four corners of the globe, as far as possible from the central glory, the disaffected ones who would rebel if only they could and dared, will begin to congregate. They are called "Gog and Magog" in the text, and the name is evidently symbolic. We still say that a man "meets his Waterloo," applying Napoleon's disastrous defeat in a metaphorical way. During the golden age, the memory of Russia's disaster will linger on, and Gog and Magog will lend their names symbolically to the dissidents of earth. Satan will seek them out and will find them only too willing to listen to his lies. They will rejoice at his bold claims, flock to his standards, and follow him headlong into rebellion. The insurrection will spread like a prairie fire fanned by a prevailing wind.

We are told of *Satan's daring approach to Jerusalem.* John says, *And they went up on the breadth of the earth, and compassed the camp of the saints about, and the beloved city.* Satan is no coward. Like a daring gambler, he stakes all on a single throw. He has nothing to lose, everything to gain. The "beloved city" is Jerusalem. The "camp of the saints" may be a reference to the headquarters of the heavenly saints who live in the heavenly Jerusalem but who have duties on the millennial earth as well.

(3) THE MILITANT PUNISHMENT OF THE LAST REBELLION (20:9b-10)

The rebellion will not succeed. In fact it never had a chance of succeeding. It is only permitted by God in order to bring to light the hidden works of darkness of the human heart. What happens is described in two stages. First, *the fiery death of the rebels* is described. John says, *And fire came down from God out of heaven, and devoured them.* The judgment is swift and sure. The invading armies, blinded by Satan, are driven forward in the grand delusion, perhaps, that they can take possession of the tree of life. There is not a word about a conflict; not a shot is fired; not a saint is harmed. With a flash, the fire of God falls, and it is all over. Nothing remains but a heap of ashes. No carrion birds are summoned to bury these dead. They are cremated in the fires that slay them. In an instant they are shivering on the other shore in sight of the great white throne.

Second, we are told of *the fiery doom of the devil.* John says, *And the devil that deceived them was cast into the lake of fire and brimstone, where the beast and the false prophet are, and shall be tormented day and night for ever and ever.* That lake of fire was prepared for him and his angels (Matt. 25:41), and there he goes headlong to make his bed in hell. His two companions in the crimes of the last days are there awaiting him. They have been there a thousand years, and far from being annihilated, they are alive and in torment and facing the same horrors for all eternity. The devil joins them, to be tormented eternally for all the wickedness and woe he has fathered since his fall.

b. THE GREAT WHITE THRONE AT THE BEGINNING OF ETERNITY (20:11-15)

Satan has persuaded mankind for centuries that there is no future punishment, no final accounting before God. That lie is now fully exposed.

(1) THE SETTING (20:11-12)

With terrible strokes of the pen, John describes the scene. He says, *And I saw a great white throne, and him that sat on it, from whose face the earth and the heaven fled away; and there was found no place for them.* Thus John describes the background. We are struck by the austere language, the remarkable economy of words. There is nothing of Dante or Milton here, no embellishments, just the stark narrative of doom.

First, John describes *the background.* There is *a terrible fact* set before us, the fact of the great white throne. It is the throne of God, dazzling to the eye, reflecting a purity so intense that before it the very seraphim shrink. Guilty men, summoned to that throne, have no place to hide, nothing behind which to cower. All the foolish little delusions behind which men hide today will be gone, and men will be confronted by a fact too terrible to contemplate—the great white throne.

There is *a terrible figure.* John sees Him at once and knows Him as the Lord. The nailprints are in His hands, the scars are upon His back and brow, the spear wound is in His side—the marks of what wicked men did to Him. There He is! Men have ignored Him, denied Him, cursed Him, disbelieved in Him, sold Him. Now He is their Judge.

There is *a terrible fear* gripping each heart. To look upon the face of Jesus is bliss beyond words for the child of God, but for the ungodly, it will be the first agonizing stab of hell. The earth and the heavens have fled already from that face, for heaven and earth have been defiled by sin and need to be made anew. Oh, what a face it is! The ungodly spat in it once and wrenched the beard from its cheeks, leaving it more marred than any man's. Now they gaze on it in fear and torment. Everything stable, solid, and familiar in the universe has gone—every landmark, every stone, every hiding place. There is nothing left but emptiness, a throne, a figure, a face, and a cramping fear.

There is *a terrible fellowship* there too. The dead, small and great, stand before God. Dead souls are united to dead bodies in a fellowship of horror and despair. Little men and paltry women whose lives were filled with pettiness, selfishness, and nasty little sins will be there. Those whose lives amounted to nothing will be there, whose very sins were drab and dowdy, mean, spiteful, peevish, groveling, vulgar, common, and cheap. The great will be there, men who sinned with a high hand, with dash, and courage and flair. Men like Alexander and Napoleon, Hitler and Stalin will be present, men who went in for wickedness on a grand scale with the world for their stage and who died unrepentant at last. Now one and all are arraigned and on their way to be damned; a horrible fellowship congregated together for the first and last time. That is the background.

Next John describes *the books*. Psychologists assure us that nothing we have ever experienced is really forgotten. The subconscious mind stores it all up in neat compartments, awaiting the appropriate trigger to recall it to the conscious mind. People saved from drowning have frequently testified to the fact that, in their last moments, their whole life has flashed back. God keeps records of everything. It is all written down.

God keeps books. There are two in particular that are mentioned by John. There is *the book of life of the Lamb*. John says, **And the books were opened: and another book was opened, which is the book of life.** This book is the Lamb's book of life, in which are written the names of all those who, from the beginning of time to the end, have been saved through faith in Christ. The book is vast, for the names are many. Every kindred and nation, people and tongue, every strata of society, every culture, and every clime are represented in that book. It contains the names of hopeless sinners who trusted in God's Son and were saved from wrath through Him. It contains the names of those long deluded by false religion who finally turned to Christ to be saved by Him alone. It contains the names of those saved in childhood's tender years and those saved with life's final breath. It contains the names of those who have gone from strength to strength and of those who have stumbled again and again. No matter! Is your name written there? That is the important thing.

There is the *book of the lives of the lost*. John says, **And the dead were judged out of those things which were written in the books, according to their works.** Nothing can save the man who is determined to stand on his record; who insists, "I'm doing the best I can." Salvation as proclaimed in the Bible is always according to faith, "for by grace are ye saved through faith; and that not of yourselves: it is the gift of God: not of works, lest any man should boast" (Eph. 2:8-9). Judgment is always according to works. The sinner can either ask God for a free pardon or demand a fair trial. If he chooses the fair trial, it will land him in the lake of fire, for he will be judged according to his works. To receive the free pardon he must plead guilty, cast himself upon the mercy of God, and accept the salvation He offers through Christ. This he must do before it is too late.

When the books are opened, God is going to judge "the secrets of men"

(Rom. 2:16), as well as the open, flagrant sins. He is going to judge the things we have left undone as well as the things we have done. Read the indictment of the nations in Matthew 25:41-46. Every count is a sin of omission. We will be judged not only for what we *do*, but for what we *are*, for we are sinners. We are not sinners because we sin; we sin because we are sinners; we do what we do because we are what we are. The lost will be weighed and measured by the holy character of Jesus and will be shown that they "have sinned and come short of the glory of God" (Rom. 3:23).

(2) THE SUMMONS (20:13)

The Holy Spirit now goes back to describe how men will be brought before the great white throne. John says, *And the sea gave up the dead which were in it; and death and hell delivered up the dead which were in them: and they were judged every man according to their works.* There will be no hiding place. The first question put to man by God was, "Where art thou?" As that word rang out across Eden, Adam and Eve came out of hiding to stand naked and ashamed before their Judge. That cry will go forth again, and out of their tombs they will come, up from the depths of the sea, forth from the arctic wastes, up from the burning sands, and out of the tropical bush. From this age and from that they will come, those newly dead and those whose bones are but dust. He knows where every speck of human dust is hidden, and at His word it will all come scurrying back to make again the forms of the departed. The bodies will rise from the dust, and the souls will come up from hades. Back they will come, with faces wrecked and ruined by sin and with souls knotted and gnarled, shriveled and shorn by lust and hate, envy and scorn, passion and pride, iniquity and crime. Back they will come to be judged—according to their works.

(3) THE SENTENCE (20:14-15)

The books have been read; every mouth has been stopped, and all at the great white throne are found guilty before God. Now the fearful sentence is read. John says, *And death and hell were cast into the lake of fire. This is the second death. And whosoever was not found written in the book of life was cast into the lake of fire.* The terrible words are spoken: "Depart from me, ye cursed, into everlasting fire, prepared for the devil and his angels" (Matt. 25:41). It was to save men from this that Christ came and suffered, bled, and died. It was to warn men of this that God wrote the Bible and for centuries has striven by His Spirit with men. The Bible leaves it at that. There is no wracking description of the horrors of the damned, no frightening drawing appended to the page, just the naked narrative, the bare sentence. Eternity itself will fill in the rest.

Part Four:
Visions of Glory (21:1–22:21)

I. THE BRIGHT NEW WORLD (21:1-8)

   A. It Is Planned as a New Creation (21:1)
   B. It Is Provided with a New Capital (21:2)
   C. It Is Prepared for a New Community (21:3-4)
   D. It Is Protected by a New Constitution (21:5-8)

II. THE BRAND NEW CITY (21:9–22:5)

   A. John's First Impressions (21:9-14)
   B. John's Further Impressions (21:15-27)
   C. John's Final Impressions (22:1-5)

CONCLUSION TO REVELATION (22:6-21)

   A. The Faithful Word of God (22:6-10)
     1. The Accuracy of the Word of God (22:6)
     2. The Authority of the Word of God (22:7-9)
     3. The Accessibility of the Word of God (22:10)
   B. The Finished Work of Christ (22:11-16)
     1. It Settles What We Are (22:11)
     2. It Settles Where We Are (22:12-15)
     3. It Settles Whose We Are (22:16)
   C. The Final Witness of the Spirit (22:17-21)
     1. The Last Welcome (22:17)
     2. The Last Warning (22:18-19)
     3. The Last Word (22:20-21)

Part Four:

Visions of Glory (21:1–22:21)

The visions of glory, which bring to an end the unfolding drama of Revelation, are in two parts. The first gives a description of the eternal state, and the second gives a description of the Millennium. The description of the Millennium is from heaven's standpoint, not earth's. The earthly view of the Millennium has already been well covered in Scripture in the Old Testament, so there is little need for John to repeat the details here.

I. THE BRIGHT NEW WORLD (21:1-8)

The vision begins with the words "And I saw," which is John's customary formula in carrying forward the chronology of this section of the book. The expression is used seven times, beginning with the appearing of the Lord on His great white horse.

A. IT IS PLANNED AS A NEW CREATION (21:1)

John says, *And I saw a new heaven and a new earth: for the first heaven and the first earth were passed away; and there was no more sea.* Peter has an interesting comment relating to this. He tells us that the first heaven and earth, "which then was," perished. That, seemingly, is a reference to the original creation mentioned in Genesis 1:1. The second heaven and earth, "which now are," are kept in store, reserved unto fire. The new heavens and the new earth will then come into being (2 Pet. 3:5-13). Paul describes an experience of being caught up into what he called "the third heaven" (2 Cor. 12:2). His expression "caught up" is sometimes rendered "raptured." Possibly Paul was actually caught away in the Spirit to this third future heaven that John now sees and describes.

It is a new heaven and a new earth. The word *new* means not merely new as to time, but also as to kind. It is a new kind of heaven and a new kind of earth, proof of which is found in the fact that the new earth will have no sea. The first heaven and the first earth are not to be annihilated; they are to be purged by fire and regenerated. Satan has defiled both spheres, and God will therefore make them anew. They are made new in the same sense that the believer is "a new man" in Christ, that is, he is a changed man, quickened and renewed by the Spirit of God.

The eternal state is not simply a spiritual condition destitute of locality. The earth and the heaven are fixed locations throughout eternity. There is something particularly comforting in that for us who, at present, know only mortality. The Lord Jesus promised to go and prepare for us a place of many mansions. "If it were not so," He said, "I would have told you" (John 14:2, cf. 1-4). The clear implication is that, could we expect to find heaven drastically, shockingly different from the earth, then He would have told us. But it is not. We shall feel as much at ease and at home in heaven as we do on earth right now. Heaven contains much with which we are fondly familiar. Paul, in describing his experience of rapture, was not sure whether he was "in the body" or "out of the body" (2 Cor. 12:3).

B. IT IS PROVIDED WITH A NEW CAPITAL (21:2)

John says, *And I John saw the holy city, new Jerusalem, coming down from God out of heaven, prepared as a bride adorned for her husband.* The heavens are literal; the earth is literal; the sea is literal; and so is the city. Many commentators view the city as symbolic of the church. There may be some justification for this because a city is often identified with its inhabitants. But primarily this is a literal city, the great heavenly capital of the renewed earth, throughout the Millennium, and the enduring home of the saints for all eternity. John later gives a detailed description of this city and tells us of its glories and its relationship to the millennial earth.

C. IT IS PREPARED FOR A NEW COMMUNITY (21:3-4)

Two things are mentioned about this blessed company. They are *blessed by the presence of God*. John says, *And I heard a great voice out of heaven saying, Behold, the tabernacle of God is with men, and he will dwell with them, and they shall be his people, and God himself shall be with them, and be their God.* In Eden before the Fall, God came and walked with Adam in the cool of the day. Now He will dwell with men forever, and they will delight in His abiding presence. The lost are without God, without Christ, and are without hope. The saved are with Him for all eternity. That presence, which is the chief horror of the lost, is the chief happiness of the redeemed. Being perfectly holy, they can enjoy the company of God.

This glorious company who make up the new community of the New Jerusalem are *blessed by the absence of grief.* John says, *And God shall wipe away all tears from their eyes; and there shall be no more death, neither sorrow, nor crying, neither shall there be any more pain: for the former things are passed away.* On earth during the Millennium, death will be rare, but it will not be banished entirely (Isa. 65:20). In the eternal state, death will be a thing of the past. There will be no more funerals, no more graves, no more hospitals, no more broken homes, no more broken hearts. What a day of rejoicing that will be!

D. IT IS PROTECTED BY A NEW CONSTITUTION (21:5-8)

When the founding fathers came to the new world, they drew up a mighty compact: "In the name of God, Amen. We whose names are underwritten, the loyal subjects of our dread sovereign Lord King James. Having undertaken for the glory of God and the advancement of the Christian faith and honour of our king and countrie, a voyage to plant the first colony in the northern parts of Virginia, do by these presents solemnly and mutually in the presence of God, and one another, covenant and combine ourselves together into a civil body politic. . ." It was a noble experiment, and it brought into being a great and mighty nation. But the dream has faded. The seeds of decay were brought over with the Pilgrims themselves, for although the Puritans were good and godly men, they were still creatures of clay, and their children were sinners like themselves. In the process of time, a remarkable Constitution was drawn up for the United States. It was one of the most impressive and enlightened documents ever penned. But the very freedoms guaranteed by that Constitution threaten to be the undoing of the nation itself. Even the best-colonized countries and the best-conceived constitutions are foiled by the sinfulness of man. But there is a country where the constitution is flawless and the countrymen perfect. That country is heaven.

There are three great guarantees built into the constitution of the New Jerusalem. First, it will be *a splendid place to live.* John says, *And he that sat upon the throne said, Behold, I make all things new. And he said unto me, Write: for these words are true and faithful. And he said unto me, It is done. I am Alpha and Omega, the beginning and the end.* Most people like to move into a brand new home; one day we shall move into a brand new world. It will indeed be a splendid place in which to live, for God will lavish the genius of His creative imagination upon it and will furnish it from resources of His unlimited power. It will take instant shape. He says, *Behold I make all things new,"* and in the next breath He says, *It is done!* He is the beginning and the ending; there is no need for anything more between. It will not take the countless ages of an imagined evolutionary process to bring that world into being. He who said in the early dawn of time, "Light, be!!"—and light was! will again put forth His power and a new universe will appear. We cannot imagine what it will be like. Even this present world, marred and spoiled as it is by sin, contains scenes of beauty that take our breath away. The landscapes of glory will be better far than these.

Second, it will be *a satisfying place to live,* and it will be so in three ways. There will be *satisfying resources* there. He says, *I will give unto him that is athirst of the fountain of the water of life freely.* Thirst is not an unpleasant sensation when it can be instantly, completely, and refreshingly satisfied. It is the raging of unsatisfied thirst that we dread, the awful lot of the damned. The saints in glory will thirst after God and will be satisfied.

There will be *satisfying responsibilities.* He says, **He that overcometh shall inherit all things.** God gave Adam a congenial occupation in Eden. Satisfying work is rewarding, challenging, and worthwhile. In heaven, the overcomer will have a special inheritance; he will be heir to all things and will administer that inheritance for the glory of God. What a challenge that should be to us! God allows the circumstances of life to test us and to put us on our mettle in order to enlarge and increase our capacity and our ability to handle responsibility. If we allow the Holy Spirit to make us overcomers down here, we shall enter into enlarged responsibilities over there; we shall inherit all things.

There will be *satisfying relationships.* He says, **And I will be his God, and he shall be my son.** How wonderful is God! First He gives us His Son; "for God so loved the world, that he gave his only begotten Son" (John 3:16). Then He gives us his Spirit. He says, "If ye then, being evil, know how to give good gifts unto your children: how much more shall your heavenly Father give the Holy Spirit to them that ask him?" (Luke 11:13). Finally He gives us Himself!

Third, heaven will be *a safe place to live.* John says, **But the fearful, and unbelieving, and the abominable, and murderers, and whoremongers, and sorcerers, and idolaters, and all liars, shall have their part in the lake which burneth with fire and brimstone: which is the second death.** It is this kind of person who has made the cities of earth centers of wickedness; all such will be banned from the new world. Sin has wrecked and ruined this world, and God is determined it will not ruin the world to come. The most sobering statement of all is that the unbelieving will be in the lake of fire. The unbelieving! Men might concede that the abominable should be there and the murderers—but the unbelieving! Yet unbelief is the father of all wickedness. It opened the gates of Eden to sin and has kept men away from God and His salvation ever since.

Here, then, is a brief but satisfying description of heaven and its eternal glory age. Just enough details are given to make our hearts hunger for home and to challenge us so to live that we shall have an abundant entrance into glory when our traveling days are done.

II. THE BRAND NEW CITY (21:9–22:5)

Now comes a change. An angel appears to give John a more extended view of the Millennium and of the relationship between the eternal state with its celestial city and the glorious reign of Christ over the renewed earth. The chronology, introduced by the words, "and I saw," is over. We are taken back to the Millennium in this, the last great parenthesis of the book. A similar visit was made by an angel to give John further details about the Babylonian city and the Babylonian system. Now John has described to him not the scarlet woman, but the bride; not Babylon, but the new Jerusalem. The purpose of this parenthesis is to show the relationship between the two Jerusalems— between the earthly Jerusalem, which will be the capital city of the nations during the Millennium, and the heavenly Jerusalem, the home of the saints during the Millennium and for all eternity.

The marvelous heavenly city is seen suspended in the heavens, flashing her rays of glory to the earth. Its peoples have great concern for what happens on earth during the thousand year reign of Christ. True, many commentators have allegorized the vision and interpreted this passage in terms of the bliss and blessedness of the saved throughout eternity. Such an application has its measure of validity, for the Scriptures are very deep. But a more literal approach seems to do better justice to the passage.

In this description of the Millennium, everything is seen in relation to the heavenly Jerusalem and in the light of that city. The first word from God in Genesis 1:1 brought heaven and earth together in perfect harmony. But then sin entered, driving its wedge between the two. Now sin has been dealt with, and the great deceiver is in bonds; once again heaven and earth are brought together in the closest harmony.

A. JOHN'S FIRST IMPRESSIONS (21:9-14)

There is an impression of *the mystery of the heavenly city.* John says, *And there came unto me one of the seven angels which had the seven vials full of the seven last plagues, and talked with me, saying, Come hither, I will shew thee the bride, the Lamb's wife. And he carried me away in the spirit to a great and high mountain, and shewed me that great city, the holy Jerusalem, descending out of heaven from God.* The city is closely linked with the bride. Babylon was set forth in a dual way as a woman and a city; so is the holy Jerusalem. The city and its inhabitants are thus closely linked.

Twice the city is said to descend from heaven. The first time, in verse 3, has to do with the eternal state. In that verse the city is seen descending toward the new earth, there to remain forever. Here in verse 9, the city descends to earth's environs to hover over the earth throughout the Millennium.

There is nothing impossible about a giant literal city hovering in the sky over the earth and located immediately over the earthly city of Jerusalem. Men have scoffed at such an idea in the past, but they can afford to scoff no more. Men themselves can now put satellites into stationary orbit over any part of the globe. The New Jerusalem is brought by God from outer space and made to hover in stationary orbit over Jerusalem. Direct communication is opened up between heaven and earth, and there will be much intercourse between the two Jerusalems. The miraculous element is present, but it is no longer the kind of thing at which men can scoff, nor is it to be regarded as science fiction.

John is impressed by *the majesty of the heavenly city.* He describes the city as *having the glory of God: and her light was like unto a stone most precious, even like a jasper stone, clear as crystal; and had a wall great and high, and had twelve gates, and at the gates twelve angels, and names written thereon, which are the names of the twelve tribes of the children of Israel: on the east three gates; on the north three gates; on the south three gates; and on the west three gates. And the wall of the city had twelve foundations, and in them the names of the twelve apostles of the Lamb.* These were his first impressions. How strange that city is! It glows with a light all its own. As we fly over the great cities of the earth at night, we see the sparkling lights of those cities illuminating the sky for miles, and beneath us, the vast panorama stretches away in millions of lights. The heavenly city will shine in the sky with a luster all its own. Men will look up from the earth and see it there flashing in the sky like a giant diamond. How secure that city is! Its twelve gates, directed toward the four points of the compass, are guarded by those mighty sentinels, one of whom in one night could destroy all of Sennacherib's host. No forbidden power will pass those strongly guarded gates. How strong that city is! Its mighty walls are bedded in twelve foundations, and the names of the apostles are blazoned there. That city is rooted and grounded in truth.

B. JOHN'S FURTHER IMPRESSIONS (21:15-27)

John has taken a swift survey of the city, taking in with a single glance its salient points and landmarks. Now he takes a closer look and gives us his second thoughts. He mentions *some of the dimensions of the city.* He says,

And he that talked with me had a golden reed to measure the city, and the gates thereof, and the wall thereof. And the city lieth foursquare, and the length is as large as the breadth: and he measured the city with the reed, twelve thousand furlongs. The length and the breadth and the height of it are equal. These dimensions can describe a pyramid, but it seems more likely that the holy city is a perfect cube, just as the Holy of Holies in the Tabernacle and the Temple were cubes. The city runs twelve thousand stadia in all directions; it is fifteen hundred miles square and high. These dimensions have puzzled past expositors, but a city this size is no longer inconceivable, especially when it is regarded as a heaven-descended satellite. The God who can orbit a moon around a planet or a family of planets around a sun can easily design a cubical satellite, create it, and then launch it into its desired orbit relative to earth.

John mentions *some of the details of the city.* He begins with a further description of the wall. The angel who was conducting John on his grand tour *measured the wall thereof, a hundred and forty and four cubits, according to the measure of a man, that is, of the angel. And the building of the wall of it was of jasper: and the city was pure gold, like unto clear glass.* Compared to the height of the city itself, the wall is quite low. The city itself was measured by God, and all is therefore vast and perfect; the wall was measured by a creature, "the measure of a man," and is therefore nothing compared with the city. The wall of an ancient city was intended for defense, but this city needs no beetling battlements to ward off attack. It is impregnable and inviolate in itself.

The wall is made of jasper (perhaps the diamond), a hard and brilliant stone. The city itself is made of gold, a precious metal usually used in Scripture to symbolize deity. The holy places of Israel's Tabernacle and Temple contained furniture of pure gold. In the Temple, the entire surface of the Holy of Holies was overlaid with gold. This heavenly city is the dwelling place of God, so all is of purest gold, clear as glass, constantly reflecting the glory of God.

John describes next the foundations and says, *And the foundations of the wall of the city were garnished with all manner of precious stones. The first foundation was jasper; the second, sapphire; the third, a chalcedony; the fourth, an emerald; the fifth, sardonyx; the sixth, sardius; the seventh, chrysolyte; the eighth, beryl; the ninth, a topaz; the tenth, a chrysoprasus; the eleventh, a jacinth; the twelfth, an amethyst.* These stones represent the glory of God in a dozen different ways. We cannot fathom the meaning of them now, but the redeemed, in their heavenly city, will appreciate their full significance. The overall impression is one of wealth and magnificence beyond anything known on earth.

In the early dawn of redemption's story, Abraham, the pilgrim patriarch, turned his back upon Ur of the Chaldees to follow the leading of God. He was seeking "a city which hath foundations." We picture Abraham shaking his head over the foundations of Jericho. In Egypt, a country where they built their giant monuments to defy the very tooth of time, we see him looking at the foundations of Thebes and shaking his head again. Abraham did not find the city of his dreams in his journeyings on earth; Jacob did not find it in Syria, nor Isaac in Canaan. To learn more about that city, we have to read through all sixty-six books of the Bible until we come to the closing chapters of the very last book. And wonder of wonders, the city has twelve founations, and each of them ablaze with the light of stones most precious!

John gives futher details about the gates. He says, *And the twelve gates were twelve pearls; every several gate was of one pearl.* How appropriate! All other precious gems are metals or stones, but a pearl is a gem formed within the oyster—the only one formed by living flesh. The humble oyster receives an irritation or a wound, and around the offending article that has penetrated and hurt it, the oyster builds a pearl. The pearl, we might say, is the answer of the oyster to that which injured it. The glory land is God's answer, in Christ, to wicked men who crucified heaven's beloved and put Him to open shame. How like God it is to make the gates of the new Jerusalem of pearl. The saints as they come and go will be forever reminded, as they pass the gates of glory, that access to God's home is only because of Calvary. Think of the size of those gates! Think of the supernatural pearls from which they are made! What gigantic sufering is symbolized by those gates of pearl! Throughout the end-less ages we shall be reminded by those pearly gates of the immensity of the sufferings of Christ. Those pearls, hung eternally at the access routes to glory, will remind us forever of One who hung upon a tree and whose answer to those who injured Him was to invite them to share His home.

John then tells us more about the street. He says, *And the street of the city was pure gold, as it were transparent glass.* All the walks and ways of that city will reflect the glory of God. Every step taken, every move made will be a step or a move along a path that brings glory to God. That is not always true down here. The very best pilgrim frequently wanders off at times into those by-paths that lead to doubting and despair. That will not be possible in glory. The streets are of transparent gold, and we shall walk forever along the highway of God's will, along the royal road of bringing pleasure to Him and glory to his name.

John tells us next of *some of the distinctives of the city.* The city is distinctive not only for the things that are there, but for the things that are missing. In that city there will be *no sanctuary.* John says, *And I saw no temple therein: for the Lord God Almighty and the Lamb are the temple of it.* The architects of our world have exhausted their greatest skill in the designing and building of shrines. Even the coldest and most prosaic person must surely be stirred by the architectural magnificence of Westminster Abbey. The intricate work in wood and filleted stone, the flying arches, the delicate tracery of marble, the carvings, the tapestry work, the rich colors, the spacious heights are all designed to stir the soul to wonder if not to worship. Such masterpieces have been called "frozen music," and so they are! Solomon's temple and Ezekiel's temple, rich with inspired symbolism and constructed by Spirit-filled men, both declare that sanctuaries may well have had a place in the scheme of things down here. But over there, John can see no temple. The very thought of a temple suggests a localizing of God. But in that city, such a thought is impossible. God will be all and in all.

In that city there will be *no substitutes.* John says, **And the city had no need of the sun, neither of the moon, to shine in it: for the glory of God did lighten it, and the Lamb is the light thereof.** When God ordered the affairs of our present world, He commanded the sun to rule the day, and the moon to rule the night. During the Millennium, "the light of the moon shall be as the light of the sun, and the light of the sun shall be sevenfold" (Isa. 30:26). But the heavenly city will have need of neither, for it is to be lighted by the glory of God and the Lamb. The light that blazed from the face of Jesus on the mount of transfiguration will be the sole illumination in the heavenly Jerusalem. We shall walk in the light of His countenance!

In that city there will be *no secrets.* John says, **And the nations of them which are saved shall walk in the light of it: and the kings of the earth do bring their glory and honour into it. And the gates of it shall not be shut at all by day: for there shall be no night there. And they shall bring the glory and honour of the nations into it.** The gates stand open forever, and in that city will be no darkness at all. Everything is open; there are no secrets. The mystery of God will be over, and everything will be plain to be seen. The light of glory, shining everywhere in that city, will enlighten mankind on the earth. The kings will bring their glory into it. They will bow in homage and acknowledge that the heavens do rule. Their faces turned upward, they will offer the only thing earth can ever give to heaven—glory and honor! The gates are open, suggesting that there will be unhindered communication between heaven and earth. The honor and glory of the kings, the royal representatives of all earth's peoples, will be brought into the city, and the blessing of God will pour down in return. The era of mystery is over; heaven is visible from earth; and men will live in the full blaze of the glory that shines visibly in the sky.

In that city there will be *no sinners.* John says, **And there shall in no wise enter into it anything that defileth, neither whatsoever worketh abomination, or maketh a lie: but they which are written in the Lamb's book of life.** All other cities have been centers of scientific activity, social action, and deliberate sophistication. They have also been great centers of sin. But not this city! Only the saved will enter into it, those whose names are in the Lamb's book of life, renewed by the Spirit of God, and living in the power of an endless, impeccable life. Sinners will be far removed from the wondrous place, and even if it were possible for them to approach it, they would detest it and would flee from it.

C. JOHN'S FINAL IMPRESSIONS (22:1-5)

In concluding this most wonderful record of our eternal home, John gives four final impressions. He mentions *the life of that city.* He says, **And he shewed me a pure river of water of life, clear as crystal, proceeding out of the throne of God and of the Lamb.** Most of earth's cities are built along the banks of important rivers that soon become polluted by the cities to which they give rise. Here, however, is a river whose streams make glad the city of God. This is no muddy, filthy stream, but a pure and crystal river containing the very essence of life itself. It flows from the throne of God. That throne, such a source of terror to evildoers, is the source of life to those who know and love the Lord. The Lord Jesus likened the Holy Spirit to a river (John 7:38), and no doubt He is the reality behind the symbol.

In numerous ways the earthly Jerusalem is a counterpart of the heavenly Jerusalem during the Millenium. Both cities are seats of government, both have a river flowing from them, and both have trees of fruit. In the earthly Jerusalem the river will flow from the Temple (Ezek. 47:1-12); in the heavenly Jerusalem the river flows from the throne.

A river is used in Scripture to symbolize both pleasure (Ps. 36:8) and prosperity (Ps. 1:3). These two great magnets are used by Satan at present to draw men away from God and into many foolish and hurtful lusts. It is only as the authority of the throne of God and the Lamb is owned that true pleasure can be enjoyed. You will remember that in C. S. Lewis's *Screwtape Letters,* Screwtape tells Wormwood about hell's philosophy of pleasure. He says that while many souls have been snared through pleasure, all the same it is God's invention, and the powers of darkness have been incapable of producing even one such pleasure. The best they can do, says Screwtape, is to encourage humans to take the pleasures God has produced at times and in ways or in degrees which are forbidden. The formula he suggests for Wormwood is "an ever increasing craving for an ever decreasing pleasure." He says that the ultimate aim of hell is to get a man's soul and give him nothing in return. Life in God's city is characterized by purity, pleasure and prosperity, but all are directly linked to a right relationship with God's throne.

John mentions *the loyalty of that city.* He says, **In the midst of the street of it, and on either side of the river, was there the tree of life, which** *bare twelve manner of fruits, and yielded her fruit every month: and the leaves of the tree were for the healing of the nations.* And there shall be *no more curse: but the throne of God and of the Lamb shall be in it; and his servants shall serve him.* This is reminiscent of the Garden of Eden where the test of loyalty had to do with a tree, the fruit of which was forbidden to men. The tree of life was not forbidden while man was sinless. But once sin entered, the race could no longer be trusted with the tree of life. Possibly Adam and his posterity, had they remained sinless, would have been enabled to live forever by means of the tree of life. God removed that tree and thus put temptation beyond Adam's reach, for had he eaten it in his fallen condition, he would have been doomed to live forever in his sins.

The tree of life now flourishes in glory. It graces the celestial city, lines the banks of the river, and runs in splendor down the central boulevard. The saints in glory can enjoy the fruit of that tree, and the nations on earth benefit from the healing properties of its leaves. We are not told what the fruit of that tree tastes like; the full delights of glory are not revealed and possibly cannot be. The throne of God is mentioned again to emphasize that it is only as we submit to the authority of God that we can enjoy anything aright. That "stolen waters are sweet" (Prov. 9:17) is a lie of the devil. "He knoweth not that the dead are there; and that her guests are in the depths of hell," is Solomon's concluding comment on the philosophy of the woman who urges fools to take what they want regardless of the consequences (Prov. 9:18).

John tells also of *the Lord of that city.* He says, *And they shall see his face; and his name shall be in their foreheads.* Here is the climax of everything! John has learned from his Master; he keeps the best wine until last! "They shall see his face," he says. The ancient mariners, sailing westward along the coastlines of the Mediterranean, came at last to the Pillars of Hercules, the Straits of Gibraltar. When they came to this point in their travels, they drew back. It was one thing to hug the coastlines and to sail from isle to isle, but it was something else to venture forth into the great unknown whence came the fearful billows of the mighty deep. *"Ne plus ultra,"* they said, "There is nothing beyond." Says John, "They shall see His face!" *Ne plus ultra!* There is nothing beyond! It is heaven's crowning joy, for what we have in the next verse is merely a repetition of what has been said before. There is nothing beyond in terms of bliss when once we have seen the face of Jesus.

Last of all, John mentions *the light of that city.* He says *And there shall be no night there; and they need no candle, neither light of the sun; for the Lord God giveth them light: and they shall reign for ever and ever.* When Saul of Tarsus met the risen Christ on the Damascus road, he was blinded by a light above the brightness of the noonday sun. The glory of it never left him. To Paul, the Lord was never "Jesus of Nazareth;" He was ever "the Lord from heaven" (1 Cor. 15:47). Paul walked in that light to the end of his days. The saints in heaven look into the face of Jesus, the same wondrous face that captivated Paul, and in the light of that shining countenance they live in endless bliss. They reign with that glorious One forever. The Millennium comes and goes, but they reign on and on. So long as Christ is on the throne, so long as He endures, they endure sharing His position and His power. They "reign in life by one, Jesus Christ" (Rom. 5:17). Joy unspeakable and full of glory awaits us on the other shore (1 Pet. 1:8).

CONCLUSION TO REVELATION (22:6-21)

John has come to the end of his book and to the end of the Bible. Most people's last words are of special interest, and God's last words before the centuries of silence descend must be of great significance indeed. Our attention is drawn to the faithful Word of God, to the finished work of Christ, and to the final witness of the Spirit. It would be hard to think of a more appropriate way of ending the Book of God.

A. THE FAITHFUL WORD OF GOD (22:6-10)

Sin entered this world when Satan questioned the word of God and when Eve, entertaining the question, was led to doubt the accuracy and the authority of God's word. God concludes the Scriptures with a fresh emphasis on both.

1. THE ACCURACY OF THE WORD OF GOD (22:6)

John's attention is again attracted by the angel. *And he said unto me, These sayings are faithful and true: and the Lord God of the holy prophets sent his angel to shew unto his servants the things which must shortly be done.* The immediate reference is to the great truths of the Apocalypse that sooner or later will all come to pass. But the statement is wider than that and embraces the whole Bible. God's Word is accurate and the truths it contains have been transmitted, recorded, arranged, and preserved exactly as God had in mind. In the original, autographed manuscripts, every jot and tittle, every word, every letter was God-breathed. Men may scoff at that fact, deride it, and deny it, but God declares that His sayings are faithful and true.

2. THE AUTHORITY OF THE WORD OF GOD (22:7-9)

John has three things to say about the book's authority. He points out *how positively this truth is declared.* The Lord says to him, *Behold I come quickly: blessed is he that keepeth the sayings of the prophecy of this book.* The words of the angel give way before the direct word of Christ. The Lord breaks in, as it were, as though what He had to say was too good to be passed along merely by an angel. "I'm coming quickly," He says. Then He adds, "Keep the sayings of this book." The spur to holy living is the imminent appearing of the Lord Jesus; the steps to holy living are given in His Word.

John reveals *how patently this truth was denied.* He says, *And I John saw these things, and heard them. And when I had heard and seen, I fell down to worship before the feet of the angel which shewed me these things.* Once already John has been told not to worship an angel, but he is so overwhelmed with the glory of the revelations entrusted to him that he does it again. Such is the heart of man! What a patent denial John's act really was of the entire message of the Word of God and especially of the message of its closing book. The whole of the book of Revelation is concerned with the unveiling and exaltation of the Lord Jesus. John, in his frail mortality, attempts to worship an angel! The Lord Himself has just burst in with the news of His imminent return, and John worships an angel! He at least has the grace to confess it for our warning and instruction. We would count John's act incredible did we not carry around in our own hearts the seeds of every imaginable form of disobedience and a whole pantheon of secret idols.

John then tells us *how plainly this truth is detailed.* He says, *Then saith he unto me, See thou do it not: for I am thy fellow servant, and of thy brethren the prophets, and of them which keep the sayings of this book: worship God.* The angel took his place with all those who govern their lives by the revealed Word of God. He says in effect, "All authority is in this Book; it speaks of God; it brings you to His feet." Courteously, conscientiously, and competently, the angel led John back to the authority of the Word of God. If we abandon that, we abandon the gold standard and bankrupt ourselves of everything worthwhile.

3. THE ACCESSIBILITY OF THE WORD OF GOD (22:10)

The angel says to John, *Seal not the sayings of the prophecy of this book: for the time is at hand.* Daniel was told to seal up one of his visions (Dan. 12:4-9) because another dispensation was to intervene before the vision would be fulfilled. But that is not the case with the great truths revealed in Revelation. They are written in an open book for all to read. In the light of the completed revelation of God, we can understand most, if not all, of what God has revealed in both Testaments. The Word is accessible to us. As Paul says, "the word is nigh thee" (Rom. 10:8)

So then, God draws our attention to His faithful Word. Visions and voices may have their place, and John has been receiving communications in both ways. But it is the Word of God, accurate, authoritative, and accessible that matters. The Word of God is our court of appeal and final arbiter in matters of faith and morals.

B. THE FINISHED WORK OF CHRIST (22:11-16)

In Eden, God slew an animal to provide the skins with which to clothe the first two naked sinners of the human race. He set before them, in prospect, the finished work of Christ. Soon after, Abel brought his lamb to God, a token of his faith in the finished work of Christ, and thus offered to God a more acceptable sacrifice than Cain did. God devotes much space in Scripture to this basic and important theme—the finished work of Christ. He closes the Book with a last, lingering look at that finished work, which for all eternity will be the wonder of heaven. The finished work of Christ settles what we are, where we are, and whose we are.

1. IT SETTLES WHAT WE ARE (22:11)

It is the great divide, the watershed between the saved and the lost. John writes, *He that is unjust, let him be unjust still: and he which is filthy, let him be filthy still: and he that is righteous, let him be righteous still: and he that is holy, let him be holy still.* The Lord Jesus on the cross separated two thieves, and He separates them still. One of them trusted in the dying Savior and went to Paradise; the other rejected Him and is lost forever in hell. Men are born in sin and shaped in iniquity. It is only through the finished work of Christ that they can be fashioned anew and fitted for heaven. Apart from faith in Christ and the regenerating work of the Holy Spirit, a person goes on sinning until, at death, his character is forever fixed and set in a final, terrible mold. The wicked go on being wicked for all eternity. The one thief died blaspheming and no doubt is blaspheming still. The lost go on sinning and therefore go on suffering. The righteous, on the other hand, continue being righteous, and because they are eternally holy, they are eternally happy. The cross of Christ stands between the sinner and the saint, separating the one from the other in time and in eternity.

2. IT SETTLES WHERE WE ARE (22:12-15)

"Where I am ye cannot come" was the solemn word of Jesus to those who rejected Him. That he would "depart and be with Christ" was the joyful testimony of Paul. Thus we find that there are *those who will be with Him.* These have two things in which to rejoice. They have *the promise of His coming to sustain them.* John says, *Behold, I come quickly; and my reward is with me, to give* [to] *every man according as his work shall be. I am Alpha and Omega, the beginning and the end, the first and the last.* What a homey, cheerful word is that! Picture a family in which the father has been away for weeks. He has told the children that if they are good, he will bring them presents when he comes home. In the light of that promise the children have put on their best behavior. Then, one night the phone rings and, sure enough, it is Father with the words "I'm coming home. I'll be there soon and I have kept my promise. I have something for you all. Have you been behaving yourselves?" That is what the Lord is saying here! He's coming back; He keeps on telling us that as the Book runs quickly toward its end; He is coming back, and His rewards are in His hands.

But those who will be with Him not only have the promise of His coming, they have also *the provision of His cross to sustain them.* John says, *Blessed are they that do his commandments, that they may have right to the tree of life, and may enter in through the gates into the city.* Some versions render the phrase "do his commandments" as "wash their robes." Here again the finished work of Christ is in view; it is in "the blood of the Lamb" that spiritual raiment is cleansed (7:14). It is the finished work of Christ alone that opens up the way through the gates of the city to the tree of life. So then, John tells of those who will be with him and who have this double anchor for their souls as they wait for His coming.

There are *those who will be without Him,* too. John says, *For without are dogs, and sorcerers, and whoremongers, and murderers, and idolaters, and whosoever loveth and maketh a lie.* The word *dogs* was an Eastern term of contempt for all vile, unclean, and injurious persons. It will be terrible enough for the lost to be in torment in the lake of fire, but their agonies will be intensified by the knowledge that they are "without." They will have full knowledge of all that might have been theirs in heaven but that is forever lost to them now. The agonies of the rich man in hell must have been greatly intensified by the sight of the bliss of Lazarus. The damned rich man was not only conscious of where he was, but of what he had missed. The lost will be exiles in the universe. The shame and the scandal of their sin will haunt them forever. They will be cut off from all that is holy and good and noble and beautiful. They will recall neglected opportunities. They will remember friends they knew of old who were saved and are now walking the streets of gold. They themselves, however, are shut out, to face the remorse, the despair, the misery, and the pain of a lost eternity. Hell will be made infinitely more unbearable by the thought of what has been lost by rejecting the finished work of Christ.

3. IT SETTLES WHOSE WE ARE (22:16)

Again the Lord Jesus speaks. He says, *I Jesus have sent mine angel to testify unto you these things in the churches. I am the root and the offspring of David, and the bright and morning star.* That is whose we are! He is the Lover of the church, the Lord of the earth, and the Light of creation; and we belong to Him! How we should thank God for the finished work of Christ, which lies behind all these magnificent statements in this closing section of this book.

C. THE FINAL WITNESS OF THE SPIRIT (22:17-21)

It is fitting indeed that the sacred canon of Scripture should close with a reference to the Holy Spirit. For He is the Author of the Book, the One who has inspired every chapter, every verse, and every line. He is the omniscient genius behind this miracle in words, the Bible. There are three last things the Spirit has to say before the inspired canon is closed.

1. THE LAST WELCOME (22:17)

John records it briefly, *The Spirit and the bride say, Come. And let him that heareth say, Come. And let him that is athirst come. And whosoever will, let him take the water of life freely.* "Come!" is the grandest word in the gospel! It first rang out in the days of Noah when God was about to pour out His wrath against the world. The ark was finished and a complete salvation provided, when God, stepping inside the ark, turned to Noah and said, "Come." Again and again the blessed word rings out, and now, before closing the book forever, the Spirit sounds it out again. The Spirit says, "Come!" and the saints say, "Come!" and the very sinners who hear the message and respond say, "Come!" It is the last welcome, and those who refuse to heed it will one day hear in its place the dread word "Depart!"

Let every lost sinner come! Let everyone within the sound of that welcoming invitation, conscious of deep thirst of the soul, come and drink of the water of life.

In his gripping classics *King Solomon's Mines*, Sir Henry Rider Haggard tells how his three heroes, hunter Quartermain, Captain Good, and Sir Henry Curtis, cross a frightful desert in their quest for King Solomon's mines. One of his heroes, Allan Quartermain, recounts the tale.

"Our only enemies," he says, "were heat, thirst and flies, but far rather would I have faced any danger from man or beast than that awful trinity. About seven o'clock we woke up experiencing the exact sensations one would attribute to a beefsteak on a gridiron. We were literally baked through and through. The burning sun seemed to be sucking our very blood out of us. We sat up and gasped."

He describes how the long day wore on as they waited for sunset before resuming their march. "There we lay," he says, "Panting, and every now and then moistening our lips from our scanty supply of water. Had we followed our inclinations we would have finished all we possessed in the first two hours, but we were forced to exercise the most rigid care, for if our water failed us we knew that very soon we must perish miserably." Presently the adventurers shouldered their packs and pushed forward further into the desert. Their one hope of survival hung on a thread. They carried with them an ancient map to guide them across the trackless sands. The desert was forty leagues wide, and the map indicated the presence of a pool of water about halfway across. Their hope was to find that pool before they perished.

"At last," says the old hunter, "utterly worn out in body and mind, we came to the foot of a queer hill, or sand koppie, which at first sight resembled a gigantic ant-heap about a hundred feet high, covering at its base nearly two acres of ground. Here we halted, and driven to it by our desperate thirst, sucked down our last drops of water. Then we lay down."

The dawn found the three white men discussing their plight as their old enemy the sun prepared for his final attack. They had with them two servants, one of whom was an old Hottentot richly endowed with the instincts of his race. Presently, Quartermain observed the Hottentot arise and begin to walk about with his eyes on the ground. Presently he spoke. "I smell water," he said.

"It was all very well," says Quartermain, "for Ventvogel to say that he smelt water, but we could see no signs of it, look which way we would." The old native insisted that he could smell water, and he sniffed with his ugly snub nose. Sir Henry Curtis suggested that perhaps the water was at the top of the hill, a suggestion scorned by Captain Good. However the desperate men decided to look, and their other black servant led the way. They trailed him up the hill.

"*Nanzia amanzi!*" cried their servant with a loud voice. "Here is water!"

Said Quartermain, "We rushed up to him, and there, sure enough, in a deep cut or indentation on the very top of the sand koppie, was an undoubted pool of water! How it came to be in such a strange place we did not stop to enquire. . . . We gave a bound and a rush, and in another second we were all down on our stomachs sucking [it] up . . . as though it were nectar fit for the gods."[1]

"Let him that is athirst come. And whosoever will, let him take the water of life freely." The water of life itself is offered here, clear as crystal, flowing from the throne of God. This world is a wilderness indeed, a desert as barren and bare to the soul as the trackless sands that led to King Solomon's mines. Men and women are dying of spiritual thirst. Yet here is the water of life, and here the invitation! How strange is the insanity that keeps men from flinging themselves on their faces before God and drinking deep of the water of life. The rich man in hell wanted just a single drop to ease the torment of his thirst. When he was alive, he might have come and received eternal access to the river of life. But he never came. Now for all eternity he must be tormented, with his cravings and longings forever unquenched. So then, this last welcome rings out from the Spirit of God—"Come!"

2. THE LAST WARNING (22:18-19)

The Bible contains many warnings. It begins with a warning to Adam before ever the serpent appeared; and it ends with a warning to us. *For I testify unto every man that heareth the words of the prophecy of this book, If any man shall add unto these things, God shall add unto him the*

1. H. Rider Haggard, *King Solomon's Mines* (London: Macdonald, 1885), pp. 60-68.

plagues that are written in this book: and if any man shall take away from the words of the book of this prophecy, God shall take away his part out of the book of life, and out of the holy city, and from the things which are written in this book. By application this warning takes in the entire canon of Scripture. God will not have His Word tampered with. Eve, when she encountered the serpent, added to what God said and subtracted from what God said. Her sin opened the door for all that followed of curse, of banishment from the tree of life, of peril and eternal doom. God's wrath abides on those who tamper with His Word, cutting out the parts that offend them and adding their own ideas thereto.

The initial scope of the warning has to do with the Apocalypse. God guards this book that so many have scorned; He guards it with a terrible warning. Thus the Apocalypse opens with a blessing for those who read it, hear it, and keep it. It ends with a curse for those who tamper with it. The closing word that guards the Apocalypse is set as a sentinel to all of Scripture, for God places this book at the end of all the rest.

3. THE LAST WORD (22:20-21)

The last word is a word about *glory.* John writes, **He which testifieth these things saith, Surely I come quickly. Amen. Even so, come, Lord Jesus.** Three times in this closing chapter, the Lord breaks in to remind us that He is coming quickly. This is His last word. It seems like a long time to us since this promise was given, as we trace the history of the past two thousand years. It is only two days to Him (2 Pet. 3:8). At any moment now, He might cleave the sky and take His saints home to glory. No wonder the church responds. *Even so come, Lord Jesus.* We address Him to the very end as Lord. He may refer to Himself as Jesus, and the Holy Spirit may call Him Jesus, but our name for Him is Lord.

The very last word is a word about *grace.* John writes, **The grace of our Lord Jesus Christ be with you all. Amen.** How like God to close His Book with a final reference to His grace! Well might we borrow the splendid lines of John Newton and celebrate that grace:

> Amazing grace! how sweet the sound!
> That saved a wretch like me;
> I once was lost, but now am found;
> Was blind, but now I see.

> 'Twas grace that taught my heart to fear,
> And grace my fears relieved;
> How precious did that grace appear
> The hour I first believed.

> Through many dangers, toils and snares,
> I have already come:

'Tis grace that brought me safe thus far,
And grace will lead me home.
When we've been there ten thousand years,
Bright, shining as the sun;
We've no less days to sing his praise
Than when we first begun.

Explore the
BIBLE
in greater depth with the
John Phillips
Commentary Series!